STUDIES
IN
EPHESIANS

STUDIES IN EPHESIANS

by

H. C. G. Moule

KREGEL PUBLICATIONS
Grand Rapids, Michigan 49501

STUDIES IN EPHESIANS, published in 1977, by Kregel
Publications, a division of Kregel, Inc. All rights reserved.

Library of Congress Cataloging in Publication Data

Moule, Handley Carr Glyn, Bp. of Durham, 841-1920
  Studies in Ephesians.

  (Kregel Popular Commentary Series)
  Reprint of the 1893 ed. published at the University Press,
Cambridge, under title: The Epistle to the Ephesians, and in
series: The Cambridge Bible for schools and colleges.
  Includes index.
  1. Bible. N.T. Ephesians — Commentaries.
I. Moule, Handley Carr Glyn, Bp. of Durham, 1841-1920. II.
  Title. III. Series: The Cambridge Bible for schools and
colleges.
BS2693.M68   1977   227'.5'077   77-79179
ISBN 0-8254-3218-9

Printed in the United States of America

First Kregel Publications edition 1977
Reprinted 1982

CONTENTS

Ephesus is the Metropolis of Asia, and was consecrated to Artemis ...Pythagoras is said to have come from Ephesus...The schools of Parmenides, Zeno, and Democritus, and many philosophers even of our time, are to be found there. This I say not for the sake of saying it, but to shew that Paul needed much earnest care in writing to the Ephesians...The Epistle overflows with lofty thoughts and doctrines. He writes it from prison at Rome...Things which he scarcely anywhere else utters, he here expounds.

ST CHRYSOSTOM, *Preamble to his Homilies on the Epistle.*

∗ The Text adopted in this Edition is that of Dr Scrivener's *Cambridge Paragraph Bible.* A few variations from the ordinary Text, chiefly in the spelling of certain words, and in the use of italics, will be noticed. For the principles adopted by Dr Scrivener as regards the printing of the Text see his Introduction to the *Paragraph Bible,* published by the Cambridge University Press.

INTRODUCTION

Chapter 1

EPHESUS: ASIA: ST PAUL'S CONNEXION WITH EPHESUS

A BRIEF notice of EPHESUS itself will be sufficient here, for the Epistle, whatever was its destination (see pp. 24, &c.), deals scarcely at all with local features and interests. Its pictures of surrounding forms of thought and life are common, if not to the world of the apostolic age in general, certainly to the then world of western Asia Minor[1].

Ephesus was colonized mainly from Athens, and the Ephesians inherited something of Athenian genius. The great painters, Parrhasius (cent. 5 B.C.) and Apelles (cent. 4 B.C.), were both Ephesians. But Asiatic elements, no doubt, largely entered into the race and thought of the people. For a great harbour and emporium the situation of the city was remarkable. It stood some miles from the open coast, on a landlocked basin, the Sacred Port. This was artificially embanked, and connected with the sea by a broad channel which communicated with the river Caÿster between the city and the shore. In primeval times the sea, not yet shut out by the alluvium of the Caÿster, had washed the buildings of the city, but long before the apostolic age a process of silting, made worse by mistaken engineering, had begun to choke the channel, and ultimately cut off altogether the waterway to the sea. It was already difficult in St Paul's time to sail into the Sacred Port.

[1] On the supposed allusion, ch. ii., to the Temple of Artemis (Diana), see the remark, p. 27.

The two architectural features of Ephesus which come up in the Scripture narrative are the Temple of Artemis (Diana), and the Theatre. The Ephesian Artemis had little if any connexion with the Huntress of Hellenic mythology. Her statue, with its many breasts, betokened the fertility of Nature, and was engraved, in Greek letters, with a magic legend. The mighty Temple, one of the Seven Wonders of the ancient world, stood facing eastward, outside the city walls. First and last, it was the work of 220 years; built of shining marble; 342 feet long by 164 feet broad; supported by a forest of columns each 56 feet high; a sacred museum of master-pieces of sculpture and painting. At the centre, hidden by curtains within a gorgeous shrine (*nâos*), stood the very ancient image of the Goddess, of wood or ebony[1], reputed to have fallen from the sky. Behind the shrine was a treasury where, as in "the safest bank in Asia," nations and kings stored their most precious things. The Temple, as St Paul saw it, subsisted till A. D. 262, when it was ruined by the Goths.

The Theatre, excavated on the western side of Mount Coressus, and, like all ancient theatres, open to the sky, was the largest in the Hellenic world, capable of containing 50,000 spectators. Not far to the north of it lay the Stadium, or Racecourse, where also the fights of beasts, and of men with beasts, were shewn. To this we can trace figurative references in the great Epistle written from Ephesus (1 Cor. iv. 9, ix. 24, 25, xv. 32).

Ephesus was the capital of Proconsular Asia. The Roman province so called included the whole western coast of our Asia Minor and a considerable interior region. It was governed by a Proconsul, chosen by lot from only the Consulars, or Past-Consuls; a distinction confined to Asia and Libya. The Proconsul was assisted, or checked, by the Agent (Procurator) of the Emperor, and by other Roman officials. But the province was permitted in a subordinate degree to administer its own affairs, through municipalities, a Senate, and a popular As-

---

[1] The material was uncertain. It may have been even an aërolite.

sembly, which Assembly met usually in the Ephesian Theatre. The President of the Senate and Assembly was the "Clerk," or "Recorder," of Acts xix. He held office for a year, and the year was dated by his name. Another important dignity was that of "Asiarch" (Acts xix. 31; "chief of Asia," A.V.; "chief officers of Asia," R.V.). The Asiarchs had for their main function, along with a priestly office, the duty of providing (in a large measure) and of controlling[1] the great public games and shows, all of which bore a quasi-sacred character.

The earliest N.T. allusion to the region of Ephesus may be found in Acts ii. 9, where we find some pious Jews from "Asia" among the crowd at Pentecost. Through these men, or some of them, the first intimations of the Gospel may have reached the plain of the Caÿster.

St Paul, in the early stages of his great second missionary circuit (A.D. 51) was divinely "forbidden to preach the word in Asia" (Acts xvi. 6). But at its close, on his way from Greece to Syria, he visited Ephesus (Acts xviii. 18—21), bringing Aquila and Priscilla with him, and leaving them there. His own stay was short, as he was hastening to keep a festival, probably Pentecost, at Jerusalem; and his evangelistic work consisted wholly in "reasonings" (perhaps in one isolated "reasoning," for the verb is aorist, ver. 19) with the Jews in their synagogue. The impression made by his message must have been favourable, for he was pressed to stay, and departed with a promise to return. During his absence, in Syria and Asia Minor (Acts xviii. 22, 23, xix. 1), Apollos visited Ephesus, received full Christian instruction from Aquila and Priscilla, and passed on to Corinth (Acts xviii. 24—28).

St Paul's second visit lasted over three years (Acts xx. 31), probably from A.D. 54 to A.D. 57. He arrived from the interior of Asia Minor (Acts xix. 1, where "upper coasts" means "inland parts"). He found, no doubt, some results already of the labours

---

[1] "The Asiarch Philip" appears in the narrative of St Polycarp's martyrdom (A.D. 166) at Smyrna (ch. xii.), as the authority to whom the populace appeal to let a lion loose upon the martyr. See the Excursus on the Asiarchate, Lightfoot's *Ignatius*, &c. vol. II. sect. ii. pp. 987 &c.

of Aquila and Priscilla, and of Apollos. But the only recorded
details of his earliest work are the discovery, instruction, baptism,
and miraculous endowment of a small group of embryo
Christians, if we may call them so (xix. 1—7), and three months
of discussion and appeal in the Jewish synagogue where he had
been so well received before (xix. 8). Opposition now developed,
and as a considerable number of "disciples" had attached themselves to the Gospel, he separated them for purposes of worship
and teaching, making the "school of Tyrannus" his Christian
synagogue. This may have been, as Alford suggests, a "private
synagogue" belonging to a Jew Tyrannus, or the lecture-room of
a Gentile convert Tyrannus, or a hall known as "Tyrannus'
hall"[1].

Here for full two years (xix. 10) he discoursed daily, just
as modern missionaries in India or China do in chapels or
wayside rooms. And such was the power of the message, with
its attendant physical miracles (xix. 12), and its victorious exposure of the magical practices[2] for which Ephesus was famous
(xix. 13—20), and such was the facility and frequency of intercourse between Ephesus and its province, that the Gospel was
"heard" during these two years by "all them that dwelt in Asia,
both Jews and Greeks" (xix. 10, and cp. 26). This doubtless
means that there was no Asiatic town or district, generally
speaking, which the Gospel did not penetrate, whether by means
of deputed missionaries, such as Epaphras probably was, sent
out by the Apostle from Ephesus, or by native visitors to
Ephesus, returning to their homes as actual converts or, at
least, "enquirers." Modern missionary work, an instructive
but neglected commentary on the Acts, can supply ample
illustrations of such an extension of the Gospel[3].

As regards St Paul's own work, it seems clear that he remained stationary, on the whole, at Ephesus. To the Ephesian

---

[1] The probable reading, Acts xix. 9, is not "*one* Tyrannus," but
"Tyrannus."
[2] See further, Appendix G.
[3] See two small but suggestive books, *The Story of the Fuh-kien
Mission of the Church Missionary Society*, and *The Story of the Cheh-
keang Mission*.

presbyters (xx. 18) he speaks of having been with them "*the whole time*" (rather than "at all times," A. V.). And in Col. ii. 1 we find him implying, in the obvious sense of the words, that he had never personally visited the missions in the vale of the Lycus—Colossæ and Hierapolis. We dwell on this double phenomenon, the Apostle's fixity of residence and wide extent of influence, as tending to explain the facts which constitute the problem of Eph. i. 1, and which are discussed more fully below, pp. 24, &c. It may help the reader to a clear conception of the geographical extent of this two years' work, to enumerate the places in Proconsular Asia named in the N. T. All the Seven Churches of the Revelation are of the number, and Troas, Assos, Adramyttium, Miletus, Trogyllium, Hierapolis, and Colossæ.

This period of extraordinary influence and success, along with constant Jewish opposition (Acts xx. 19), was closed somewhat sooner, perhaps, than the Apostle had planned, by the tumult raised by Demetrius (Acts xix.); itself a direct testimony to the extent and depth of the work of the Gospel in the city and province.

The First Epistle to the Corinthians was written from Ephesus, at some time during this long stay of the Apostle. Its date lies close to the end of the stay. The writer (ch. xvi.) evidently contemplates a speedy visit to Macedonia on the way to Corinth. We have referred already to the Ephesian allusions to be found in that Epistle.

On St Paul's last voyage to Syria (A.D. 58) he touched (Acts xx. 15) at Miletus, on the coast of Caria, some 30 miles south of Ephesus. Avoiding on purpose a visit to Ephesus, where in so large a Christian community causes for delay would inevitably have arisen[1], he sent for the presbyters (called *episcopi*, ver. 28) of Ephesus to meet him at Miletus, and there addressed to them the pathetic and noble "charge" recorded by St Luke, Acts xx. 18—35. We point out elsewhere (p. 32) some resemblances between the Charge and the Epistle. Here it is

---

[1] See Prof. Lumby's notes on Acts xx. in this Series.

enough to say that this remarkable passage in the Acts is specially interesting as indicating the early organization of the Christian ministry at Ephesus, a fact only remotely suggested in the Epistle; and as supplying an interior view of the persistency, thoroughness, and profound affection and earnestness of the Apostle's personal work in the city.

We hear no more of Ephesus till near the close of St Paul's life, the period of the "Pastoral Epistles." Probably in A.D. 63[1] we find him (1 Tim. i. 3) exhorting Timothy to "stay on at Ephesus," when Paul himself was on the way to Macedonia. And Timothy's work was to be, besides the superintendence of church order, the correction of a type of false doctrine, in the outline of which we can detect the same combination of Judaistic and theosophic elements which seems to have formed the "heresy of Colossæ" when our Epistle and that to the Colossians were written[2]. Ephesus is twice named in 2 *Timothy*, the Apostle's last letter. He speaks (i. 18) of the Ephesian Onesiphorus as having "served him in many things" at Ephesus; possibly during the long stay of three years, possibly during the later visit indicated 1 Tim. i. 3[3]. And finally (iv. 12) he says that he has "sent Tychicus to Ephesus." We cannot know why this was done. Perhaps the "beloved brother and faithful minister" of Eph. vi. 21 was dismissed by the Apostle from the dangerous duty of personal attendance on the way to Rome, in order to return to Ephesus, there to build up and encourage the now endangered Church.

Ephesus is mentioned twice more in the N. T.; Rev. i. 11, ii. 1. We cannot here discuss the question, who and what were the "Angels of the Churches." But on any theory the Epistle to the Ephesian Angel is addressed by implication to the Ephesian Church also, and it is deeply interesting to gather

---

[1] This is not the place to examine the date of the Pastorals. To us it seems certain that they are the work of St Paul's latest years, and of a period following the imprisonment at Rome recorded Acts xxviii.

[2] See further, p. 20.

[3] Very possibly St Paul was seized at Ephesus and carried thence to his death at Rome. Onesiphorus may have done him loving service at that crisis.

from the words of the glorified Lord[1] what was the spiritual condition of that Church at the distance of about a generation[2] from the date of St Paul's writing. The merits and the faults are alike those of a highly enlightened and mature community, deeply taught in Divine truth and jealous for its purity, but allowing the chill to which a traditional faith, however exalted in its creed and theory, is liable, to infect their love to Christ. It is instructive to remember how amply the Pauline Epistle had provided the Ephesians with the antidote (ch. iii. 14—21) to this decline of love, while labouring for their fullest apprehension of the great theory of truth.

See further, on the Apocalyptic Epistle, p. 33.

"Asia" appears among the regions of our Asia Minor, 1 Pet. i. 1. The passage suggests that St Peter, as well as St Paul, worked as an Apostle in the countries indicated. But his headquarters appear to have been in the extreme east, not west, of the great district (ch. v. 13). Not with St Peter but with St John do we find Ephesus itself connected in the latest apostolic history; as the reference to the Epistles of the Revelation has already reminded us. Whatever there may be of mere legend in the stories of St John's old age, we may be quite reasonably sure that Ephesus was the abode of his last years, the scene of his influence on Polycarp, Ignatius, and Papias, and the place of his burial. Here, probably, his Gospel and his Epistles were written, and, within sixty miles of the Ephesian coast, the Revelation.

Ephesus long remained the seat of a Christian Church, and was the place of the great Christian Council (A.D. 431) which dealt with the heresy of Nestorius. Eighteen years later it was the scene of the "Robber Synod," an assembly occasioned by controversies indirectly connected with the same heresy, and specially infamous for the outrageous violence of the dominant party.

The Bishop of Ephesus, at the end of cent. 4, bore the

---

[1] Surely we are bound by the explicit language of the Seven Epistles to read them as His direct words, in a sense altogether peculiar.

[2] See Abp Trench, *Epistles to the Seven Churches*, p. 78.

title of Exarch (or Grand Metropolitan) of Asia; but the Patriarch of Constantinople ultimately annexed the primacy of Asia.

Ephesus, after a long gradual decline, is now an almost total solitude. A small Turkish village, Ayasaluk (a corruption of *Hagios Theologos*, the Holy Divine, St John), stands upon a part of the site.

For further particulars of Ephesus, or Asia, or both, see Smith's *Dictionaries, of Classical Geography* and *of the Bible;* Falkener's *Ephesus;* Lewin's *Life and Epistles of St Paul,* vol. I., ch. xiii., with the *Addenda,* pp. xxii, xxiii; and especially J. T. Wood's *Discoveries at Ephesus.*

Chapter 2

ST PAUL AT ROME : OCCASION AND DATE OF THE EPISTLE

ST PAUL arrived in Rome, from Melita, in the spring of A.D. 61, probably early in March. There he spent "two full years" (Acts xxviii. 30), at the close of which, as we have good reason to believe, he was released.

In the long delay before his trial[1] he was of course in custody; but this was comparatively lenient. He occupied lodgings of his own (Acts xxviii. 16, 23, 30), probably a storey or flat in one of the lofty houses common in Rome. It is impossible to determine for certain where in the City this lodging was, but it is likely that it was either in or near the great Camp of the Prætorians, or Imperial Guard, outside the Colline Gate, just N.E. of the City[2]. In this abode the Apostle was attached day and night by a light coupling-chain to a Prætorian sentinel, but was as free, apparently, to invite and maintain general intercourse as if he had been merely confined by illness.

[1] Due probably to procrastination in the prosecution and to the caprice of the Emperor. See Lewin, vol. II. p. 236, for a parallel case.
[2] See Bp Lightfoot, *Philippians,* pp. 9 &c., 99 &c.

The company actually found in his rooms at different times was very various. His first visitors (indeed they must have been the providers of his lodging) would be the Roman Christians, including all, or many, of the saints named in a passage (Rom. xvi.) written only a very few years before. Then came the representatives of the Jewish community (Acts xxviii. 17, 23), but apparently never to return, as such, after the long day of discussion to which they were first invited. Then from time to time would come Christian brethren, envoys from distant Churches, or personal friends; Epaphroditus from Philippi, Aristarchus from Thessalonica, Tychicus from Ephesus, Epaphras from Colossæ, John Mark, Demas, Jesus Justus. Luke, the beloved physician, was present perhaps always, and Timotheus, the Apostle's spiritual son, very frequently. One other memorable name occurs, Onesimus, the fugitive Colossian slave, whose story, indicated in the Epistle to Philemon, is at once a striking evidence of the perfect liberty of access to the prisoner granted to anyone and everyone, and a beautiful illustration both of the character of St Paul and the transfiguring power and righteous principles of the Gospel.

No doubt the visitors to this obscure but holy lodging were far more miscellaneous than even this list suggests. Through the successive Prætorian sentinels some knowledge of the character and message of the prisoner would be always passing out. The right interpretation of Phil. i. 13[1] is, beyond reasonable doubt, that the true account of Paul's imprisonment came to be "known in the Prætorian regiments, and generally among people around"; and Phil. iv. 22 indicates that a body of earnest and affectionate converts had arisen among the population of slaves and freedmen attached to the Palace of Nero. And the wording of that passage suggests that such Christians found a welcome meeting place in the rooms of the Apostle; doubtless for frequent worship, doubtless also for direct instruction, and for the blessed enjoyments of the family affection of the Gospel. Meanwhile (Phil. i. 15, 16) there was a section of the Roman Christian community, probably the

---

[1] See Bp Lightfoot, *Philippians*, pp. 99 &c.

disciples infected with the prejudices of the Pharisaic party (see Acts xv., &c.), who, with very few exceptions (see Col. iv. 11 and notes), took sooner or later a position of trying antagonism to St Paul; a trial over which he triumphed in the deep peace of Christ.

It is an interesting possibility, not to say probability, that from time to time the lodging was visited by inquirers of intellectual fame or distinguished rank. Ancient Christian tradition[1] actually makes the renowned Stoic writer, L. Annæus Seneca, tutor and counsellor of Nero, a convert of St Paul's; and one phase of the legend was the fabrication, within the first four centuries, of a correspondence between the two. It is quite certain that Seneca was never a Christian, though his language is full of startling superficial parallels to that of the N.T., and most full in his latest writings. But it is at least very likely that he heard, through his many channels of information, of St Paul's existence and presence, and that he was intellectually interested in his teaching ; and it is quite possible that he cared to visit him. It is not improbable, surely, that Seneca's brother Gallio (Acts xviii. 12) may have described St Paul, however passingly, in a letter; for Gallio's religious indifference may quite well have consisted with a strong personal impression made on him by St Paul's bearing. Festus himself was little interested in the Gospel, or at least took care to seem so, and yet was deeply impressed by the *personnel* of the Apostle. And, again, the Prefect of the Imperial Guard, A.D. 61, was Afranius Burrus, Seneca's intimate colleague as counsellor to Nero, and it is at least possible that he had received from Festus a more than commonplace description of the prisoner consigned to him[2].

Bp Lightfoot, in his Essay, "St Paul and Seneca" (*Philippians*, pp. 270, &c.), thinks it possible to trace in some of the Epistles of the Captivity a Christian adaptation of Stoic ideas.

---

[1] The first hint appears in Tertullian, cent. 2—3.
[2] We cannot but think that Bp Lightfoot (*Philippians*, p. 301) somewhat underrates the probability that Gallio and Burrus should have given Seneca an interest in St Paul.

The Stoic, for example, made much of the individual's *membership* in the great Body of the Universe, and *citizenship* in its great City. The connexion suggested is interesting, and it falls quite within the methods of Divine inspiration that materials of Scripture imagery should be collected from a secular region. But the language of St Paul about the Mystical Body, in the Ephesian Epistle particularly, reads far more like a direct revelation than like an adaptation; and it evidently deals with a truth which is already, in its substance, perfectly familiar to the readers[1].

Other conspicuous personages of Roman society at the time have been reckoned by tradition among the chamber-converts of St Paul, among them the poet Lucan and the Stoic philosopher Epictetus[2]. But there is absolutely no evidence for these assertions. It is interesting and suggestive, on the other hand, to recall one almost certain case of conversion about this time within the highest Roman aristocracy. Pomponia Græcina, wife of Plautius the conqueror of Britain, was accused (A.D. 57, probably), of "foreign superstition," and tried by her husband as domestic judge. He acquitted her. But the deep and solemn seclusion of her life (a seclusion begun A.D. 44 when her friend the princess Julia was put to death, and continued unbroken till her own death, about A.D. 84), taken in connexion with the charge, as in all likelihood it was, of Christianity, "suggests that, shunning society, she sought consolation in the duties and hopes of the Gospel"[3], leaving for ever the splendour and temptations of the world of Rome. She was not a convert, obviously, of St Paul's; but her case suggests the possibility of other similar cases.

At what time of the Two Years the Epistle to the Ephesians was written, we cannot hope to determine with precision. It is

---

[1] It appears in the First Ep. to the Corinthians, written a few years before the Ep. to the Ephesians. See 1 Cor. xii.

[2] For the curiously Christian tone of Epictetus' writings here and there, see Bp Lightfoot, *Philippians*, pp. 313 &c. The *Manual* of Epictetus is a book of gold in its own way, but still that way is not Christian.

[3] Bp Lightfoot, *Philippians*, p. 21.

a prevalent theory that the Ephesian and Colossian Epistles date somewhat early in the period, and the Philippians late. Bp Lightfoot (*Philippians*, pp. 30, &c.) has given some strong reasons for the reversal of the order. The strongest, in our view, is the consideration of style in the respective Epistles. The Philippian Epistle, so far as it is dogmatic, approaches certainly much nearer to the type of the Roman than the Ephesian does; and this suggests a comparative nearness in date. The test of style demands caution, certainly, in its application, in the case of a writer of such compass and versatility as St Paul; circumstances might suggest similarity of subject to his mind at widely dissimilar times, and the subject rather than the time would rule the style, within certain limits. But in this case we have further to observe that the style of the Ephesian Group (so to call it) is manifestly, in some aspects, a new style, and charged with dogmatic materials in many respects new. And this suggests at least the probability of an interval between the Roman and Ephesian Epistles as long as the chronology will reasonably allow.

We may conjecture that it was at some time in A.D. 62, perhaps even early in A.D. 63, that the Ephesian Epistle, with its companion Epistles, was written. Epaphras had arrived from Asia, and Tychicus was ready to travel thither, with Onesimus. The news from Asia had conveyed encouragement and anxiety at once. Life and love were abundant in the Churches. But a subtle danger was abroad, in the form of a pseudo-Christian teaching in which were blended ritual Judaism and a theosophy from the further East, dealing much with unhealthy theories of body and spirit, and with hierarchies of angelic powers set in the place due to Christ alone. With this error the Apostle deals explicitly in the Colossian Epistle, in which we can surely see, in some respects, the sketch or germ of the Ephesian[1]. In writing to the Ephesians he is not unconscious of this special need, which seems to give point to his repeated allusions to the spiritual hierarchies, good and evil, and their relation to Christ. But he was guided to make of his

---

[1] See further, p. 32.

Ephesian Letter far more than the treatment of a single phase of truth. As in the *Romans*, so here, he addresses himself to the mighty theme of the whole Gospel ; from the point of view not now of the justification of the saints but of their life in and union with their Redeeming Head, and the consequent oneness of the whole organism of the true Church in time and in eternity. Faithful to the genius of the Gospel, he applies these transcendent truths with great minuteness to the realities of common life, especially that of the Christian Home.

Some scholars, notably Meyer, have placed the Ephesian and its companion Epistles in the two years' imprisonment at *Cæsarea Stratonis* (Acts xxiv. 23—27). But the reasons for this date (which may be seen carefully stated in Alford's[1] Prolegomena to the *Ephesians*) are met by some obvious considerations which seem to us altogether conclusive. The Roman imprisonment, far more than the Cæsarean, was a time likely *à priori* to be one of stimulated energy and administrative as well as doctrinal action on the Apostle's part. And the language used in the *Philippians* about the progress of the Gospel in the Imperial Guard and Household points almost in so many words to Rome. And if this be so, and if it is granted, as it is, that the *Philippians* and *Ephesians* are not to be dated far apart, and above all if it is granted that the *Philippians* is the earlier Epistle, the *Ephesians* must be assigned of course to the Roman captivity. For this conclusion Bp Lightfoot decides without reserve.

It may not be uninteresting to enumerate briefly some events of Roman secular history which fall within, or nearly within, the two years of St Paul's residence at Rome.

A.D. 61. Boadicea revolts in Britain ; 70,000 Romans and allies perish, and, in the suppression of the revolt, 80,000 Britons.

Pedanius Secundus, a senator of Rome, is murdered by one of his slaves. As the legal consequence 400 slaves, the number under the master's roof at the time, are put to death.

Agrippa (the Agrippa of Acts xxv.) raises the structure of his

---

[1] Alford controverts them with convincing force. See also Harless' Commentary on the Epistle, *Einleitung*, pp. lxii, &c.

palace at Jerusalem so as to command a view of the Temple courts. The Jews raise a counter-wall. Festus orders its demolition. The Jews send an embassy to Rome, which is successful by the favour of Nero's mistress Poppæa, a proselyte.

Festus dies, and is succeeded in Judæa by Albinus.

A.D. 62. Afranius Burrus, Prætorian Prefect, dies. This begins the decline of the influence of his colleague Seneca, who is compelled to retire into private life. Nero is more than ever his own master.

Tigellinus, the Emperor's favourite, becomes the supreme influence at court.

Octavia, Nero's wife, is divorced, and soon after put to death. Before her death Nero's concubine Poppæa is made his wife.

The High Priest Ananus procures, at Jerusalem, the martyrdom of St James the Just (the James of Acts xv.). The Roman Governor Albinus, appealed to by the moderate Jewish party, reprimands the High Priest. It appears that the High Priest possessed no power of life and death without the Procurator's sanction.

The *Quinquennium* of Nero, the first five years of his reign, during which, under good advice and guidance, the Empire had been singularly happy, had closed about three years before St Paul's Roman residence.

Chapter 3

AUTHENTICITY OF THE EPISTLE

THERE is no trace in early Christian literature of doubt about the authenticity of the Epistle. Not to enumerate more passing references, *St Irenæus* (cent. 2), quotes ch. v. 30 as the words of "the beatified Paul in his Epistle to the Ephesians," and ch. v. 13 as "the words of Paul"; *St Clement of Alexandria* (cent. 3), quotes *inter alia* ch. iv. 21—25, as St Paul's; and *Tertullian* (cent. 2—3) names (*de Præscriptione*, c. xxxvi.) Ephesus among the Churches which possess original apostolic (and, by context, Pauline) Epistles.

To give further detail would be needless, as there is absolutely no adverse ancient voice on the authorship and authority of the Epistle. We only add, for the great interest of the
passage, the possible allusion to this Epistle by *St Ignatius*
(early cent. 2) in his Ep. to the Ephesians, ch. xii. The passage,
undoubtedly genuine, admits of translation either thus :—"Ye
are initiated into mysteries with Paul,...who *in every part of his
letter* makes mention of you in Christ Jesus"; or thus :—"...who
in every letter makes mention &c." The former rendering is
advocated by Dean Alford, and by Prof. Westcott (*Canon of the
N.T.*, ed. 1866, p. 44 note), the latter by Bp Lightfoot in his
recent edition of St Ignatius. In our view the rendering "*in
every Epistle*" is preferable, for the reason that (being abundantly safe grammatically) it is somewhat nearer to the facts.
It is scarcely the case that St Paul "mentions" the Church
he addresses, *in any unusual way*, "in every part of" our
Epistle ; while it is remarkable that he does "mention"
Ephesian Christians in the *Romans*, 1 and 2 *Corinthians*, and
1 and 2 *Timothy;* often enough to account for the phrase "in
every Epistle" in a rather hyperbolic passage.

In quite modern times doubt has been cast on the authorship, by some great critics of the liberal school in Germany.
De Wette took it to be an amplification of the Epistle to the
Colossians[1] by an imitator in the apostolic age ; Baur, to be full
of Gnostic thought and phraseology proving it to belong to a
time when Gnosticism was developed, and to be the work of a
writer of Gnostic tendencies. It is surely reply enough to both
lines of attack to say, "*Take up and read*"[2]. Few indeed must
be the readers who, whatever their view of the dogmatic authority of the Epistle, will not recognize in it the thought and
diction of a mighty master. And who, with any knowledge of

---

[1] An argument in this direction has been drawn from the words "*If
ye have heard*" (iii. 2), which, it is alleged, could not have been
naturally written by St Paul. But an able imitator would instinctively
avoid just such a verbal difficulty.

[2] "To all such difficulties there is the one sweeping reply, that no one
but St Paul *could* have been the writer." Howson, *Character of St
Paul*, p. 146, note.

Gnostic theory and practice, will believe that an Epistle so full of humbling precepts for the conduct of daily life in common homes, to mention that feature only of the Epistle, could have come from a Gnostic quarter?[1]

The Epistle is both sublimely and practically Christian. It is the work of a writer whose intellect and affections were of the highest order. His words have proved an inexhaustible mine of spiritual truth and light for eighteen centuries in every branch of the Christian Church. But the extant writings of the Fathers of the first two centuries, to say the least, shew no trace of the existence among them of such a personage as would be thus required, on the theory that the Epistle is not St Paul's. It seems needless to say more, unless to remark that a very deliberate fabrication is inconceivable, on any reasonable moral theory, in the case of a writer who was at once of a high type of mental character and emphatically earnest in the inculcation of absolute truthfulness.

Chapter 4

IN WHAT SENSE WAS THE EPISTLE ADDRESSED TO THE EPHESIANS?

THIS question arises immediately out of the critical problem of ch. i. 1, where see the note. And the answer will be best given in the form of a discussion of that problem.

[1] M. Renan, in the Introduction to his *Saint Paul*, discusses the character and authorship of the Epistle at some length. He wavers, apparently, between the alternatives that it is a fabrication based on the *Colossians*, and that it is a letter written, under St Paul's eye, by Tychicus, or more likely Timothy, as a circular for the Asiatic churches. He does not hesitate to call it "*une Épître banale*", a very mediocre, almost a vulgar, Epistle, and to describe its style as "diffuse, nerveless, loaded with repetitions and useless words, entangled with foreign incidental matter, full of pleonasms and confusion." On the other hand he is prepared to regard it as forming, with the *Colossians*, "a pendant to the *Romans*, as a sort of theological exposition intended to be transmitted by way of circular to the different churches founded by the Apostle." (*Saint Paul*, Introduction, pp. xviii, &c.)

What, then, is the evidence, favourable and adverse, about the presence in the original Epistle, ch. i. 1, of the words "*at Ephesus*"?

A. *Evidence for omission:*

a. External:—Two uncial Gr. MSS. (only two, but both of the greatest importance) Bℵ (cent. 4), shew no trace of the words. One cursive MS. (67 of St Paul's Epp., cent. 12), as corrected by a later scribe, omits them. The reading of such copies has to be rendered, "To the saints that are, and to the faithful, &c.," or, just possibly[1], "To the saints that are also faithful, &c." Besides this MS. evidence there is much more considerable evidence for omission in the way of patristic quotations and allusions. The earliest witness (an indirect one) is *Tertullian* (cent. 2—3), who states (*adv. Marcion.* v. 11, 17) that "the heretics," i.e. the Marcionite Gnostics, certainly Marcion himself, tampered with (*interpolare*) the title, reading *To the Laodiceans* before the Epistle which the Church knew as *To the Ephesians*. This certainly suggests the high probability that copies existed in cent. 2 which did not contain the disputed words in ver. 1; and although Marcion was a ruthless and most uncritical emendator, or rather lacerator, of the Scripture text, it is not likely that he was guilty here, where the change would have served no dogmatic purpose. All that Tertullian asserts is that he changed *the title*. Would he have done this, or would Tertullian have said no more of it, if "*at Ephesus*" had notoriously stood *in ver.* 1? Again, *Origen* (cent. 3), in a fragment, quotes this verse as presenting the phrase, absolutely, "the saints that *are*," and conjectures that it indicates the truth that in Christ believers have attained *real being*, as partakers of the Life of the I AM. *St Basil the Great* (cent. 4) alludes to the shorter reading as "handed down by those before us," and as "found by himself in the more ancient copies." And he remarks on the absolute phrase in the same sense as Origen's, and perhaps with allusion to his opinion. To the same interpretation *St Jerome* (cent. 5) alludes in his

[1] This is suggested in the admirable statement of the case in Westcott and Hort's *N. T. in Greek*, II. 124. But surely the improbability is great.

commentary on the verse, describing it as more recondite (*curiosius*) than was necessary. In the context, indeed, he says that some think the reading to be "to them that are *at Ephesus*." But St Jerome's received text must have run otherwise.

These facts leave the impression, on the whole, that an uncertainty, to say the least, attached very early and very widely indeed to the two words. Renan boldly says, " The words ἐν Ἐφέσῳ were inserted towards the end of cent. 4" (*Saint Paul*, Introd., p. xvi).

And to turn now to

b. Internal Evidence: it is plain that the Epistle does not bear an Ephesian destination on the face of it. Only one Christian's name occurs, Tychicus (vi. 21), besides St Paul's own. The salutations are of the most general kind, and the topics of the Epistle the highest and least local. The obvious connexion of the contents with those of the Colossian Epistle, and the name Tychicus in both Epistles, fix the destination to Roman Asia, but scarcely to a narrower area. This phenomenon is the more noticeable when St Paul's peculiarly intimate and prolonged relations with Ephesus are considered. And the suggestion has been made accordingly[1] that the Epistle is a Circular, an Encyclical, designed perhaps for the Churches of Asia Proper, if not for a wider range; and that we have a probable allusion to it in Col. iv. 16, where observe the wording, "The Epistle" not "*to*," but "*from*, Laodicea;" a phrase well suited to a circular upon its round. If so, it is suggested, the letter may have left Rome with an unfilled blank, so to speak, after the words "*which are*," a blank which Tychicus would fill up for various Churches as copies were made and carried to them. And the pre-eminence of Ephesus in its Province would readily explain how the address "*to Ephesus*" in one copy, or some copies, came to be thought the sole address of the Epistle.

B. *Evidence for retention:*

a. External:—Every known MS. (in its uncorrected form), save two, reads "*at Ephesus*." So does every ancient Version (the oldest Syriac version is of cent. 2), a most important class of

[1] First by Abp Ussher (cent. 17), *Annales N. T.*, A. M. 4068.

witnesses in a case like this. Every known MS. again, without exception, reads "*To the Ephesians*" as the *title* of the Epistle, and though this does not carry direct proof higher than early in cent. 4, it practically proves a much older tradition; a tradition, as we have already seen, which to Tertullian appeared to be broken only by Marcion's "tampering." And it is most remarkable that no hint appears anywhere, unless in the case of Marcion's opinion, that the Epistle was ever claimed by any other Church, or by the collective Churches of Asia. As against the suggestion that St Paul, designing the Epistle to be an Asiatic Circular, left out the name of any Church in the very place where in other Epistles a name is found, it may fairly be asked whether it is not far more likely that he would have written, in such a case, "*in Asia*," or, "*in the Churches of Asia*." Cp. 2 Cor. i. 1; Gal. i. 2.

b. Internal:—Here we can say little but what is negative. Some may find a local reference to the Ephesian *Temple* in the great passage at the close of ch. ii. But surely to the Hebrew Apostle's mind one Temple, and one only, the House of the Messiah's Father at Jerusalem, would be allowed to suggest such imagery in such a connexion. And this apart, there is literally no trace of "local colouring." But on the other hand, the very greatness of the Ephesian Church and the vast area of the influence which St Paul had exerted from it (Acts xix.) lessen the unlikelihood that he should have dealt wholly with the highest and most permanent topics while yet, in the first place, addressing Ephesus.

One interesting piece of evidence on this side, halfway between the external and internal, may be seen in the long and remarkable Epistle to the Ephesians, written (about A.D. 110) by the martyr St Ignatius. Several passages in that Epistle read like allusions to St Paul's Epistle, and, if so, raise some probability that this Epistle was regarded by Ignatius as written *to Ephesus.* We subjoin the Ignatian passages which seem to us to be fairly in point[1].

[1] See further Bp Lightfoot's *Ignatius* &c. vol. II. pp. 15—89; and on an important passage in St Ignatius' Epistle, ch. xii. see above, p. 23.

(1) Ch. i. "Ignatius...to the Church blest in greatness, by the fulness (*plerôma*) of God the Father, predestinated before the worlds (*aiônes*) to be always unto abiding and unchangeable glory, joined in one and chosen in the true Passion in the will of the Father and of Jesus Christ our God, &c." Cp. generally Eph. i. 1—11, iii. 19, &c.

(2) Ch. ix. "[Ye are] stones of the temple, prepared beforehand for the abode of God the Father, &c." Cp. Eph. ii. 22.

(3) Ch. xiii. "In peace is annulled all war of *celestial* and terrestrial enemies;" i.e., apparently, Christian concord is an antidote to the attacks of *evil spirits* and evil men. The word here rendered "celestial" is the same as that rendered "heavenly," Eph. vi. 12; see note there.

(4) Ch. xv. "Let us do all things as (remembering that) He dwelleth in us, that we may be His temples and He may be the God in us." Cp. Eph. iii. 17.

(5) Ch. xvii. "The Prince of this world (*aiôn*)." Cp. Eph. ii. 2.

(6) Ch. xx. "I will further expound to you the dispensation (stewardship) concerning the New Man, Jesus Christ." Cp. Eph. i. 10, iv. 24, and notes in this latter place. To us this Ignatian passage is confirmatory of the reference there (advocated in those notes) to Christ as the "New Man."

(7) *Ibid.* "Ye all meet together in one faith and in one Jesus Christ." Cp. Eph. iv. 5.

On reviewing the evidence, it is plain that the true theory must embrace the phenomena, on the one hand, of a very early variation in the reading of i. 1, and of the non-local tone of the Epistle; on the other hand, of the universal tradition of its destination to Ephesus, and the immense documentary evidence for it, and the total absence of any serious rival claim. In constructing such a theory it will be useful to remember, what is indicated by the *Acts*, that the City stood in the closest possible relation to the Province, both politically and in regard of St Paul's three years' work (see above, pp. 10—12). Ephesus, more than many another Metropolis, may well have represented its Province to the writer's mind.

We believe that the facts are fairly met by the view that St Paul actually addressed the Epistle, in its first words, "to the saints that are at Ephesus," but designing it also for the other Asian Churches, and that the transcripts dispersed through the Province frequently omitted this precise original address accordingly, but without introducing any other. It was well understood to be the property of Ephesus, but in trust for the Province.

See further on Col. iv. 16. We have there a very probable reference to this Epistle; but it will be better to discuss the question there.

Chapter 5

PARALLELS BETWEEN THE EPISTLE TO THE EPHESIANS AND THE EPISTLE TO THE COLOSSIANS

THE parallelism of the two Epistles can be fully appreciated only through the comparative study of both the details and the whole of each ; a study which will also bring out many important differences between the points of view and modes of treatment in the two. In the following table all that is offered is a view of the chief doctrinal parallels, and a few out of the very many instances of parallelism of subject, or expression, not necessarily connected with doctrine.

1. *Christ the Head of the Church:*
        Eph. i. 22, iv. 15, v. 23=Col. i. 18, ii. 19.
This view of the Lord's position and function is practically confined to these Epistles.

2. *Christ supreme over angelic powers:*
        Eph. i. 21 = Col. ii. 10.

3. *The Church Christ's Body:*
        Eph. i. 23, iv. 12, v. 23, 30, &c. = Col. i. 18, 24.

4. *Articulation and nourishment of the Body:*
        Eph. iv. 16 = Col. ii. 19.
The imagery is peculiar to these Epistles.

5. *Growth of the Body:*
   Eph. iv. 16 = Col. ii. 19.

6. *The Body one:*
   Eph. ii. 16, iv. 4 = Col. iii. 15.

7. *Christians once dead in sin:*
   Eph. ii. 1, 5 = Col. ii. 13.

8. *Once alienated from God and grace:*
   Eph. ii. 12, iv. 18 = Col. i. 21.
The Greek verb is confined to these Epistles.

9. *Once in darkness:*
   Eph. iv. 18, v. 8 = Col. i. 13.

10. *Now risen with Christ:*
    Eph. ii. 6 = Col. ii. 12, iii. 1.
The Greek verb is confined to these Epistles.

11. *Made alive with Christ:*
    Eph. ii. 5 = Col. ii. 13.
The Greek verb is confined to these Epistles.

12. *Reconciled through the Death of Christ:*
    Eph. ii. 13—16 = Col. i. 20, 21.
The Greek verb is confined to these Epistles.

13. *Redeemed, in the sense of pardon of sin, in Christ:*
    Eph. i. 7 = Col. i. 14.
The exact phrase is peculiar to these Epistles.

14. *In the light:*
    Eph. v. 8, 9[1] = Col. i. 12.

15. *Rooted in Christ:*
    Eph. iii. 17 = Col. ii. 7.
The Greek verb is confined to these Epistles.

16. *Built up as a structure:*
    Eph. ii. 20 = Col. ii. 7.

17. *On a foundation:*
    Eph. iii. 17 = Col. i. 23.

18. *Spiritually filled:*
    Eph. i. 23, iii. 19, v. 18 = Col. i. 9, ii. 10.

[1] See note on ver. 9.

19. *The Fulness:*
      Eph. i. 23, iii. 19 = Col. i. 19, ii. 9.

20. *The Old Man and the New Man:*
      Eph. iv. 22—24 = Col. iii. 9, 10.

21. *Similar classes of sins reproved:*
      Eph. iv. 2, 3 = Col. iii. 12—14.
      Eph. iv. 25, v. 5 = Col. iii. 5—8.

22. *The wrath of God coming:*
      Eph. v. 6 = Col. iii. 6.

23. *The duties of home enforced, in the same order and similar words:*
      Eph. v. 22–vi. 9 = Col. iii. 18–iv. 1.

24. *The Walk of sin:*
      Eph. ii. 2, iv. 17 = Col. iii. 7.

25. *The Walk of holiness:*
      Eph. ii. 10, iv. 1, v. 2, 8, 15 = Col. i. 10, ii. 6, iv. 5.

26. *Redemption of opportunity:*
      Eph. v. 16 = Col. iv. 5.

The phrase is peculiar to these Epistles.

27. *Spiritual songs:*
      Eph. v. 19 = Col. iii. 16.

This precept is peculiar to these Epistles.

28. *Prayer and intercession:*
      Eph. vi. 18 = Col. iv. 2.

29. *The Mystery revealed:*
      Eph. i. 9, iii. 3, 4, 9, vi. 19 = Col. i. 26, 27, ii. 2, iv. 3.

30. *Riches:*
      Eph. i. 7, 18, ii. 7, iii. 8, 16 = Col. i. 27, ii. 2.

31. *Ages and generations:*
      Eph. iii. 21 = Col. i. 26.

"Generation" occurs, in St Paul, only in these Epistles and the *Philippians.*

32. *The word of truth:*
      Eph. i. 13 = Col. i. 5.

33. *Character and commission of Tychicus:*
      Eph. vi. 21 = Col. iv. 7.

Many other parallels, more or less exact, can be collected. Meanwhile it will be observed, from the above table, that the distribution of the points of likeness is, so to speak, complicated and capricious in many instances. A study of this phenomenon will fully refute the conjecture (see pp. 23, 24) that the Ephesian Epistle is an elaborate and artificial expansion of the Colossian, by a personator of St Paul.

Chapter 6

THE CHARGE OF ST PAUL TO THE EPHESIAN ELDERS: THE
EPISTLES TO TIMOTHY: THE APOCALYPTIC EPISTLE TO
THE EPHESIAN ANGEL

IN the Milesian Charge (Acts xx. 18—35) a few similarities of expression to the Ephesian Epistle may be traced:

α. "*With all lowliness of mind:*"

Acts xx. 19 = Eph. iv. 2.

The precise phrase does not occur elsewhere.

β. *The Divine counsel:*

Acts xx. 27 = Eph. i. 11.

The word "counsel," with reference to the Divine Plan, occurs nowhere else in the Pauline Epistles (not reckoning Heb. vi. 17).

γ. *Divine ability:*

Acts xx. 32 = Eph. iii. 20.

δ. *Building upon:*

Acts xx. 32 = Eph. ii. 20.

ε. *The inheritance of the saints:*

Acts xx. 32 = Eph. i. 14, 18.

The two Epistles to St Timothy (dated by Dr Howson A.D. 67, A.D. 68, respectively) are in a sense Epistles to Ephesus, for the recipient was the Apostle's delegate there for superintendence of doctrine, life, and organization. But it is difficult to trace any distinct resemblances in these Epistles to the surroundings indicated in our Epistle, except in the probable allusions (1 Tim. i. 4, vi. 20) to the growth of Judaic Gnôsis (see above, ch. ii.). Doctrinal parallels with our Epistle can be seen here and there; e.g. 2 Tim. i. 9, 10, ii. 1. But they are scarcely significant.

In the Epistle to the Ephesian Angel (Rev. ii. 1—7) we may perhaps trace a reference not to our Epistle but to its spiritual purpose, in the words, "Thou hast left thy first love." In no Pauline Epistle is the experience of the Divine Love, and its result in the saint's walk of love, so fully in view as in the Ephesian. It may not be wholly fanciful to see in this searching reproof of the glorified Lord a word specially appropriate to the Church where, a generation before, such teaching and such experience had had a special place. See further, p. 14.

Chapter 7

ARGUMENT OF THE EPISTLE

CH. I. 1—2. PAUL, a divinely commissioned messenger of Jesus Christ, greets the Christians of Ephesus, invoking blessing on them from the Father and the Lord Jesus Christ.

3—14. He gives adoring thanks to God the Father, as he contemplates the origin and issues of the salvation of the Church; its possession of all the gifts of Divine Love in Christ, consequent upon a pre-mundane Choice and Appointment to acceptance and adoption in Him, and secured by the possession in Him, as the atoning Sacrifice, of actual Redemption, in the sense of Remission. This Divine Plan and Work is now at length unveiled to the illuminated minds of the saints, who are permitted to know that Christ is the predestined Head of a Church one and universal, the crown of the purposes of God; in which Church both writer and readers have now found their appointed place, on their way to the consummation in which God will be glorified in those who shall have believed. In Christ the Ephesians now thus stand, having entered into union with Him by faith, faith verified by the presence of spiritual gifts; yea, by that Holy Spirit Himself who is the pledge of the full and glorious realization of Redemption.

15—23. In view of such position and possessions, and of the good report of the Ephesians' actual life in Christ, he prays incessantly for a development in them of Divine light, love, and hope; especially, that they may enter more deeply into the eternal prospect, the sequel of present grace, measuring its glorious hope by the power exercised in the Resurrection of their Lord, raised by the Father from the dead to the supreme Throne itself, there to preside with absolute lordship over all angelic powers for ever, to be the universal Conqueror, and to be Head of the living organism of His true Church, His Body, filled in all its parts with Him, and itself, with Him, the embodiment of the ideal of the grace of God.

Ch. II. **1—10.** [As an example of the ways of grace, he dwells on the regeneration of the Ephesians in particular.] They once were spiritually dead, following the tendencies of fallen humanity and the leading of the great personal Evil Spirit, master of an invisible system of evil agencies, and powerful still in men who reject God. Yes, such had been the position of the writer and the readers; they had lived willingly the life whose law [in the true analysis] is self, (whether manifested in grosser modes or not), and they had stood exposed, by the very condition of their nature [antecedent to all outcome in act] to the Wrath of God. Thus once spiritually dead, they had been raised by an act of sovereign love, and not raised only, but, (in virtue of their life and interest in the now ascended Christ,) exalted to the sphere of glory, and destined to be monuments of eternal kindness in the great ages to come. Gratuitous indeed that Kindness is! Salvation, including the faith that accepts it, is the *gift* of God. The believer, in his new life in Christ, is God's creation; and his path of service is altogether God's plan.

11—22. This wonderful salvation is most wonderful of all, in view of the antecedent position of the Ephesians as non-Israelites. Pharisaic contempt for "the uncircumcised," [however false in spirit,] was yet an index of the fact that apart from incorporation into Israel there is no true connexion with the commonwealth, the covenant, the hope, the life, of God. This connexion has been now effected for them, by their incorporation into Christ, the great Covenant Sacrifice. He has brought Jew and Gentile together, in Himself, in one developed and true Israel, [the old Israel and yet another,] one New Race; annulling the ancient antipathy by altering the relations of both parties to the Law through His atoning Death, and by uniting them to Himself the Risen Lord, the Messenger of peace [with one another, because of peace with God]. Through Him equally, with equal gifts and graces of the Spirit, they now approach the Eternal as His covenant children. The Ephesian believers are no mere resident aliens [in the mystic Jerusalem], but lawful citizens at home. They are integral parts in the great Temple of the true Church, based on apostolic doctrine, and held together in living coherence by Jesus Christ as the great angle-stone [in which the lines of structure meet]; Him, in vital contact with Whom the whole vast building, ever rising, ever more profoundly cohering, prepares for its eternal destiny as the Sanctuary of the Presence of God. Into such a structure the Ephesians are being incorporated, and for such a purpose, under the Spirit's power.

CH. III. 1—13. [The Apostle is about to dilate on the Divine Indwelling in the spiritual Temple, but the mention of his commission to the *Gentiles* leads him to a digression.] He appeals to the acquaintance of his readers with his special work as an inspired and empowered "steward of the mystery" already indicated, the secret long kept, now at last revealed, of the full and true incorporation of Gentile believers into Christ (Messiah) and His Promise. Yes, entirely unworthy in himself, he has yet been chosen to unfold to the Gentiles the labyrinth of the wealth of Christ ; to throw the broad light of a mighty proclamation on the now ample distribution of the long-hidden blessings of the world-wide Gospel; a distribution designed to illustrate even to the angelic world, in accordance with the great progressive Plan of Redemption, the Divine wisdom [in its dealings with the problem of human sin]. In Christ that Plan is embodied, and we Christians, actually, in Him, are examples of it in respect of our freedom of spiritual access to God.

In such a heraldry the herald may well be content to suffer. Let not the Ephesians, then, deplore Paul's persecutions and captivity. Rather, these things are "their glory," [as proving that God willingly spends on their incorporation the sufferings of a chosen servant].

14—19. And now, [returning to the imagery of Temple and Shechinah,] he tells them of his prayer to the One Father of the great spiritual Family. It is that He would apply His Divine resources, in granting to them, by the immediate action of the Holy Spirit, power to welcome into their hearts, without reserve, evermore, Christ as the Indweller ; [power personally to accept all that His Presence means];

and this, in order that they may be able, resting on and rooted in the Love of God, to grasp, in the sense of a new realization, the illimitable greatness of that Love, the Love of Christ, which eternally transcends the knowledge it invites; and that they may thus be *ful*-filled with grace and God.

20—21. [The special treatment of the great Theme of the In-dwelling closes with] an ascription of praise to Him who is supremely ABLE, with an ability indicated already in experience by the life of regeneration, to do things in the soul which pass all actual articulate prayer and thought. To Him, for His glory manifested in the Church and in His Son, be all thanksgiving through all developments of the eternal Future !

CH. IV. **1—16.** [He has hitherto dealt with spiritual facts and principles concerning the True Church, as in themselves. Now, without leaving them behind, or closing all further exposition of them, he comes to their application in the life and walk of the saints.] Let the first result of this transcendent salvation be a course of entire unselfishness, gentleness, and love, and of watchful resolves not to break up the spiritual unity of the Church by the opposite temper. This holy Unity pervades their new life and position everywhere; they form one Organism, animated by One Divine Spirit, with one glory in prospect, belonging to One Master, united to Him by one quality of faith, faith verified by one baptismal Seal ; children of One Divine, supreme, all-immanent Father. Of this great Truth the other side, [equally needful to a life of holy unity,] is the diversity of endow-ments and works. This diversity is divinely suggested in the prophetic Psalm (lxviii.) which depicts [in its ultimate import] the Messiah's largess of gifts after conflict and victory; (a passage whose wording suggests, in passing, the truth of the Descent of the Redeeming King in order to His infinite Ascent and His Omnipresence as actual Redeemer). What were those gifts? They were regenerated men, commissioned and qualified for ordered work for Him, apostles, pro-phets, evangelists, pastor-teachers, [different from each other per-sonally and officially in very many ways, and] designed to work above all things for the equipment of the saints in general for *their* [varieties of] active service, in the doing of which lies one great means to the growth of the mystic Body. For the developed life and activity of the members will ever promote that of the Body, in its progression towards the eternal maturity [of the glorified state], in which CHRIST will be all that is intended by that great word—the Head and the Members alike perfect and perfectly one for ever. [On the way to this, the unity in diversity of active spiritual life will secure] that the disciples shall not stand exposed, in childish weakness, to every shifting fashion of delusive teaching, but with a holy and loving instinct for Divine truth shall ever deepen their communion with their Head, the Vital Source from which, through contact of each with It, (such is the life-power of the Head, ministered to the varied receptacles of the Limbs,) the Body derives its secret of ever-developing coherence and growth, in the atmosphere of the love of God.

17—25. [Again to come to the point of practice;] their daily life is to break away for ever from the old unregenerate line, the line of moral and resulting mental delusion, in which the Divine Life was lost in the guilty blindness of fallen nature and whose manifestation in act had been the terrible surrender of the man to willing wickedness. The Ephesians, in their conversion, had learned far other principles in learning CHRIST, JESUS CHRIST, the holy Embodiment of all reality. In His school they had learnt the truth of a spiritual break of con- nexion with the "Old Man"; [in other words, that they had quitted the position of condemnation and spiritual impotence proper to the morally decaying member of the First Adam, and had taken the position of acceptance and of spiritual victory proper to the living and developing member of the Second Adam;] a divestiture of the "old self" and its status and an investiture of a "new self" and its status—that self whose Basis and whose Ideal is He who is the personified Righteousness and Holiness of His own Gospel.

25—32. [Such being their position and possessions, let them put them into action. Let their acceptance, life, and union, in Christ come out in] mutual truthfulness, entire avoidance of unhallowed wrath, strictest honesty, total abstinence from polluting words, and uniform pure and helpful use of speech, lest the Holy Comforter, their Seal of final glory, should be grieved. All displays of anger, all self-asserting claims, all evil-speaking, all malice, are to be decisively ejected from their lives. They are to shew themselves always kindly, sympathetic, mutually forgiving, after the glorious Pattern of HIM Who had as a fact forgiven them, in Christ, [the Reason and the Sphere of Divine Forgiveness].

CH. V. **1—14.** Of such a God, as His true born children, let them be imitators. And let their life be one of self-sacrificing love, after the example of the Saviour whose love led Him to the supreme sacrifice of atoning Death. And, of course, let all *gross* transgressions be banished from their very lips; impure act, and impure word, however witty. Lovers and doers of such things have no part in the kingdom of Redemption. No, let falsehood say what it will, for such sins the wrath of God is on its way to visit the impenitent. Let them make sure of exemption from such a doom, by making sure of holiness. Let them walk in the new-found light, and bear its pure, sound fruit; testing everything by the touchstone of God's will; and not only avoiding the darkness and its unnamable shame, but exposing it, in the contrasted light of Christ. Nothing less than that light is needed in order to the rescue of [the victims of] darkness. They become light only when found by light. And so runs the prophetic word; "Arise—shine—awake."

15—21. Let them be in earnest, then, in the details of life: spending watchfulness to purchase opportunity for good; cultivating in practice a sanctified intuition into God's will. Let them avoid indulgence in wine, but seek the "calm excess" of a life which is lived in the Spirit, and in which the Spirit lives. Let them use for their musical expression of truth and joy [not the songs of the reveller but] the rich varieties of holy psalm, song, and ode, employed in spiritual truth. Let them meet God's will, expressed in circumstances, with unvarying thanksgiving. Let them, [with the sweet instinct of the thankful,] be ever yielding to one another.

22—32. [And now, to come to the grand, primary, special instance —the Christian Home, the sphere in which above all the spirit of the Gospel of unity in Christ must have its way.] Let the *wife* thus ever yield, in the Lord, to the *husband's* headship, after the great example of the Church's subjection to Christ, her Head, in the supreme Matrimonial Union; (He being the very Saviour of the mystic Body). And let the *husband* love the *wife* after the Lord's own perfect example; with a love akin to that with which He gave His life for her, in order to her holy separation to Himself in the New Birth, signified and sealed by the baptismal Rite [of the New Covenant]; and in order ultimately to the Bridal Festival of Eternity, when He shall welcome her in her sinless glory to Himself. Yes, with love kindred to this let the husband love. Let the wife be seen to be part of his very body, claiming a no less tender and instinctive care; for so cares the Lord for us His Church, for us His limbs, us, who derive from Him our true being [as veritably as did the Primal Woman derive her physical being from the Primal Man]. To this His union with us mysteriously pointed the words of Genesis, about the man's leaving parents to be joined to bride. Great is this revealed secret, this Archetype of every true marriage, this bridal Union of the Lord and the Church, and her derivation, as to second life, from Him. But [to sum up the matter of such marriage and its holy duties], let the husband love the wife with entire devotion, and the wife see that she reverence the husband.

CH. VI. 1—4. [Next among the relations of Home stands that of *child and parent*.] Let Christian children, as members of Christ, obey their parents as a sacred duty, a duty emphasized by the Promise of the Fifth Commandment. And let Christian parents temper with sympathetic kindness their sacred office of discipline and warning.

5—9. [Last comes the relation between *servant and master*.] Let the Christian servant, [and now especially, as the prominent case at Ephesus,] the Christian slave, obey his earthly master with conscientious care and holy singleness of aim, not only when watched, or in hope of gain, but as recognizing and loving the will of God in the hourly task, and as looking for the heavenly Master's impartial "Well done" hereafter. And let the Christian master, as the slave of Christ, laying the old harsh ways aside, be as faithful to the slave's interests as he asks the slave to be to his.

10—20. And now to sum up the whole teaching of the Epistle, [including the practical directions for common life just given,] let the Ephesians *use* the vast resources of spiritual strength secured to them by their union with Christ. Let them, [as if for the first time,] arm themselves completely with these resources against the crafty Enemy [whose great aim is to dislodge the believer from his vantage-ground]. Yes, our conflict, hand to hand, is with no mere human foes. We have to deal with the princes and marshals of the dark spiritual Empire of the Unseen. Let the Ephesians, then, take up the panoply of God, that they may stand, and still stand, in each crisis of the strife. Let them *gird* themselves with spiritual reality; put on the *cuirass* of loyalty to the will of God; *sandal* their feet, for foot-hold, with the calm certainty of peace [with Him and in Him]; meet every assault with the *shield* of simplest reliance on Him, thus quenching, as it were, before they can wound, the fire-arrows [of polluting or doubting thought]; receive [from the Lord's hand], as a *helmet*, the fact of deliverance [in Him from doom and sin], and, as the *sword* of the Spirit's forging, the inspired Word of God. And let spiritual prayer, in every variety of its exercise, be their constant practice, followed up with persevering watching; especially let them use intercessory prayer for all their fellow Christians, and not least for the Apostle, that he may deliver with more freedom of utterance than ever the revealed Secret whose chained ambassador he is.

21—22. And now to conclude. The Ephesians, as well as Paul's other converts, must be kept informed of his position; and Tychicus, so well known as a devoted Christian labourer, is on his way to report on this and to encourage them.

23. So may the Divine gift of love, with that of faith, from the Father and the Son, be on the Ephesian brethren. Yea, let the grace of Christ be with all, everywhere, who love Him in the reality secured by the gift of the life of God. Amen.

The Epistle to the Ephesians...is one of the divinest compositions of man. It embraces every doctrine of Christianity;—first, those doctrines peculiar to Christianity, and then those precepts common to it with natural religion.

S. T. COLERIDGE, *Table Talk.*

The Epistle to the Ephesians embraces, in its brevity, the whole field of the Christian religion. It expounds now its doctrines, now its morals, with such conciseness and such fulness combined that it would be difficult to name any great doctrine, or any essential duty, which has not its place marked in this Epistle.

ADOLPHE MONOD, *Explication de l'Épître aux Ephésiens,* Introduction, p. i.

There shall arise from my seed in the latter times one beloved of the Lord, hearing upon earth His voice, shedding the light of new knowledge upon all the Gentiles...And unto the consummation of the ages he shall be, in the synagogues of the Gentiles and among their rulers, like a musical strain in the mouth of all, and shall be recorded in holy pages, both his work and his word, and shall be the chosen of God for ever.

TESTAMENTS OF THE TWELVE PATRIARCHS
(cent. I or 2), '*Benjamin*', ch. xi.

COMMENTARY ON EPHESIANS

Paul, an apostle of Jesus Christ by the will of God, to 1
the saints which are at Ephesus, and to the faithful in

TITLE

The oldest known form is the briefest, To (THE) EPHESIANS. So
in the "Subscription" to the Epistle, which see. The title as in the
Authorized Version agrees with that adopted in the editions of the
Greek Testament printed (1624, 1633), at Leyden by the brothers
B. and A. Elzevir.

CH. I. 1—2   GREETING

1. *Paul*] See Acts xiii. 9 for the first occurrence of this name
of the Apostle. He probably bore, from infancy, both the two names,
Saul (*Saoul, Saulus*) and *Paulus*, the first as a Hebrew home-name,
the latter for use in the Gentile world. Paulus (Paul) would thus
naturally become the prevalent name during the Christian life-work of
the bearer.

an apostle] Lit., **an envoy, a missionary**; in the Gospels and Acts
always in the special sense of an immediate Delegate from the Saviour;
except perhaps Acts xiv. 14, where Barnabas bears the title. In Rom.
xvi. 7 the sense is perhaps more extended; certainly so in 2 Cor. viii. 23.
It always, however, in N. T., designates at least a *sacred* messenger,
not excepting Phil. ii. 25, where see note in this Series. St Paul
needed often to insist on the fact and rights of his apostleship in the
highest sense of the word; 1 Cor. ix. 1, 2; 2 Cor. xii. 12; Gal.
i. 1.—See further, Appendix F.

of Jesus Christ] **Of Christ Jesus** is the order in many documents.
The sacred name (JESUS) and title (CHRIST) occur *together* in the
Gospels five times, in the Acts often, in the Epistles perpetually. It is
most important to remember that *Christ* is merely the Greek version of
the Hebrew *Messiah* (*Anointed*). In the N. T. it thus constantly refers
back to O. T. prophecy and to the truth (uttered by the Messiah
Himself, John iv. 22), that "salvation is of the Jews."

2 Christ Jesus: grace *be* to you, and peace, from God our Father, and *from* the Lord Jesus Christ.

by the will of God] So, in the same connexion and position, 1 Cor., 2 Cor., Col., 2 Tim. In 1 Tim. (and Tit. i. 3) we have "according to the commandment" of God. See Gal. i. 1 for the deep certainty of a direct Divine commission which underlay such a phrase in St Paul's mind. He *knew* himself to be "a vessel of choice, to bear the name" (Acts ix. 15) of his Lord.

saints] **Holy ones**; persons possessed of holiness, separated from sin to God. It is true that this is "the language of charitable presumption" (Pearson, *Exposition of the Creed*, Art. IX); when a community is thus described, St Paul does not thereby positively assert that each individual answers the description. But observe that this presumptive use of the word "saint" does not lower the true sense of the word, so as to make it *properly* mean, e. g., *merely* a member of a Christian community, a possessor of visible Church privileges.

which are at Ephesus] "Some very ancient authorities omit *at Ephesus*" (margin of Revised Version). On the question thus raised, see *Introduction*, ch. iv.

and to the faithful] I.e. "the saints," under a different aspect. For the word as used, of Christian believers, see Acts x. 45 ("the faithful of the circumcision"); xvi. 1 ("a faithful Jewess"); 2 Cor. vi. 15 ("the faithful with the unfaithful," i.e. the believer with the unbeliever); Col. i. 2; 1 Tim. iv. 3 ("them who are faithful and know, &c.), iv. 12 ("the faithful"), v. 16 ("any faithful man or faithful woman"), vi. 2 ("faithful," i.e. Christian, "masters"); Tit. i. 6. These and similar passages, and the contrast of the word "unfaithful" (*infidelis*, infidel), shew that as a designation of Christians it means not trustworthy but trustful; *full of faith*, in the Christian sense. On its application to the community, see on "saints," above.

in Christ Jesus] See, for parallels to this all-important phrase, Rom. viii. 1; 1 Cor. xv. 18; 2 Cor. v. 17, &c. And compare the Lord's language, Joh. vi. 56, xiv. 20, xv. 2—7; and the illustration given by e.g. Eph. v. 30. The "saints and faithful" are regarded as *solidaire* with their Lord, in respect both of inseparable interest, holy dearness, and oneness of spirit (1 Cor. vi. 17); specially the latter. The Epistle itself is a large comment on the phrase.

2. *Grace* be *to you, and peace*] So in the opening words of Rom., 1 Cor., 2 Cor., Gal., Phil., Col., 1 Thess., 2 Thess., Philem., 1 Pet., 2 Pet., and Rev. In the Pastoral Epistles, and in 2 John, the remarkable addition "mercy" appears; in Jude, "mercy, peace, and love." In these salutations, "Grace" is all the free and loving favour of God in its spiritual efficacy; "Peace" is specially the complacency of reconciliation with which He regards His people, but so as to imply also its results *in* them; repose, serenity of soul; spiritual happiness, in the largest sense. See further on vi. 23, 24 below.

from God our Father] To St Paul God is the *Pater Noster* of Christians, in the inner sense of their union by faith with His Son.

Blessed *be* the God and Father of our Lord Jesus Christ, 3
who hath blessed us with all spiritual blessings in heavenly

The Scriptures, while not ignoring a universal Fatherhood of God
towards mankind, always tend to put into the foreground the Fatherhood and Sonship of special connexion; that of covenant, of grace, of
faith. Among many leading passages see, in N. T., Joh. i. 12; Rom.
viii. 14, &c.; Gal. iii. 26; 1 Joh. iii. 1, 2.

and from *the Lord Jesus Christ*] He, equally with His Father, is
the Giver of eternal blessing, and the Lord of the soul. Incidental
phrases of this kind form a testimony to the Proper Deity of the
Saviour weightier, if possible, than even that of direct dogmatic
passages. They indicate the drift *of the main current* of apostolic
belief. See further on iii. 19 below.

3—14 ASCRIPTION OF PRAISE, IN VIEW OF THE ELECTION AND REDEMPTION OF THE SAINTS

3. *Blessed* be *the God*, &c.] The same Benediction occurs (verbatim
in the Greek, nearly so in A. V.), 2 Cor. i. 3; 1 Pet. i. 3. Observe
the different motive of the same phrase in each case.—The word rendered "Blessed" occurs eight times in the N. T., and always of a
Divine Person. In Mar. xiv. 61 "The Blessed" appears without an
explicit Name, as often by the Rabbis.

For the sacred Formula "the God and Father of, &c." cp. further
Rom. xv. 6 (where the Greek, though not the A. V., is the same);
and see Joh. xx. 17; Heb. i. 8, 9; and note below, on ver. 17.

who hath blessed us] Better, **Who blessed us**. The reference is to
the heavenly world and the eternal purpose of God towards the saints.
See just below, on *"before the foundation*, &c." This Benediction on
the New Creation may be illustrated by that on the Old; Gen. i. 22,
28, ix. 1. It is the utterance (in whatever way) of a fixed Divine
purpose of good. "When we bless God, we speak well of Him; when
He blesses us, He powerfully confers blessings on us" (Scott). "*Us*":—
the members of the New Race; "the saints and faithful;" those who
"are Christ's."

with all spiritual blessings] Better, **with** (lit. **in**) **all spiritual blessing.**—"*Spiritual:*"—the Benediction supremely affected the "*spirit*"
of its objects, not merely their externals. It bore upon their *spiritual*
Birth (Joh. iii. 6); Life (Rom. viii. 9, 10); and Consummation (Rom.
viii. 11; 1 Cor. xv. 44).

in heavenly places] Lit., "*in the heavenlies*"; an adjective without a
noun. So below, ver. 20, and ii. 6, iii. 10, vi. 12. The noun is
rightly supplied in A. V. The region of utterance of the Blessing was
heaven; the eternal abode of the Covenant-Head of the blessed ones
is heaven; and the final issue of the blessing will be their own abode
there "in glory." See Heb. xi. 16. The form of the adjective suggests
not only a heavenly origin, or nature, but a heavenly locality.

4 *places* in Christ : according as he hath chosen us in him before the foundation of the world, that we should be holy

in Christ] as the Covenant-Head, Root and Source of Life, and
Representative, of the saints. Cp. 2 Tim. i. 9.

4. *According as he hath chosen*, &c.] Better, **According as He
chose,** &c. The time-reference is the same as just above; to the Divine
premundane deed of purpose.—"*Chosen*":—out of mankind. See Rom.
viii. 33 and its context for commentary on the idea of the word. The
word "elect" (chosen) is generally used in N. T. in connexions where
the highest level of Divine purposes, or spiritual privileges, is in view.
In the O. T., Israel is " My people, My chosen " (Isai. xliii. 20). In
the N. T. the chosen are "the Israel of God " (Gal. vi. 16 ; cp. Gal.
iii. 29; Rom. iv. 11). As with the Old so with the New Israel the
choice is emphatically sovereign ; "not according to our works " (2 Tim.
i. 9). On the other hand, it *takes effect through means ;* a truth perfectly
harmonious with sovereign purpose, while often conveyed in the language of ordinary contingency. Cp. 2 Tim. ii. 10; and, by way of
illustration, Acts xxvii. 22 with 31.

before the foundation of the world] For the identical phrase, cp.
Joh. xvii. 24; 1 Pet. i. 20. "*From* the foundation, &c." occurs,
among other places, Luke xi. 50; Heb. iv. 3, ix. 26, where the apparent meaning is "since the beginning of *human* time." But with the
word "before", as here, the context always suggests the highest reference;
"before *any created* being began." Cp. the parallel phrases "before
the ages (*æons*)" (1 Cor. ii. 7); "before eternal (*æonian*) times " (2
Tim. i. 9; Tit. i. 2); and see Rom. xvi. 25. Every genuine scientific
discovery of vast antiquity in material nature throws a true though faint
light on the grandeur of such words of Revelation.

that we should be, &c.] This clause, taken in itself, is of ambiguous
reference. It may bear either (1) on the intended personal spiritual *state* of
the elect, whether in this life, or in the life eternal, or in both; or (2) on
their intended *standing*, as they are viewed as "in Christ," their
Covenant Head. In the first case it would convey the undoubted truth
that the intention of the electing Father is a real and universal personal
holiness, perfect in this life in principle and motive (cp. e.g. Matt. v. 48;
below, iv. 24; Col. iii. 12; 1 Thess. v. 23; 1 Pet. i. 15, 16; 1 Joh. iii.
3, 6, 9), and, in the life eternal, in attainment (cp. e.g. ch. v. 27; Rom.
iv. 22; 1 Joh. iii. 2; Jude 24). Cp. 1 Thess. iv. 7 (where the "*call*"
closely corresponds to the "*choice*" here, as to the persons in view),
and 2 Thess. ii. 13, a remarkable parallel. In the second case the
clause would mean that the elect are to be viewed as holy and spotless
because identified, for purposes of acceptance, with their absolutely
holy Head and Representative, "in Whom" they stand. Cp. for
illustration the whole range of passages where believers are said to
have "died and risen with Christ," in respect of atonement and justification, e.g. Rom. vi. 2, &c.; Col. iii. 1, 3. (And see Article XI. of
the Church of England.) On the whole the powerful argument of
context decides the ambiguity for the *second* alternative. The thought

and without blame before him in love : having predestinated 5
us unto the adoption of children by Jesus Christ to himself,

throughout this passage is of the relation of the elect to Christ as
their Head and Representative in the pre-mundane Covenant of the
Father and the Son. We may explain accordingly, "that we should
stand, in the judgment of eternal and absolute Holiness, accepted
and satisfactory because united to Christ." Such a truth is only one
aspect, but an all-important one, of the great Truth of Salvation.

in love] I.e., in the embrace of that Divine Love which gave, and
sustains, our position (1 Joh. iii. 1). If we connect "in love" with
the words previous (as A. V.), and explain those words as above,
this must be the meaning. Many expositors, however, ancient and
modern, and the important Peshito Syriac Version (cent. 2), connect
"in love" with the words *following;* "in love having predestinated, &c."
So margin, R.V. But the cadence of the Greek is in favour of the
ordinary connexion.—In questions of punctuation in the Greek Testament it must be remembered that the oldest MSS. are scarcely punc-
tuated at all, and the decision must rest accordingly with grammar,
context, or the like.

5. *Having predestinated us*] Again an aorist, not a perfect, in the
Greek; referring to a definite past act. For the same word, in the
Greek, cp. ver. 11; Acts iv. 28 (E. V. "determined "); Rom. viii. 29,
30; 1 Cor. ii. 7 (E. V. "ordained "). It is lit. "to define, mark out,
set apart, beforehand." All idea of *blind destiny* must be excluded;
the "pre-ordination" is the act of the Living and Holy God. But
while we can thus repose upon its justice, it is none the less sovereign.
And it is a cause, not an effect, of good desires and holiness in the
saints.

the adoption of children] For the (one) word rendered thus, cp. Rom.
viii. 15, 23, ix. 4; Gal. iv. 5. The sacred truth of the *filial* relation of
the saints to their Lord's Father (see above on ver. 2) comes out further
iii. 15, iv. 6, v. 1. This sonship has two aspects in the N. T. ; the
generative aspect, a change in the state of will, character, nature, a new
birth; and, as here, the *adoptive* aspect, a divinely legal institution into
filial position and privilege. In the eternal Idea this latter may be
said to be first in order; and thus it stands here, in this account of the
heavenly origin of our salvation.

by Jesus Christ] Lit., **through Jesus Christ**; Representative and
Mediator. As in the Old Creation (see e.g. Joh. i. 3, "all things came
into being *through Him*" ; and cp. Heb. i. 2) so in the New, the Father
works through the Son, Whom He "gives," "anoints," "sanctifies,"
"sends."

to himself] As the Father is the Origin of the process of Redemption, so He is continually presented as its End. See the Lord's dis-
courses in St John's Gospel, *passim*, and e.g. 1 Cor. xv. 28; Phil. ii. 11.
This fact makes it on the other hand the more deeply significant that
the same language is used also with reference to the Son; e.g. below
ch. v. 27. And cp. "*for* Him," Col. i. 16.

6 according to the good pleasure of his will, to the praise of
the glory of his grace, wherein he hath made us accepted in
7 the beloved : in whom we have redemption through his blood,

according to the good pleasure &c.] The ultimate account of all
Divine procedure, from the creature's point of view. Nothing in that
Will is capricious; all is supremely wise and good. But it enfolds an
"unseen universe" of reasons and causes wholly beyond our discovery;
and here precisely is one main field for the legitimate exercise of faith;
personal confidence as to the unknown reasons for the revealed action
of a Known God. Cp. Matt. xi. 26; 1 Cor. i. 21. The word rendered
"good pleasure" means specially (in N. T.) deliberate beneficent
resolve.

6. *To the praise*, &c.] I. e., that the *grace* of Redemption might be
adored and *praised* in respect of that *glory* of God which is the harmony
of His attributes, His Character. See Rom. iii. 23 and note in this
Series. Possibly, but far less probably, the meaning is "that praise may
be rendered for the (coming) *glory given by* His grace."

wherein he hath made us, &c.] The tense is aorist; so that if the
A. V. is otherwise retained it should be modified **wherein He made,**
&c. But the rendering of the Greek verb is a question. It is a very
rare verb, and occurs elsewhere (in N. T.) only Luke i. 28 (A. V.
"highly favoured"). Analogy of verb-forms suggests the meaning "to
make gracious," "to *make (us) recipients of grace*," and as the "grace"
specially in view here is that of *adoption and acceptance* in Christ, the
A. V. would thus be very nearly in point, though rather as a paraphrase
than as a translation.—R. V., "which He freely bestowed on us;"
margin, "wherewith He endued us."

in the beloved] of the FATHER.—This designation of the Son (cp.
Isai. xlii. 1; Matt. iii. 17, xvii. 5; Mark xii. 6; Joh. i. 18, xvii. 24;
Col. i. 3, where lit. "the Son of His love;" &c.) is specially appropriate here, where the greatness and graciousness of salvation is in
view. Cp. Rom. viii. 32.—"The Son, loveable in Himself, is essentially *The Beloved*; we, unloveable in ourselves, are accepted because of,
and in, the Beloved; and if we are called *beloved* in our turn (ch. v.
1, &c.), it is because God sees us in His Son" (Adolphe Monod[1]).

redemption] Lit., "*the redemption*." The Greek article (often refus-
ing transference into English idiom) is here probably to be represented
by **our redemption**, as R. V.—"*Redemption :*"—this word and its Greek
equivalent point by derivation to the idea of *rescue by ransom*, whatever the ransom may be. This meaning in usage often vanishes, or at
least retires, as where in O. T. a deliverance by mere force is called a
redemption (Exod. vi. 6, &c.). But it is always ready to assert itself as
the native meaning, and certainly so here, close to the mention of the
Redeemer's *blood*. Cp. esp. Rom. viii. 24, 25; and for illustration see
Matt. xx. 28; Heb. ix. 15; 1 Pet. i. 18, 19.

The order of thought at this point descends from the pre-mundane

[1] *Explication de l'Épître aux Éphésiens* (Paris, 1867); a book often referred to in
these notes.

the forgiveness of sins according to the riches of his grace ; wherein he hath abounded toward us in all wisdom and 8

Covenant to the actual Work of Redemption; the accomplished deliverance of the saints through the Death of Christ.

through his blood] I.e. through, by means of, His *Death*, viewed as the ransom-price. Cp. for the supremely important thought, Matt. xxvi. 28; Acts xx. 28; Rom. iii. 25, v. 9; Heb. ix. *passim ;* 1 Pet. i. 18, 19; Rev. v. 9, &c.

We are now (see last note) on the level of the actual state and needs of the persons contemplated in vv. 3, &c. They are found to need *redemption,* rescue by ransom, and the ransom must be *death.* In other words, their *lives are forfeit,* for they are sinners; and a sacrificial Death is needed, and is provided. On this great subject it is enough here to say that a careful review of N. T. passages under the word *Blood* will shew that the *prevalent and leading* ideas associated with it, in religious connexions, are expiation of guilt, ransom of person, and ratification of covenant. In all these can be traced the uniting idea of forfeiture of life as the due of sin. Cp. further the great range of passages, in both O. T. and N. T., where the Death of Christ (apart from the special phrase " His *Blood*"), is seen in prophecy, history, or doctrine, as not one great Incident of His redeeming Work, but its absolute Essential.

the forgiveness of sins] Lit., **of the (our) trespasses.** See last note but one. Observe this account of Redemption ; it is Forgiveness, Remission. Not that it does not involve immensely more, both for soul (Tit. ii. 14) and body (Rom. viii. 3); but all else is so inseparably bound up with Forgiveness as its *sine quâ non,* (a fact which gives a colour of its own to all the rest,) that the *whole* is often practically identified with this great *part.* For illustration of this primary position of Forgiveness, cp. Matt. xxvi. 28; Luke i. 77, xxiv. 47; Acts ii. 38, v. 31, x. 43, xiii. 38, xxvi. 18; Col. i. 14.—"*Sins :*"—better, **trespasses,** as above. The original word, by derivation, means "a falling out"—of the way, or the like; and is occasionally used for sin or fault in its lighter aspects. But this cannot be pressed ; and very often, as here, the reference is to all kinds and degrees of sins, which are all "fallings out" of the straight line of the will of God. For this deep and universal reference of the word cp. Rom. iv. 25 ; 2 Cor. v. 19 ; Col. ii. 13. In Heb. vi. 6 the cognate verb is used to indicate very grievous sin, as apostasy. See further on ii. 1 below.

the riches of his grace] "Riches" is a frequent idea with St Paul, in reference to Divine grace and gifts. Cp. ver. 18, ii. 4, 7, iii. 8, 16 ; Rom. ii. 4, ix. 23, x. 12, xi. 12, 33 ; 1 Cor. i. 5 ; 2 Cor. viii. 9, ix. 11 ; Phil. iv. 19; Col. i. 27 ; ii. 2.

Observe in this verse the contrasted but harmonious aspects of the gift of Redemption : it flows from a Divine wealth of love and goodness; it flows through, not any channel, but the Death of Christ.

8. *Wherein he hath abounded*] Better, probably, **Which He made to abound;** at the time of manifestation and impartation, the great

9 prudence; having made known unto us the mystery of his
will, according to his good pleasure which he had purposed
10 in himself: that in the dispensation of the fulness of times

crisis of the Gospel proclamation. This time-reference is fixed by the
next verse. Ideally, and for the Church as a body, this time was *one;*
actually, for individuals, it is the time in each case of personal illumination sealed by baptism.

in all wisdom and prudence] In themselves, these words are of ambiguous reference. They may mean either that God largely exercised His
wisdom and prudence, or that He largely gave wisdom and prudence
to the saints. The context of ver. 9 favours the latter; He "made
known the mystery," in part by granting the spiritual power to read it.
The word rendered "prudence" is the same as that rendered "the
wisdom of the just," Luke i. 17; a passage in point here. It does not
occur again in N.T. On the thought and fact, cp. e.g. Jas. i. 5.

9. *Having made known*] An aorist participle. The time-reference
is to the actual revelation of the Gospel. Cp. e.g. Rom. iii. 21, xvi.
25, 26; 2 Tim. i. 10. And see last note.

unto us] the believing Church; as throughout this passage. No
special reference to St Paul, or other Apostles, is intended. The "us"
of ver. 9 must be identical with the "we" of vv. 11, 12.

the mystery] I.e., as always in N.T., a truth undiscoverable except by
revelation; never necessarily (as our popular use of the word may suggest)
a thing unintelligible, or perplexing, *in itself.* In Scripture a "mystery"
may be a fact which, when revealed, we cannot understand in detail,
though we can know it and act upon it; such a fact as that of 1 Cor.
xv. 51, where we have it revealed that an inconceivable change will
take place, at the last day, in the bodily condition of the then living
saints; a change quite beyond the inferences of reason and *also* beyond
the reach of imagination. Or it may be, as here, something much
more within our understanding. But in both cases it is a thing only
to be known when revealed. What this "mystery" is will be seen
just below.

which he had purposed in himself] Better, **which He purposed in
Him,** i.e. in the Son. The "purpose" of the Father was "in the Son,"
inasmuch as it was to take effect through the Son, incarnate, sacrificed,
and glorified; and further, as it concerned a Church which was to
be incorporated "into Christ." The whole context illustrates this
phrase. For the "purpose," cp. ver. 11; Rom. viii. 28, ix. 11; 2 Tim.
i. 9.

10. *in the dispensation,* &c.] Lit., **in view of the stewardship
of the fulness of the seasons.** The word rendered "dispensation"
is lit. "stewardship, house-management." Its special meaning here
seems to be that the eternal Son is the True Steward in the great
House of the Father's spiritual Church; and that into His hands is to
be put the actual government of it as it stands complete in the "fulness, or, fulfilment, of the seasons" (cp. for the phrase Gal. iv. 4); i.e.
in the great Age of the Gospel, in which the universality of the Church,

he might gather together in one all *things* in Christ, both which are in heaven, and which are on earth ; *even* in him : in whom also we have obtained an inheritance, being pre- **11**

long indicated and prepared for by successive "seasons," or stages, of providence and revelation, is at length a patent fact. In other words, the Father " purposed " that His Son should be, in a supreme sense, the manifested Governor and Dispenser of the developed period of grace, of which " glory " is but the outburst and flower.

gather together in one all things *in Christ*] This clause explains the clause previous; the "stewardship" was to be, in fact, the actual and manifested Headship of Christ. The Gr. may be literally represented by "that He might *head up* all things in Christ." The verb is only used elsewhere (in N. T.) Rom. xiii. 9, where A. V. reads "it is briefly comprehended," summed up. The element "head" in the compound verb *need* not appear in translation; as it does not in either A. V. or R. V. (which reads "sum up"). But the Lord is so markedly seen in this Epistle (i. 22, iv. 15, v. 23; and see 1 Cor. xi. 3; Col. i. 18, ii. 10, 19) as the Head of the Church that a special reference to the thought and word seems to us almost certain here. We render, accordingly, **to sum up all things in Christ as Head.**—"*In Christ*" will here import a vital and organic connexion; as so often.

both which are in heaven, &c.] Here, and in the close parallel, Col. i. 20, the context favours the reference of "all *things*" to the subjects of spiritual redemption who are in view through the whole passage; not explicitly to the *Universe*, in the largest sense of that word. More precisely, regenerate men are specially intended by "the things on earth," as distinguished from "the things in heaven," the angelic race, which also is "made subject" to the glorified Christ (1 Pet. iii. 22, and see Col. ii. 10). The meaning here will thus be that under the supreme Headship of the Son were to be gathered, with the "elect angels" (1 Tim. v. 21), all "the children of God scattered abroad" (Joh. xi. 52); the true members of the universal Church. So, nearly, St Chrysostom interprets the passage; making the meaning to be that "both to angels and to men the Father has appointed one Head, according to the flesh, that is Christ." (He has previously explained the verb (see last note) to mean "sum up," "gather together;" but here recognizes an additional reference to the *Headship* of Christ.)—See further Appendix A.

11. *In whom also we*] "We" is not emphatic. The emphasis ("also" or "even") is on the actual attainment, not on the persons attaining. Not only was the "mystery made known to us," but we came *in fact* to share its blessing.

have obtained an inheritance] Better, **were taken into the inheritance,** made part of "the Lord's portion, which is His people" (Deut. xxxii. 9). The Gr. verb occurs here only in N. T. and not at all in LXX. In later Church language the verb was used of ordination, reception among the *clergy* (*clêros, lot*; men selected by lot).

predestinated] to this admission among the Lord's own.—On the word, see note above on ver. 5.

destinated according to the purpose of him who worketh all
12 *things* after the counsel of his own will : that we should be
13 to the praise of his glory, who first trusted in Christ : in
whom ye also *trusted*, after that ye heard the word of truth,

according to the purpose of him who worketh, &c.] The stress is
not only upon the sovereignty but upon the effectuality of the Divine
purpose. He Who supremely wills, going in His will upon reasons
which are indeed *of His own*, also in fact carries out that will; so that
with Him to preordain is infallibly to accomplish.—The Gr. verb
rendered "worketh" is a compound; lit. *"in-worketh."* The usage of
the verb warns us not to press this, but on the other hand the *"in"*
comes out more often than not in the usage. This suggests the explanation, "worketh in *us;"* a special reference of Divine power to the
process of grace in the soul and the Church. Cp. Phil. ii. 13.

12. *That we should be*, &c.] On the *time when* of this, see next
note but one, at the end.

his glory] His revealed Character, of which the Gospel of the Son
is the grand illustration; being thus "the Gospel of the glory of the
blissful God" (1 Tim. i. 11; and cp. 2 Cor. iv. 4, "the Gospel of the
glory of Christ, who is the image of God").

who first trusted in Christ] Lit. **who have** (or, **had) hoped beforehand in Christ**. *"Trust"* here nearly represents "hope" (as perhaps
quite, Joh. v. 45; Rom. xv. 12); but, unless context forbids, the reference
of hope to the *future* should always be recognized. And this is emphasized here by the "beforehand," which in the Gr. is a part of the
verb-form. What then is the precise *expectation about Christ* in view
here? It may be either (1) that of Jewish believers, as e.g. the O. T.
saints, and Symeon, &c., up to the First Advent; or (2) that of all
believers up to the Second Advent; a view of Christ specially as
the Coming One, in either case. Both interpretations find some
support in the context. If (1) is adopted, the reference will be to Jewish
believers as against Gentile, and their priority both in time and, in
a certain sense, in claim, as holders of the great Messianic Hope; as if to
say, "that we, who as Israelites had inherited and cherished that hope
before it was fulfilled, and before it was imparted to you, should be, &c."
If (2) is adopted, the reference will be to the expectant attitude of all
Christians till the Lord's Return (cp. e.g. Rom. viii. 24, 25, and note);
at which Return they, in a final sense, will "be to the praise of His
glory" (cp. 2 Thess. i. 10). To this reference we incline. The
grandeur and universality of the scope of the whole passage favours it
rather than the other; though it must not be forgotten on the other
hand that this Epistle is often specially occupied with contrasts between
Jew and Gentile.—Thus paraphrase; "That we should contribute to the
glory of God, at the appearing of Christ; welcomed then as the once
patient and expectant believers in His promise while still it tarried."

13. *In whom ye also* trusted] Here then (see last note) the thought
moves from the general case of Christians to the particular case of the
Ephesian Christians; *"we"* includes *"you."* The verb "trusted" is

the gospel of your salvation : in whom also after that ye
believed, ye were sealed with *that* holy Spirit of promise,

supplied by A.V. In R.V. we have :—"In Whom ye also, having heard
the word of the truth, the gospel of your salvation—*in Whom, having
also believed, ye were sealed.*" Here the second "in Whom" is treated as
the resumption and repetition of the first, and the verb "ye were sealed"
is connected with both. But a simpler explanation than either is possible ;
—"*In Whom* [*are*] *ye also, having heard,* &c." And this adapts itself
well to the repeated "in Whom"; as if to say, "In Whom you enjoy
acceptance, attained by your reception of the message of salvation; in
Whom further you experienced the special 'seal' of the Spirit"—as an
additional aspect of the privilege of union with Christ. But the grammatical difficulty does not affect the main import of the verse.

after that ye heard] Better, **on hearing**; without the strong
suggestion of *sequence* of time given by A.V. On the all-importance
of "hearing," in order to salvation, cp. Rom. x. 14. The hearing may
of course be literally with the ear, or not; but it must be the reception
ab extra of a message, no mere result of thought or aspiration.

of truth] Better, perhaps, **of the truth**; the Eternal Verity of
Christ. So often in N. T. "truth" is truth not in general but in
special; spiritual truth, Christian truth (cp. Joh. xvi. 13, where lit.
" He shall guide you into all *the truth*"); a thing in harmony, of course,
with all truth, scientific or other, but capable of being quite separately
studied.

salvation] The one place in the Epistle where the Gr. noun occurs;
another noun being used vi. 17; which see. On the threefold aspect of
"salvation" in Scripture see on ii. 5.

In whom also, &c.] Better, **In Whom moreover, on believing, ye
were sealed,** &c. The Gr. does not forbid the rendering, "*on believing
in Whom;*" but this demands an unusual construction.—The Christian
is here viewed as "*sealed in Christ;*" that is, as receiving a Divine
attestation of his union with his Lord.

"*On believing*":—better than "*after* believing," because the Gr.
does not emphasize sequence. It rather combines into one idea the
facts of the *faith* and the *seal.* In experience, the latter might markedly
follow the former; but not necessarily in the Divine ideal.

sealed] So again iv. 30; and cp. 2 Cor. i. 22. The idea of the
phrase is a double one ; attestation of reality (cp. Joh. iii. 33; Rom.
iv. 11; 1 Cor. ix. 2), and claim of property (cp. Rom. xv. 28). "The
Spirit" was at once the proof of the presence of Divine faith in
the recipient, and the mark of Divine ownership over him. The
latter view is the leading one in iv. 30. In the Fathers, the word
"seal" is a frequent equivalent for Baptism; one explanation (given by
Gregory of Nazianzus, cent. 4) being that Baptism was the "badge of
lordship;" the mark of the Lord's ownership. In the N. T. however
the reference is plainly to something usually subsequent to Baptism,
and we turn for illustration to the Acts. There we find many cases in
which baptized converts receive supernatural powers, visible (Acts viii.

14 which is the earnest of our inheritance, until the redemption
of the purchased possession, unto the praise of his glory.

18) in their effects; which gifts in 1 Cor. xii. xiv. are treated as things
preeminently (in a certain sense) *spiritual*, the work of the *Spirit*. We
find as a fact that these powers were conferred not in the ordinary
ministry of the Church but in special connexion with the Apostles; at
least, no clear case is to the contrary. So it is in Samaria (Acts viii.
14—18); at Cæsarea (x. 44—46); at Ephesus (xix. 5, 6). We do not
find e. g. Philip the Evangelist (Acts viii.) conveying these gifts.
Ananias (ix. 17) *apparently* does so to Saul at Damascus; but the circumstances in that case are unique. As a fact, the possession of Spiritual Gifts, in this sense, became early rare; a phenomenon falling in
with this limitation of conveyance. And in one remarkable passage
(1 Cor. xiii. 8) we have inspired intimation that they were *meant* to
cease. On these manifestations it will be here enough to remark that it
is impossible in all details to lay down a precise theory, for instance as
to the demarcation of the "gifts" from the "ordinary" graces of faith,
hope and love, things equally due, in their regenerate exercise, to
Divine agency; while on the other hand we soon, in observation, practically reach a point where the "gifts" and the "graces" (to use convenient though inexact terms) diverge. The connexion is always close,
for both are effects of the same Power; the difference is real, for the
"gifts" are limited by many circumstances, and are rather means to
ends than ends, while the "graces" are universal and essential in the
regenerate character, and in fact constitute that character, and are thus
true ends. Cp. especially 1 Cor. xii. 31, xiii. 1, 2, xiv. 22.

that *holy Spirit of promise*] Lit. **the Spirit of the promise, the
Holy One**; the Personal Paraclete, the great burthen of the *promises* of
the Son (Luke xi. 13; Joh. vii. 39, xiv. 16, 26, xv. 26, &c.), and of
the Father (Luke xxiv. 49; Acts i. 4, 5).

14. *the earnest*] The Gr. word is *arrhâbôn*. It appears in the
LXX. (only in Gen. xxxviii. 17, 18, 20); in the later Greek classics
(e.g. Aristotle); and in the Latin classics. It is Shemitic (Heb.
'*êrâbhôn*, Gen. xxxviii.) by derivation. See further, Additional Note,
p. 164. It probably reached the Greeks and Latins through the (Shemitic) Phenician traders. By derivation it has to do with *exchange*, and
so first means a *pledge* (the word used here by the ancient Latin versions)
to be exchanged between two parties to an agreement—first given, then
on fulfilment returned. But usage brought it to the kindred meaning of
an *earnest;* a part of a price, given as a tangible promise of the payment
of the whole in time. Thus it is defined by the Greek lexicographers.
It was used for the bridegroom's betrothal-gifts to the bride; a case
exactly in point here. In ecclesiastical Latin, prose and verse, it appears usually in the shortened form *arra*. It survives in the French
arrhes, the money paid to strike a bargain.—*Arrhâbôn* occurs elsewhere
in N. T. 2 Cor. i. 22, v. 5. There, as here, it denotes the gifts of the
Holy Spirit given to the saints, as the part-payment of their coming
"weight of glory," the inmost essence of which is the complete attain-

Wherefore I also, after I heard of your faith in the Lord 15

ment (1 Joh. iii. 2) of that likeness to their Lord which the Spirit begins and developes here (2 Cor. iii. 18). A kindred expression is *"the first-fruits* of the Spirit," Rom. viii. 23, where see note in this Series.

our inheritance] The "enjoyment fully for ever" of God in Christ; the final Canaan of the true Israel, His "heirs" because His children (Rom. viii. 17).

until] Better, perhaps (as the more usual meaning of the Gr.), **unto**; with a view to; as the spiritual means to the glorious end.

redemption] See note on ver. 7, and on Rom. viii. 23. The saints already "have redemption," in the radical sense of Acceptance, rescue from condemnation into sonship. But they still look forward to redemption, in the developed sense of actual emancipation from the last effects of sin, which is to come when the body is glorified along with the spirit.

the purchased possession] The R. V. renders *"God's own* possession." "Purchased" is an idea not necessary to the Gr. noun (though such passages as Acts xx. 28 readily suggest it as a kindred idea here), which denotes simply "acquisition," however made.—The explanatory word "God" is doubtless a true interpretation.—The noun is the same as that in 1 Pet. ii. 9, where "peculiar" means (literally from the Gr.) "intended for (His) *personal property*". Thus the thought here is not of "glory" as the "property" of the saints, but of the saints, the Church, the New Israel (cp. Exod. xix. 5; Psal. cxxxv. 4), as the property of God, to be hereafter actually "bought back" from the grave for His eternal use and pleasure.

unto the praise of His glory] Cp. note on ver. 12. Here perhaps the word "glory" has a special reference to the manifestation of the Divine Character, as the Object of praise, in the *glorified* world.

15—23. PRAYER, THAT THE SAINTS MAY FULLY REALIZE THEIR DIVINE PRIVILEGES AND PROSPECTS IN CHRIST

15. *Wherefore, &c.*]. The Apostle now passes from the adoring view of Divine Redemption to prayer that its treasures of grace may be realized in the whole experience and life of the saints. And this he does, as elsewhere (Col. i.; 2 Thess. i.) in close connexion with thanksgiving for what they had already found[1].—"*Wherefore*":—because such is the greatness of Redemption, in fact and prospect.

I also] as well as others who have you in their hearts; a touch of gracious modesty.

heard] in his Roman lodging, doubtless through Epaphras (Col. i. 7) among others.

your faith] More lit., **the faith among you**, *la foi chez vous*.

in the Lord Jesus] Reposed on and *in* Him, as an anchor in the ground. It is questioned whether "faith," "believe," &c. with the

[1] In Dean Howson's admirable *Lectures on the Character of St Paul* (Lect. IV.) it is pointed out that St Paul always, in opening an Epistle, joins prayer to thanksgiving, except in Epistles (1 Cor. ; Gal.) marked by a certain severity.

16 Jesus, and love unto all the saints, cease not to give thanks
17 for you, making mention of you in my prayers; that the

preposition "in," do not rather mean "faith, &c., *maintained in* and
by connexion with Christ." But there are passages which fully prove
the possibility of the simple meaning given above (e.g. Mar. i. 15,
where lit., "believe *in the Gospel*;" and cp. in LXX. Psal. lxxvii.
(lxxviii.) 26; Jerem. xii. 6); and in most passages where the construction occurs a remote and elaborate meaning would in the nature of the
case be unlikely.

and love unto all the saints] Cp. Col. i. 4 for an exact parallel.
Here, however, the reading is disputed. Some very important MSS.
omit "love," and R. V. reads accordingly "*the faith...which ye shew
toward all the saints*." But the external evidence for the received
reading is very strong. All the ancient Versions give it, as well as some
of the oldest MSS., and the vast majority of others. And it is internally
very much more likely than a phrase which is *without any real parallel*,
and which couples together, under closely kindred terms, "faith in"
Christ and "faith towards" Christians. And the parallel in Col. i. 4
is strongly in favour of the received reading; for though it is likely
enough that St Paul may have *omitted* in one Epistle a whole phrase
which he used in the other (as in ver. 7 above, where the Colossian
parallel omits "through His blood"), it is far from likely that he should
have *varied* the easy and obvious phrase in the one for a curiously
difficult one in the other. The true probability is that we have here an
early mistake of transcription, due to certain phenomena in the Gr.
words.

The Apostle has heard with joy of their personal trust in the Divine
Redeemer, and their consequent love to all who are His; "faith
working by love," coming out, developing itself, in a life of holy love.

It is obvious that this "love to the saints" does not negative "love
towards *all* men." But it is love of another order, love of endearment,
not only of good will; a necessary sequel of the family connexion of
the saints; "*brotherly* love." The N. T. is full of this supernatural
family affection.—See 2 Pet. i. 7 for "love" (to all men) "*added to*," or
rather "*supplied in*, love to the brethren."

16. *cease not*, &c.] For similar thanksgivings cp. Rom. i. 8; 1 Cor.
i. 4; Phil. i. 3; Col. i. 3; 1 Thess. i. 2, ii. 13; 2 Thess. i. 3, ii. 13;
Philem. 4. The thanks were literally "unceasing" in principle, and,
in practice, came out on *every* fit occasion.

making mention of you] For parallels, see the contexts of the passages
just quoted, and 2 Tim. i. 3. The phrase implies the *expression* of
individual remembrance. It might be literally "by name," or not.
How much of the Apostle's work for his converts consisted in the holy
labour of special intercessory prayer, with thanksgiving! In his Roman
lodging this was the case, perhaps, even more than ever.

The recorded prayers of St Paul form in themselves one of the richest
of Scripture studies. Most observable in them is their almost invariable
intercessory direction. He thinks of others, not of self, upon his

God of our Lord Jesus Christ, the Father of glory, may
give unto you the spirit of wisdom and revelation in the

knees.—On that which now follows Bengel remarks, "*Argumentum
precum pro veris Christianis*," "heads of prayer for true Christians."

17. *the God of our Lord Jesus Christ*] Cp. the Saviour's own words
on the Cross, "ELI, ELI" (Matt. xxvii. 46); and after Resurrection (Joh.
xx. 17), "I ascend unto...my God." See also Joh. iv. 22.—The Father
is the GOD of the Son Incarnate, in a sense which, however partially,
we may be said to understand. Hence in the two passages just
quoted, where the Death and the Resurrection of the Incarnate One
Who could not "taste death" except as Incarnate (Heb. ii. 9), are
respectively in view, the thought is specially in point ; and so also
in a passage like this, where the Saviour's exaltation *after death* is
before us. There *may* also lie in the phrase here the thought that He
is "the God of our Lord" in the sense of being the God revealed and
known through our Lord.

the Father of glory] Not merely "the glorious Father," but the
Father who is the Origin and King of all that is meant by eternal "glory."
Cp. the words "the Lord of glory" (Jas. ii. 1), used of the Son. Alford
suggests that the "glory" here involves the thought of Christ as the
true Shechinah, in whom the true glory of Godhead shines forth; who
is thus the true "Glory of God." But the suggestion, beautiful and
true in itself, appears far-fetched here. Cp. the phrase "Father of
mercies," 2 Cor. i. 3, to illustrate the interpretation above.

may give] Lit., **might give**. The writer records his object as it *was*
when he last prayed.

the spirit] R. V., "*a spirit*." The Gr. has no article, but this does
not settle the question, for (not to speak of other grammatical reasons)
the article is often omitted with well-known words, such as God,
and Christ. And in passages where certainly "*the* Holy Spirit" is
meant, we have the same omission; see esp. the LXX. of Isai. xi. 2,
where lit., "*A* spirit of God shall rest upon Him, *a* spirit of wisdom and
intelligence, &c. ;" a close verbal parallel to this passage.—The Scripture
use of the word "spirit" seems to us to favour the reference here to the
Holy Spirit. The word is rarely if ever in Scripture used in the loose
modern sense of "sentiment," "tendency," or the like, but far rather of
personal spirits—the spirit of man, in or out of the body; spirits, good
or evil, not human; and THE SPIRIT of God. And the idea of *Gift* is
deeply connected with this last, very usually betokening the impartation
to man, in whatever mode, of the Holy Spirit in His presence and
power, whether for lower effects and purposes (as e.g. Exod. xxviii. 3),
or for the highest.—Rom. xi. 8 is an exception; "God hath given them
the (or a) spirit of slumber." But even there the reference is probably
to a *personal* spiritual agent.

It may be asked, was not the Holy Spirit already "given" to these
saints? Yes, undoubtedly. But where *spirit* is concerned we must be
cautious how we insist too much on logical inferences from forms
of expression. We are not to think of the "coming" of the Spirit as a

18 knowledge of him : the eyes of your understanding being enlightened; that ye may know what is the hope of his

literal passage through space to a locality, but a manifestation of His power in human subjects in a new way. Similarly we are not to think of the "giving" of the Spirit as of an isolated deposit of what, once given, is now locally in possession. The first "gift" is, as it were, the first point in a series of actions of which each one may be expressed also as a gift. Not infrequently in Scripture spiritual processes are viewed as *beginning* at what is more precisely a point of new development.

Practically, the bearing of this passage is not greatly affected by the question of "*a*" or "*the*". The work would in any case be immediately done by the Holy Spirit, and would take the form of a developed experience in the spirit of the Christian.

in the knowledge of him] Precisely, **in full, or thorough, knowledge**; *epignôsis*, more than *gnôsis*. The same word is used, e.g. Rom. iii. 20, x. 2; Col. ii. 2; and the cognate verb, e. g. 1 Cor. xiii. 12.—The tendency of the word in N. T. usage is to denote knowledge which is not merely intellectual, but of the nature of spiritual experience.— "*Of Him*":—of the Father, to Whom similar pronouns throughout the passage plainly refer. To know HIM (in and with the Son) is the inmost secret of "life eternal" (Joh. xvii. 3; cp. Matt. xi. 27). "Philosophy, taking, as it must, man for its centre, says to him, *Know thyself*. But the inspired Word, which alone can originate with God, is alone able to say to man, *Know God*" (Monod, after Pascal).

This Divine knowledge is the region, so to speak, "*in*" which the "wisdom and unveiling" just spoken of are to grow and work.

18. *The eyes*, &c.] The Gr. grammar here is free, and difficult to analyse. We may explain it either, "[that He may grant you to be] enlightened in your eyes," or, "[grant] your eyes enlightenment." But the meaning is unmistakable, and well conveyed in A. V. For the metaphor, cp. Psal. cxix. 18; Matt. xiii. 15; Joh. xii. 40; Acts xxvi. 18; Rev. iii. 18; and see esp. 2 Cor. iii. 12—iv. 6.—The thought of ver. 17 is now illustrated and developed in detail.

understanding] Read, **heart**. The MS. and other documentary evidence is conclusive. The word is highly significant, when we remember that "heart" in Scripture includes affections without excluding intelligence. (See further on iii. 17.) The illumination is to be of that deep and subtle kind which, in the light of supreme *truth*, will shew the *affections and will* their supreme objects and attractions.

that ye may know] as the immediate effect of the illumination. Observe, they "knew" these things already. The experience in view is novel not in kind but in degree.

what] in its true essence, its "quiddity."

the hope of his calling] The eternal Prospect opened by, and connected with, the Effectual Call of Divine grace; "that blessed hope" (Titus ii. 13), resurrection-glory with the Lord. See, among the wealth of references, Psal. xvi. 9; Acts xxiii. 6, xxiv. 15; Rom. viii. 24; Col. i. 5, 27; 1 Thess. v. 8; 1 Pet. i. 3, 4; 1 Joh. iii. 2, 3.

calling, and what the riches of the glory of his inheritance
in the saints, and what *is* the exceeding greatness of his 19

"*His calling*":—the Voice of Divine Grace, prevailing upon the
will. This is the ruling meaning of "call," "calling," &c. in the
Epistles; while in the Gospels it means no more *necessarily* than the
audible invitations of the Gospel; see e.g. Matt. xxii. 14. Abp
Leighton, on 1 Pet. ii. 9, writes of the inner call: "It is an operative
word, that effects what it bids. God calls man; He works with him
indeed as a reasonable creature; but sure He likewise works as Himself,
as an almighty Creator. His call…doth, in a way known to Himself,
twine and wind the heart which way He pleaseth." See esp. 1 Cor. i.
24; and Rom. viii. 28, xi. 29.

riches] See note on ver. 7. There the "wealth" was "of grace,"
here it is "of glory." The two are of one piece, developments of one
process. In this whole passage the main reference is to the eternal
prospect, the life of the glorified. Cp. Rom. ii. 7, 10, v. 2, viii. 17—
23, ix. 23; 1 Cor. xv. 43; 2 Cor. iv. 17; Phil. iii. 21, &c.—See below
on iii. 16 for another reference of this same phrase.

his inheritance] The same word as in ver. 14, where it is "*our* inheritance". It is the same thing from another aspect. There, the
saints' "inheritance" of heavenly glory is before us; here, the state of
the glorified as the "inheritance" of the King of glory. The O. T.
often describes Israel as JEHOVAH'S "inheritance;" "the people whom
He hath chosen for His own inheritance," Psal. xxxiii. 12.—In such a
phrase the special thought of "*heir*-ship" is not to be pressed; nor do
the original words, Gr. or Heb., insist upon it. That thought is always
ready, wherever context favours (as e.g. Rom. viii. 17); but the word
may import no more than actual possession, however acquired. The
Heb. word constantly means "possession," merely, and is so rendered
in A. V.

in the saints] "Amongst them;" manifested in their heavenly life.
The Gr. leaves us free to connect these words with either "riches of
glory," or "inheritance"; and we advocate the latter, as the far more
natural construction. A fair paraphrase will be, "What is the wealth of
the glory of the New Israel in the eternal Canaan, as it will be
manifested in the saints".

"*The saints:*"—see note on ver. 1. The ref. here is to the "all
saints" of the heavenly state. Not that the word "saint" is limited
to them; on the contrary, the N. T. habitually uses it of Christians
in this life. It is context here (as in 1 Thess. iii. 13) which lifts it to
the sphere of glory.

19. *And what* is *the exceeding greatness*, &c.] The Gr. word
rendered "exceeding" is, with its cognates, found in the N. T., in St
Paul's writings only; a characteristic of the ardour of his style. The
passages are Rom. vii. 13; 1 Cor. xii. 31; 2 Cor. i. 8, iii. 10, iv. 7, 17,
ix. 14, xi. 23, xii. 7; Gal. i. 13; Eph. ii. 7, iii. 19, and here.

his power] exercised in the whole work of grace and glory, from
regeneration onward to resurrection. Cp. for various aspects of its

power to us-ward who believe, according to the working of
20 his mighty power, which he wrought in Christ, when he
raised him from the dead, and set *him* at his own right

exercise, Rom. i. 16; 1 Cor. vi. 14, xv. 43; 2 Cor. iv. 7, xii. 9, xiii. 4;
Eph. iii. 16, 20; 2 Thess. i. 11; 2 Tim. i. 8; 1 Pet. i. 5. We take its
main reference here to be to the coming resurrection, believing the
whole context to refer mainly to the future, and finding a special and
suggestive mention of the Lord's Resurrection just below. But the deep
and strong continuity of process in the Divine work makes it impossible
to *restrict* the reference so. The same "power that worketh in us"
(iii. 20, see note) is that whereby we shall be glorified. See the significant words of Rom. viii. 11.

to us-ward who believe] whose "faith stands in the power of God"
(1 Cor. ii. 5), which gave it; and who, as believers, are now in a state
of *receptivity* towards that power (Mar. ix. 23); and who, by faith,
touch the "things hoped for" (Heb. xi. 1) of the blessed prospect.

according to the working of his mighty power] Lit., **according to the
working of the strength of His might**; a magnificent accumulation.
Here is the *scale* by which to measure the possibilities of the Divine
power; it is the surpassing victory of its exercise in the Lord's Resurrection. See next note; and see further, on vi. 10.

20. *which he wrought*] The verb is aorist. Another reading, but
without equal support, gives the perfect: "He *hath* wrought."—The
time-reference is to the actual past crisis of the Lord's exaltation.

in Christ] In the supreme instance of Christ. Cp. *"in me"* 1 Tim.
i. 16.—Olshausen (quoted by Bp Ellicott) remarks that this passage, with
Phil. ii. 6—11 and Col. i. 14—19, gives us "the entire Christology of St
Paul." In them we find His essential and glorious Deity; His eternal
Sonship; His immediate action in Creation; His Headship over the
created Universe; His Divine free-will in Incarnation and Humiliation;
His atoning Death, "making peace by the blood of His Cross;" His
Resurrection, and Exaltation as the Incarnate, by the Father's power;
His Headship over the Church, and animation of it with His Spirit.
See further, Appendix J.

when he raised him] I.e., in the act of raising Him. *This* was the
act of almighty power, embodying the wonders at once of a triumph
over the physical mystery of death, of the manifestation of an "eternal
redemption" from condemnation and sin, and of the ministration of the
Life of the Risen One to His people.

From another point of view the Resurrection was the act of the Son's
own will; "I have power to take it again," Joh. x. 18. But where it
is viewed as the Father's acceptance of the work of the Son, or as
the Father's testimony to Him, it is always attributed to the Father
as His act. Cp. Acts ii. 24, iii. 15, v. 30, x. 40, xiii. 30—37, xvii. 31;
Rom. i. 4, iv. 24, &c.; 1 Cor. vi. 14; Gal. i. 1; 1 Thess. i. 10; Heb. xiii.
20; 1 Pet. i. 3.

and set him *at his own right hand*] The Ascension is directly recorded only thrice (Mark xvi.; Luke xxiv.; Acts i.), but it is constantly

hand in the heavenly *places*, far above all principality, and ²¹

taken for granted and dealt with, in the Acts and Epistles, as a fact as
objective and literal as the Resurrection. Cp. Acts ii. 33, iii. 19, 20,
v. 31, vii. 55; Rom. viii. 34; 1 Cor. xv. 25; Phil. ii. 9, iii. 20; Col. iii.
1; 1 Thess. i. 10, iv. 16; 2 Thess. i. 7; Heb. i. 3 and *passim;* 1 Pet.
iii. 22; Rev. iii. 21, v. 6, &c.

"*His own right hand:*"—the glorious metaphor betokens a share *in*
the throne (Rev. iii. 21), not merely session *near* it. From eternity
the Divine Son had been "*with* God" (Joh. i. 1); "*beside* the Father"
(Joh. xvii. 5; A.V. "*with* thee"); now also as the Incarnate after Death
and Resurrection He appears in *the same* exaltation; "the *Son of Man*
at the right hand of God" (Acts vii. 55). In *this* Capacity, as well as
in that of Filial Godhead, He now "reigns;" wields "all power in
heaven and earth." And this Session, like Resurrection, is the act of
the Father's accepting and glorifying will.—Observe that in Scripture
imagery the ascended Lord is always *on* the throne; "a Priest *upon* his
throne" (Zech. vi. 13); not pleading before, but exalted upon, "the
throne of grace" (Heb. iv. 16). Cp. Ps. cx. 1, 4.

in the heavenly places] See note above on ver. 3. A Region is
spoken of, in which the glorified Lord locally is. Local conceptions,
indeed, soon fail us in thoughts of the eternal world. But the fact of
the Lord's veritable ascended *Body* binds us to them, in a real degree;
for where body is in question there also is locality.

far above] The same word as in iv. 10, and in Heb. ix. 5 (A. V.,
"over"). The Gr. does not necessarily denote *distance;* see Heb. ix.
5. But the compound form *admits* the idea, and in St Paul's style,
especially in a passage like this, we are right to see it.—The Saviour's
eminence is measured by the height of the Creator's throne above
Creation.

all principality, &c.] More strictly, **all government, and authority,
and power, and lordship.** For similar phrases cp. Rom. viii. 38; Col.
i. 16 (a close parallel), ii. 15; below, iii. 10, vi. 12; 1 Pet. iii. 22 (a
close parallel). Two thoughts are conveyed; first, subordinately, the
existence of orders and authorities[1] in the angelic (as well as human)
world; then, primarily, the imperial and absolute Headship of the SON
over them all. The additional thought is given us by Col. i. 16 that
He was also, in His preexistent glory, their Creator; but this is not in
definite view here, where He appears altogether as the exalted Son of
Man after Death. In Rom. viii., Col. ii., and Eph. vi., (quoted above,)
we have cognate phrases where *evil* powers are meant; (and see note
below on vi. 12, on the remarkable wording, "in the *heavenly* places").
But the context here is distinctly favourable to a *good* reference. That
the Redeemer should be "exalted above" powers of *evil* is a thought
scarcely adequate in a connexion so full of the imagery of glory as this.
That He should be "exalted above" the holy Angels is fully in point.
1 Pet. iii. 22 is our best parallel; and cp. Rev. v. 11, 12. See also Matt.
xiii. 41: "The Son of Man shall send forth *His* angels."

---

1 "The mighty kingdoms angelical," as S. T. Coleridge (*Omniana*) has it in a
sentence of extraordinary depth and beauty.

power, and might, and dominion, and every name that is named, not only in this world, but also in that which is to

We gather from the Ep. to the Colossians that the Churches of Asia Proper were at this time in danger from a quasi-Jewish doctrine of Angel-worship, akin to the heresies afterwards known as Gnosticism. Such a fact gives special point to the phrases here. On the other hand it does not warrant the inference that St Paul repudiates all the ideas of such an Angelology. The idea of order and authority in the angelic world he surely endorses, though quite in passing.

Theories of Angelic Orders, more or less elaborate, are found in the *Testaments of the Twelve Patriarchs*, cent. 1—2; Origen, cent. 3; St Ephrem Syrus, cent. 4. By far the most famous ancient treatise on the subject is the book *On the Celestial Hierarchy*, under the name (certainly assumed) of Dionysius the Areopagite; a book first mentioned cent. 6, from which time onwards it had a commanding influence in Christendom. (See article *Dionysius* in Smith's *Dict. Christ. Biography*.) "Dionysius" ranked the Orders (in descending scale) in three *Trines;* Seraphim, Cherubim, Thrones; Dominations, Virtues, Powers (Authorities); Principalities, Archangels, Angels. The titles are thus a combination of the terms Seraphim, Cherubim, Archangels, Angels, with those used by St Paul here and in Col. i.

Readers of *Paradise Lost*, familiar with the majestic line,

"Thrones, Dominations, Princedoms, Virtues, Pow'rs,"

are not always aware of its learned accuracy of allusion. The Dionysian system powerfully attracted the sublime mind of Dante. In the *Paradiso*, Canto XXXVIII., is a grand and characteristic passage, in which Beatrice expounds the theory to Dante, as he stands, in the ninth heaven, in actual view of the Hierarchies encircling the Divine Essence :

"All, as they circle in their orders, look
Aloft; and, downward, with such sway prevail
That all with mutual impulse tend to God.
These once a mortal view beheld. Desire
In Dionysius so intensely wrought
That he, as I have done, ranged them, and named
Their orders, marshal'd in his thought."

Cary's Dante.

and every name that is named] Cp. Phil. ii. 9, "the Name that is above every name." To the words suggestive of celestial ranks in detail, St Paul adds this more absolutely inclusive phrase, like the "any other creature" of Rom. viii. 39. "Name," in such a phrase, is, practically, state and place of dignity. Whatever such there are, and however justly recognized ("named"), the exalted Christ sits infinitely above them.

not only in this world, but &c.] Lit. **this age**, *aiôn*. The word is used in the following passages more or less kindred, Matt. xii. 32; Luke xvi. 8; 1 Cor. i. 20, ii. 6, 8, iii. 18; 2 Cor. iv. 4; Gal. i. 4; 1 Tim. vi. 17; 2 Tim. iv. 10; Tit. ii. 12. See also on ii. 2 below. The root-idea of the word is duration, a period; then, by transition, the contents or

come : and hath put all *things* under his feet, and gave ²²
him *to be* the head over all *things* to the church, which is ²³

condition of the period, an order of things. Here "this age" is the
period of mortality, probation, preparation for "the age to come," the
spiritual and eternal *régime*, the final development of "the Kingdom of
God " (1 Cor. xv. 50). All superhuman authorities recognized now,
all that may be set up and recognized then, alike are absolutely inferior
to Christ. We have here a suggestion of the truth (to which 1 Cor. xv.
28 is no real contradiction) that "of His Kingdom there *shall be no
end.*" The eternal throne will be that "of God *and of the Lamb*"
(Rev. xxii. 1, 3).

22. *and hath put*] Lit. **and did put**; at the great act of En-
thronement after Resurrection. Cp. 1 Cor. xv. 27 &c., where we have
explicit reference to Ps. cx. 1, and in a way which suggests here the
interpretation that the subjection of all things was then accomplished in
the *earnest*, but is not to be accomplished in final *act* till the "destruc-
tion of death."—The phrase here carries the thought of Christ's Lordship on from His relations to angels as their King to His attitude
towards all opposition as its Conqueror.

and gave him] "Him" is emphatic by position ; He *and no other* is
the Head.

head] A word combining the idea of exaltation with that of the
vital union necessary to an organism. The ascended Lord presides
over His Church, but more—He is to it the constant Cause and mighty
Source of spiritual vitality. "Because He lives, it lives also." Its
organization grows from Him, and refers to Him. Cp. 1 Cor. xi. 3 ;
Col. i. 18, ii. 10, 19; and below, iv. 15, v. 23. The idea, it will be
seen, appears in this precise form (the Headship of the *Body*) only in
Eph. and Col.; unless 1 Cor. xii. 21 is to be added.

over all things] I.e., immeasurably *beyond* anything else that can
seem to claim headship ; any fancied Power of quasi-philosophic
systems.

the church] This great word appears here in its highest reference,
the Company of human beings "called out" (as the word *Ecclêsia*
implies) from the fallen world into vital union with the glorified Christ.
The word occurs nine times in this Epistle (here, iii. 10, 21 v. 23, 24,
25, 27, 29, 32) and always in the same high connexion. Cp. for parallels
Col. i. 18, 24 ; Heb. xii. 23; and, in a measure, Acts xx. 28; 1 Cor.
xv. 9. As it stands here, the word rises above the level of visibility
and external organization, and has to do supremely with direct spiritual
relations between the Lord and the believing Company. In is, in fact,
(see ch. v.), "the Bride, the Lamb's Wife," of the Revelation, only
not as yet manifested in bridal splendour. It is "the called, justified,
and glorified," of Rom. viii.; "the Church of the Firstborn," of Heb.
xii.; "the royal priesthood, the people of possession," of 1 Peter.
All other meanings of the word Church are derived and modified
from this, but this must not be modified by them. "The Church
of Christ, which we properly term His body mystical, can be but

2 his body, the fulness of him that filleth all in all.   And you

one...a body mystical, because the mystery of their conjunction is
removed altogether from sense.   Whatsoever we read in Scripture
concerning the endless love and saving mercy which God sheweth
to His Church, the only proper subject thereof is this Church.
Concerning this flock it is that our Lord and Saviour hath promised,
'I give unto them eternal life, and they shall never perish, neither
shall any man pluck them out of my hand.'   They who are of this
Society have such marks and notes of distinction from all others as
are not objects unto our sense; only unto God who seeth their hearts...
they are clear and manifest" (Hooker, *Eccles. Polity*, III. 1.)   See
further Appendix B.

which is his body]   A metaphor which suggests not only vital union
with the Head, but that the will of the Head is exercised through the
members.   They are His *instruments.*—A kindred but not identical
use of the metaphor appears Rom. xii. 5; "members *one of another;*"
and 1 Cor. x. 17.   For closer parallels cp. Col. i. 24, ii. 19; and below,
ii. 16, iv. 4, 12, 16, v. 23, 30.

the fulness of him, &c.]   This mysterious phrase has been much
discussed.   On the whole the inferences have taken one or other of
two main lines.   The word "fulness" (*plerôma*), has been (1) explained to mean the *receptacle of fulness*, or *filled receptacle;* the
vehicle, so to speak, in which the resources of the grace of Christ
manifest their greatness, and which is filled by them.   Among other
pleas for this view is the fact that in some schools of the Gnosticism
which so soon followed the apostolic age the *Plerôma* was the recognized term for the *home*, or *sphere*, of the great Emanations (*Æons*)
of the Absolute Being (*Bythus*), and in one theory, of the Absolute
Being Itself also.   The word has been (2) held to mean, in all
doctrinal passages of the N. T., substantially, the ideal fulness, or
totality, of Divine attributes or graces; as certainly in Col. ii. 9.   Bp
Lightfoot (*Colossians*, pp. 323—339) discusses the word in an ex-
haustive essay.   He shews that *plerôma* cannot naturally mean
(as it has been taken to mean in some passages) *the thing which fills
a void*.   It is *the filled condition of a thing*, whether the thing be a rent
to be mended, an idea to be realized, or a prophetic plan to be "fulfilled."   He shews further that the word had acquired a technical theological meaning in St Paul's time, probably in the Palestinian schools
of Jewish thought; a meaning connected especially with the eternally
realized Ideal of Godhead; the Divine Fulness.   This Fulness resides
(by the Father's will, yet necessarily,) in the Eternal Son (Col. i. 19);
and the Son, Incarnate, Sacrificed, and Risen, is so conjoined in spiritual
Union to His regenerate Church that what is true of Him is true,
within sacred limits, of her.   As He without measure is the Fulfilment,
or Ideal, of Divine Attributes, so she in measure is the Fulfilment, or
Ideal, of Divine Graces; which are, we may venture to say, the Attributes in their reception and manifestation by the regenerate Church.
She is the Body through which is realized the Will of the Head, the

hath he quickened, who were dead in trespasses and sins;

Fulfilment in which is realized the Grace of the Head.—It will be observed that the two interpretations of the word indicated in this note have an underlying connexion. See this curiously illustrated by Bp. Lightfoot (*Colossians*, pp. 331, &c.), from the history of Gnostic theories.

that filleth all in all] The reference is to the Son, Who is in view through the immediate context. His vital connexion with His true Church is such that it not only is the Receptacle of His Divine grace, but is actually pervaded everywhere by His spiritual omnipresence. The form (middle) of the verb suggests intensity and richness of action; a power which is indeed living and life-giving.

"*All in all:*"—in other words, He is the Cause of all the holiness that is in all His members; whatever in them is filled with grace, He fills it.—It seems needless to seek a remoter meaning, as, "filleth all things (*the universe*) with all things " (Alford).

The true Church, in its glorious Ideal, which is meanwhile its proper Reality, only not yet fully manifested, is thus presented in spiritual and eternal union with its exalted Head. The Apostle is now about to descend to the special instance of the bringing into it of its Ephesian members. Cp. Col. i. 21, &c.

CHAPTER II

1—10 REGENERATION OF THE EPHESIANS, AN INSTANCE OF GRATUITOUS SALVATION

1. *And you* hath he quickened] The construction is broken, and the gap is filled by the inserted verb, inferred from ver. 5 below, where however "*we*" has taken the place of "you." Better, perhaps, **did He quicken** (as R. V.); the Gr. verb in ver. 5 being the aorist. Ideally, in their slain and risen Lord's triumph, actually, in their spiritual regeneration, "believing on His name," they had definitely received "eternal life."—The English reader will remember that in the A. V. "to quicken " means seldom if ever to excite what already lives, but to bring from death to life.

Observe here the great theme of the Church and its Head treated in the special aspect of entrance into the Body by Divine regeneration of persons. For close parallels, though they treat the matter more from the side of Christ's atoning work, cp. Col. i. 21, ii. 13; passages which, if written shortly before this, may have suggested the form of the opening phrase of this.

who were dead] Lit. **being dead**, "when you were dead;" devoid of spiritual and eternal life; see the next words. Obviously this weighty phrase needs to be read in the light of other truths; such as the existence of *spirit*, and the full presence of conscience, and of accountability, in the unregenerate. But those truths must not be allowed unduly to tone down this statement, which distinctly teaches that the

² wherein in time past ye walked according to the course of

state of the unregenerate has a true analogy to physical death; and that that analogy on the whole consists in this, that (1) it is a state in which a living principle, necessary for organization, growth and energy, in reference to God and holiness, is entirely lacking; (2) it is a state which has no innate tendency to develope such a principle of life. The principle must come to it altogether *ab extra*.—The latest researches into nature confirm the conviction that *dead matter* has absolutely no inner tendency to generate life, which must come into it *ab extra* if it is to live; a suggestive analogy.

On the doctrine of spiritual death as the state of unregenerate man, cp. ch. v. 14; Joh. v. 24; 1 Joh. iii. 14, v. 12; and see Joh. iii. 3, vi. 53. There are passages where "death" is used as a strong term to denote a *comparatively* lifeless state of the regenerate soul, needing (if it is to be escaped) not new birth, which is a thing once accomplished, but revival. But this modified sense of "death" must not be allowed to lower the absolute sense in a passage like this, with its peculiar doctrinal emphasis on the contrast of death and life. The state here described is not one of suppressed life, but of absence of life. Cp. 1 Tim. v. 6; Rev. iii. 1.

2 Cor. v. 14, sometimes quoted of spiritual death, is not in point: translate, "then did all die," and interpret of the death, representatively in Christ, of "all" at Calvary.

in trespasses and sins] Better, **in respect of your trespasses**, &c. —The Gr. construction is the dative without the preposition "in," (so Col. ii. 13); and indicates conditioning circumstances.—What is the distinction between "trespass" and "sin"? It has been held that "trespass" is more of the conception, and "sin" of the act; or again that "trespass" is more of omission, "sin" of commission. But usage forbids any certainty in such inferences. In Ezek. xviii. 26 the LXX. use the word *paraptôma* (trespass) of the sin which the "righteous" commits and in which he dies. Etymologically, it is a *fall over;* and this may be either over a pebble or over a precipice. In actual usage, however, there is a slight occasional tendency in "trespass" towards a mitigated idea of sin, a "fault," as in Gal. vi. 1; and it is possible that we have this here; as if to say, "in every form of evil-doing, whether lighter (trespasses) or heavier (sins)." But it is more probable still that the phrase is used designedly for accumulation's sake alone, without precise distinction; as if to say, "evil-doing, however described."

See Abp. Trench, *N. T. Synonyms*, under the word ἁμαρτία, &c. And above, note on i. 7.

2. *Wherein...ye walked*] The transgressions were the road, or region, of the moral "walk," i.e. the successive acts and practices of life. Contrast below, ver. 10, the region of the regenerate "walk." The Gr. verb is aorist. The whole past experience, however long, is gathered up in memory into a *point.*

the course] Lit. **the age.** But the A. V. perfectly represents the meaning. See above on i. 21.

this world, according to the prince of the power of the air,

this world] This present sinful order of things, as characterized by discord with the will of God. Cp. for the precise phrase Joh. viii. 23, ix. 39, xii. 25, 31, xiii. 1, xvi. 11, xviii. 36; 1 Cor. i. 20, iii. 19, vii. 31; 1 Joh. iv. 17; (and see Gal. i. 4, where however "world" is *aiôn*). In almost all the above passages the word (*cosmos*) will be seen clearly to mean not the physical world, (or certainly not it alone,) but the sinful human race, as now conditioned on earth. Full illustration will be found in very many passages where "*the* world," (not as here, "*this* world"), occurs, and which context will distinguish from others (*e.g.* i. 4 above) where the Cosmos of Creation is intended. The Gr. word rendered "world" in some passages of A. V. (Matt. xxiv. 14; Luke ii. 1, iv. 5; Acts xvii. 31; Rom. x. 18; Heb. i. 6, ii. 5; Rev. iii. 10, xii. 9, xvi. 14; are the most important) is different, meaning literally "the inhabited earth," and so either the Roman empire and its surroundings, or the mystic empire of the Messiah, according to context.

the prince, &c.] Lit., **the Ruler of the authority of the air**; the great Personal Evil Spirit, Satan ; whose existence, sparingly indicated in the O. T., is largely dwelt upon in the N. T. To the Lord and the Apostles he was assuredly no mere personification of evil, but an evil personality, as truly as for example "Gabriel, who stands in the presence of God," is a good personality. As such, his existence is a fact-mystery, so to speak, not greater in kind, though in degree, than that of the permitted existence of an evil man who tempts and influences others. There is a strong prejudice in our time against the recognition of the personality of Satan; but it must stand on the level of other mysteries of Revelation; and the prejudice should never be fostered by exaggeration. Some food for prejudice has perhaps been found in the grotesque terrors of medieval art and legendary demonology; but this is not Scripture, rather the deepest contrast to Scripture.—The belief of a Devil has been called (*Westminster Review*, April, 1865, in an article on the Positive Philosophy), "a thoroughly polytheistic conception;" but what excuse is there for this statement in the *Scripture* portrait of the Enemy, save the solitary and quite explicable phrase, "God of this age" (2 Cor. iv. 4)?

For St Paul's recognition of the great fact, cp. Acts xiii. 10, xxvi. 18; Rom. xvi. 20; 1 Cor. v. 5, vii. 5; 2 Cor. ii. 11, xi. 14; 1 Thess. ii. 18; 2 Thess. ii. 9; 1 Tim. i. 20, iii. 6, 7, v. 15; 2 Tim. ii. 26; and below, iv. 27, vi. 11.

"*The authority of the air:*"—"The ruler of the authority" means the chief of all that is in power, the general of subordinate governors ; an allusion to the organization of the evil spiritual world, of which much more is said below, vi. 12.—The word rendered "authority" does not necessarily mean *lawful* authority; indeed it often inclines to mean usurped or arbitrary authority. But it is authority as distinguished from mere dynamic *force.* See Bp. Lightfoot on Col. i. 13.

"*Of the air:*"—on this phrase much has been written. It here stands

the spirit that now worketh in the children of disobedience :

alone (as connected with spiritual mysteries) in the N. T., and hence is the more difficult to analyse with certainty. In studying it we must dismiss the thought (Wetstein) that St Paul is speaking "the language of Pythagorean philosophy, in which his readers were versed," or the like; no where is his tone more dogmatic. And we must seek a meaning of "air" literal and local, rather than otherwise, looking at his usage elsewhere (1 Cor. ix. 26, xiv. 9; 1 Thess. iv. 17). This however does not mean a narrow localization, or hard literality, only that "air" is not a mere figure of speech for "mystery," "darkness," or the like. On the whole we gather, as the revelation of this passage, that as earth is the present abode of embodied spirits, mankind, so the airy envelope of earth is the haunt, for purposes of action on man, of the spirits of evil, which, if not bodiless, have not "animal" bodies (cp. 1 Cor. xv. 44). Observe our Lord's use of "the *birds of the sky*" (Luke viii. 5) as the figure for the Tempter in the parable of the Sower.

Abundant illustrations of such a view may be found in quotations from classical, Jewish, and medieval literature. But it would be a hasty inference either that the Apostle *derived* his doctrine from previous extraneous sources, or that below the wildest exaggerations there lay no fact.

the spirit] This word is in grammatical apposition, in the Greek, with that rendered "power" or "authority" just before. That "authority" meant, as we have said, "those in authority," the unseen lords of evil, including their head. "*The spirit*" seems accordingly to mean, practically, "*the spirits*," summed up into one idea, and used by one central power.

that now worketh] "*Now*," as opposed to the "*then*" of its former action on those now rescued from it.—For illustrations of its "working" cp. the language used of Satan's power on Judas (Luke xxii. 3; Joh. xiii. 2, 27), and Ananias (Acts v. 3), and of his energies (through men) at a time of persecution (Rev. ii. 10). See also 2 Thess. ii. 9. The subtle power of human personal influence may well prepare us to believe in the mysterious depth, force, and variety, of Satanic influences.

in the children of disobedience] I.e., in men characterized by moral resistance to the Holy God; a "disobedience" which, whether explicit or implicit, patent or latent, marks fallen man as such. There is that in the central Ego of fallen man which is antagonistic to the true claims of *the God of Revelation*, and which waits only the presentation of those claims to come out in action.—For the phrase, **sons of disobedience,** cp. ch. v. 6, and Col. iii. 6. It is an example of the frequent Hebrew phrase, "son of," "child of," in the sense of close connexion, whether a connexion, as here, of principle and motive, or, as Luke xx. 36 ("sons of the resurrection"), and 2 Pet. ii. 14 ("children of a curse"), of result and reward.—"*Disobedience:*"—the Latin versions have *diffidentia*, unbelief; and so the A.V. renders the same word, Rom. xi. 30, 32; Heb. iv. 6, 11. But the proper meaning of the word is *resistance of the will*. This is deeply connected with spiritual unbelief, but not identical.—The same remarks apply to the kindred *verb*, which occurs Joh. iii. 36; Acts xiv. 2, xvii. 5, xix. 9; Rom. xi. 30, 31, xv. 31; Heb. iii. 18, xi. 31; places where A.V. has "believe not," &c.

among whom also we all had our conversation in times past 3
in the lusts of our flesh, fulfilling the desires of the flesh and

3. *also we all*] Better **we also all**, the "also" emphasizing the
"**we.**"—"*We all:*"—all present Christians, whether Jews or heathens
by origin. St Paul often insists on this *one level of fallen nature*,
wholly unaffected by external privilege. Cp. Rom. iii. 9, 23; Gal.
iii. 22. It is met by the glorious antithesis of *equal grace*. Cp. just
below, and Rom. i. 16, iii. 29, 39, x. 12, &c.—Observe the emphatic
statement that man as (fallen) man, whether within or without the pale
of revelation, begins as a "child of disobedience."—Observe too the
change of person, from the second (ver. 2) to the first. The Apostle
willingly, and truly, identifies his own experience with that of his
converts.

had our conversation] Lit., **moved up and down**; engaged in the
activities of life. *Conversatio* in Latin, like the Gr. word here, means
precisely this; the goings in and out of human *intercourse;* not specially
the exchange of *speech*, to which the word "conversation" is now restricted.—In Phil. iii. 20 the Gr. original is different.

the lusts of our flesh] Better, **the desires.** "Lusts" is narrowed in
modern usage to a special class of sensual appetites, but the older
English knew no such fixed restriction; see *e.g.* Psal. xxxiv. 12, in the
Prayer Book (Cranmer's) Version; "what man is he that *lusteth to
live?*" and Gal. v. 17, where the Spirit, as well as the flesh, "lusteth."—
Sinful "lusts" are thus *all desires*, whether gross or fine in themselves,
which are against the will of God.

"*Our flesh:*"—this important word, wherever it occurs in N.T. in
connexion with the doctrine of sin, means human nature as conditioned
by the Fall, or, to word it otherwise, either the state of the unregenerate
being, in which state the sinful principle dominates, or the state of that
element of the regenerate being in which the principle, dislodged, as it
were, from the centre, still lingers and is felt; not dominant in the
being, but present. (For its permanence, till death, in the regenerate,
see the implied statements of *e.g.* Gal. v. 16; Phil. iii. 3.) We may
account for the use of the word *flesh* as a symbol for this phenomenon by the fact that sin works so largely under conditions of bodily,
fleshly, life in the literal sense of those words. See further, note on
Rom. viii. 4 in this Series.

fulfilling the desires] Lit., **doing the wishes.** This (see last note)
does not mean that "we" were loose livers, in the common sense; we
might or might not have been such. But we followed the bent of the
unregenerate Ego, whatever on the whole it was.

of the mind] Lit., **of the thoughts**; in the sense generally of reflection and impression. The word is used (in the singular) *e.g.* Matt.
xxii. 37; "with all thy mind," representing the Heb. "heart" in Deut.
vi. 5; and 1 Joh. v. 20; "He hath given us an understanding." Here
probably the distinction is between sin in imagination and sin in positive
action ("of the *flesh*"); one of the many warnings of Scripture that
moral evil lies as deep as possible in the texture and motion of

of the mind; and were by nature the children of wrath,

the fallen nature. Cp. Matt. xv. 19; 2 Cor. vii. 1, and see Prov. xxiv. 9.

by nature the children of wrath] On the phrase "children of wrath" see last note on ver. 2. "By nature we were connected with, we essentially were exposed to, wrath, the wrath of God." It has been suggested that "children of wrath" may mean no more than "beings *prone to* violent anger," or even to "ungoverned *impulse*" generally. But the word "wrath" is frequent with St Paul, and in 13 out of the 20 places it unmistakably means the Divine wrath, even where "of God" is not added, and where the definite article is absent. See for passages specially in point Rom. iv. 15, v. 9, ix. 22; below, ch. v. 6; 1 Thess. v. 9. Add to this that this passage deals with the deepest and most general facts, and it is thus unlikely that any one special phase of sin would be instanced.—N. T. usage gives *no* support to the suggested explanation "ungoverned *impulse*" mentioned above. The word must mean "wrath," whether of man or of God.—Translate, certainly, with A.V. and R.V.—On the truth that the fallen being, as such, lies under Divine "wrath," see Joh. iii. 36, where "the wrath of God *remaineth* against" the soul which does not submit to the Son. Not to "possess eternal life" is to have that "wrath" for certain still impending.

And what is the Divine wrath? No arbitrary or untempered passion in the Eternal, but the antagonism of the eternal Holiness to sin; only—the antagonism of an Eternal PERSON. Von Gerlach, quoted by Monod on this verse, writes: "The forgetfulness at the present day of the doctrine of the wrath of God has exercised a baneful influence on the various relations in which man holds the place of God, and in particular on the government of the family and the state." The antithesis to the truth about it is the *dictum* of the "Absolute Religion," that "there is nothing in God to fear;" words in complete discord with great lines of revelation.

"*By nature:*"—i.e., by our unregenerate state in itself, not only by circumstances. For illustration see Gal. ii. 15, ("Jews by nature") and iv. 8, ("by nature no Gods"). Such was our state antecedent to the new process, *ab extra*, of regeneration. We have here the doctrine of "Original or Birth Sin," as given in Art IX. of the Church of England. "That which provokes the wrath of God is not only in the individual, but in the race and in the nature" (Monod). A greater mystery we could not state; but neither could we name a surer fact. "Original sin is, fundamentally, simply *universal* sin. That is the fact which is at once the evidence and the substance of it...Universal sin must receive the same interpretation that any other universal does, namely that it implies a *law*, in consequence of which it is universal. Nobody supposes that anything takes place universally by chance...we know there must be some law working in the case...What we *call* the law is a secondary question. The great thing is to see that there is a law. If all the individuals who come under the head of a certain nature have sin in them, then one mode of expressing this law is to say that it

even as others. But God, who is rich in mercy, for his 4
great love wherewith he loved us, even when we were dead 5
in sins, hath quickened *us* together with Christ, (by grace

belongs to the nature, the nature being the common property and ground
in which all meet" (J. B. Mozley, *Lectures*, ix. pp. 136, &c.). See
further, Appendix B.

even as others] Lit., **as also the rest**; the unregenerate world at
large.

4. *But God*] The Divine counter-fact now comes in, brighter for the
awful contrast.

who is rich in mercy] See note on "riches," i. 18.—The *ultimate
motive* of the work of regeneration is here given, and it is simply the
Divine Mercy. No claim or obligation is in the question, nor right
inherent in the alienated race, nor "fitness of things" in the abstract;
only the uncaused and supremely free choice of the God of mercy. Cp.
Tit. iii. 5; 1 Pet. i. 3.

for his great love, &c.] **On account of**, &c.; another aspect of the
same fact.

loved us] the New Israel, the Church. Not the Philanthropy of
God, His "love toward man" (Tit. iii. 4), but His inner and special
love, is here in view; *affection* rather than *benevolence*. The whole
context shews this.—Observe the change from *"you"* (ver. 1) to *"us."*—
For similar words regarding the Old Israel see Deut. vii. 8; "Because
the LORD loved you, &c."

5. *dead in sins*] Better, **in respect of our trespasses**. See on ver.
1, where the construction is the same.

hath quickened] **Did quicken**, i.e., bring from death to life; ideally,
when our Lord and Head rose to life; actually, when we, by faith,
were united to Him.

together with Christ] As vitally and by covenant one with Him. For
all His true "members," His Death of propitiation is as if theirs; His
Life of acceptance before the Father, and of spiritual triumph and
power, is as if theirs also. As it is to *Him* the Divine pledge of the
finished work of satisfaction, that pledge is *theirs;* as *He* appears in it
"in the power of indissoluble life" (Heb. vii. 16), *they*, "because He
lives, live also" (Joh. xiv. 19). For the phrase cp. Col. ii. 13, which
fixes the main reference to Acceptance. See accordingly Rom. iv. 25;
"He was raised again by reason of *our justification*."—Another reading, but not well supported, gives, "He quickened us together *in*
Christ."

(by grace ye are saved)] Lit. **ye have been saved**; and so ver. 8.
The verb is perfect. More usually the present tense appears, "ye are
being saved;" *e.g.* 1 Cor. xv. 2; 2 Cor. ii. 15 ("them that are being
saved; them that are perishing"); the Christian being viewed as under
the *process of preservation* which is to terminate in glory. See 1 Pet. i.
5. And again a frequent meaning of the noun "salvation" is that glory
itself, as in the text just quoted and Rom. xiii. 11. Here, where the
whole context favours such a reference, the reference is to the *complete-*

6 ye are saved;) and hath raised *us* up together, and made
7 *us* sit together in heavenly *places* in Christ Jesus: that in
the ages to come he might shew the exceeding riches of his
8 grace in *his* kindness towards us through Christ Jesus. For
by grace are ye saved through faith; and that not of your-

ness, in the Divine purpose and covenant, of the rescue of the members
of the true Church. From the Divine point of view that is a *fait ac-
compli* which from the human point of view is a thing in process, or in
expectation.—"*By grace:*"—for commentary, see the Ep. to the
Romans, esp. cch. iii. iv. and xi. 5, 6. The emphatic statement here
is due to the whole context, (so full of the thought of a salvation which
the saved could not possibly have generated, *dead* as they were,) and,
immediately, to the phrase "quickened *with Christ*," which involves
the thought of the entire dependence of their "life" on Him.

6. *and hath raised* us *up together*, &c.] Better, **did raise**, &c.—The
radical idea of *new life* is here put into more detail, as a resurrection
and ascension; the special form of the Lord's Revival.— "*Together:*"
—the Gr. grammar allows this to refer to either (1) union with *the
Church*, or (2) union with *the Lord;* (1) "as a united company," or (2)
"as united to Him." And the words just below "*in* Him," not "*with*
Him," may seem to favour the former. But the previous verse, and
Col. ii. 12, iii. 1; are strongly for the reference to Christ. His resurrection and ascension are the basis of the spiritual (as well as future
bodily) resurrection and ascension of His Church.

made us *sit together*, &c.] Our great Representative is there, "*sitting*
at the right hand of God" (Col. iii. 1). We, as "in Him," vitally
united to Him, are there also, in the sense of a supreme acceptance and
welcome by the Eternal Father, and of the sure prospect of heavenly
"glorification together [with Christ]" (Rom. viii. 17).

in heavenly places] See on i. 3.

7. *the ages to come*] All future periods of development in His Kingdom. The phrase must not be restricted to the future history of the
Church on earth; it is akin rather to the frequent formula for the eternal
future, "unto the ages of the ages," and cp. esp. Jude 25, "both now
and unto *all the ages*". "The King of the Ages" (1 Tim. i. 17) alone
knows what great "dispensations" are included in the one Eternity.

shew] to other orders of being, angelic or other. Cp. iii. 10, and
note.

exceeding riches] A phrase intensely Pauline. See on i. 7.

through Christ Jesus] Lit., and better, **in.** Vital union with the
Lord is the never silent key-note of the passage.

8. *For by grace*, &c.] The connexion of thought ("*for*") is with
the leading truth of vv. 4—7; the *gratuitous* "loving-kindness of the
Lord" in the salvation of the Church. This, we have just read, will
be the great future lesson of that salvation to the intelligent Universe;
and this accordingly is re-stated here.

This important ver., and ver. 9, are rendered lit., **For by grace ye**

selves : *it is* the gift of God : not of works, lest any *man* ₉

have been saved, by means of faith; and that, not of you—God's is the gift; not of works, that no one should boast. Here the main teaching is clear in itself, and clearer than ever as illustrated by *e.g.* Rom. iii.; Phil. iii. The salvation of the soul, and of the Church, is essentially and entirely a matter of sovereign Divine mercy in purpose and accomplishment. It is deliberately meant that no exception or reserve is to be made to that statement. But in detail, the verse presents a problem. Does it distinctly state that "faith" is the "gift of God," or does it state, more generally, that "gratuitous salvation" is the "gift of God," leaving it open whether the faith which accepts it is His gift or not? The question is largely occasioned by the construction of the Greek, in which "*that*" (neuter) does not agree with "*faith*" (feminine).—Many great expositors, Calvin at the head of them, accordingly take "that" to refer to the main previous idea, and "through faith" to be a separate inserted thought. Alford, who takes this view, states the case for it briefly and well. Nevertheless we recommend the other explanation, and for the following simple reason : the phrase "*and that*" (lit., "*and this*") is familiar in N.T. Greek to introduce an *addition of thought*, enforcing or heightening what has gone before. See 1 Cor. vi. 6, 8; "*and that* before the unbelievers;" "*and that,* your brethren;" Phil. i. 28; Heb. xi. 12, (A.V., "*and him*, &c."). But if it here refers only to the general previous idea, gratuitous salvation, it is hard to see what *new force of thought* it adds to the words "*by grace*." If on the other hand it refers to the last special statement, "*through faith*," there is a real additional point in the assertion that even the act of believing is a gift of God; for thus precisely the one link in the process where the man might have thought he acted alone, and where therefore, in St Paul's sense, he might claim to "boast," is claimed for God. Let the clauses, "and that, not of you; God's is the gift," be taken as a parenthesis, and the point of the interpretation will be clear; while the Greek amply admits the arrangement.

That "faith" *is* a matter of Divine gift is clear from *e.g.* 2 Cor. iv. 13; Phil. i. 29. Not that a new faculty of trust is implanted, but gracious manifestations—of the soul's need and the Saviour's glory—prevail upon the will to choose to repose trust in the right Object. The "gift" of faith is but one phase of the Divine action which (Phil. ii. 13) "worketh in us to will." And it may be said to be one aspect of the "gift of repentance" (Acts v. 31; 2 Tim. ii. 25), for repentance is no mere preliminary to faith; it is the whole complex "change of mind" which *includes* faith.

See Bp O'Brien's *Nature and Effects of Faith*, Note I.

9. *lest any* man *should boast*] Lit., **any one**; there is no emphasis on "man."—For the thought, cp. Rom. iii. 27, (and see iv. 2); 1 Cor. i. 29, iv. 7; Gal. vi. 14; Phil. iii. 3; in all which passages the Gr. word is the same. The Apostle is everywhere jealous for the sovereign claim of God to the whole praise of our salvation.

10 should boast. For we are his workmanship, created in Christ Jesus unto good works, which God hath before ordained that we should walk in them.

11 Wherefore remember, that ye *being* in time passed Gentiles

10. *For, &c.*] The connexion is, "works are not the antecedent, but the consequent, of your acceptance in Christ; *for* the true statement of the case is, that you were re-made, re-born, *in order to* work the will of God."

his] Strongly emphatic. "It is HE that made us, and not we ourselves" (Ps. c. 3).

workmanship] Better, **making**. The Gr. word (*poiêma*) is not akin to that rendered "works" (*erga*) in the passage, so that there is no intended *antithesis.*—"*Making:*"—i.e., He has made us what we are, members of His Son. The noun does not necessarily give the precise idea of a new "creation;" it may mean only an appointment to position. But the two, as a fact, coincide in this matter.—In Rom. i. 20 (its only other place in N.T.) the word is used of God's handiworks in nature.

created] A frequent word, in spiritual connexions, with St Paul. Cp. ver. 15, iv. 24; 2 Cor. v. 17; Gal. vi. 15; Col. iii. 10. As in the sphere of nature, so in that of grace, it means essentially the making of a new state of things, whether in a Universe or a personality; implying indeed the omnipotence which originally willed the very material into existence, but not necessarily dwelling on this; rather giving the thought of first, or new, *arrangement.*—In practice, the thought of the *sovereignty of the Worker's will* lies in the use of the word.

in Christ Jesus] The third occurrence of these words within five verses.—The Church was "created *in*" Him, in that its very existence as such depends on vital union with Him.

unto good works] Lit., "*upon good works,*" i.e., as interpreted by usage, "with a view to them." The same construction and meaning appear Gal. v. 13; 1 Thess. iv. 7 (A.V., "*unto* uncleanness); 2 Tim. ii. 14 (A.V., "*to* the subverting").

hath before ordained] Lit., and better, **did prepare beforehand**; on the ideal *occasion* of His planning the salvation and the function of His true Church. The phrase does not state, but surely implies, the happy truth that the Divine pre-arrangement so maps out, as it were, the duties and the sufferings of the saint that his truest wisdom and deepest peace is to "do the next thing" in the daily path, in the persuasion that it is part of a consistent plan for him. There are some admirable remarks in this direction in Monod's *Adieux à ses amis et à l'Église*, no. 14; "*Le secret d'une vie sainte, active et paisible*[1]".

11—22. REGENERATION OF THE EPHESIANS, AN INSTANCE OF THE EQUAL WELCOME OF GENTILES TO THE COVENANT CHURCH, THE TRUE TEMPLE

11. *Wherefore remember*] Here first the Apostle deals with the special fact of the previous Gentilism of his converts. Hitherto he has

[1] The book has been translated, as *A. Monod's Farewell.*

in the flesh, who are called Uncircumcision by that which is called the Circumcision in the flesh made by hands ; that ¹²

spoken of their regeneration, and incorporation into Christ, with regard to the state of *fallen humanity* in general ; "when *we* were dead...He quickened *us*," &c. The further element in the phenomenon now appears, that the recipients of the Epistle had been "outsiders" as regarded any explicit covenant of redemption. *In itself*, spiritual regeneration was equally gracious and sovereign for Jew and for Gentile. But as to any *previous intimations*, it must needs come with a greater surprise to the Gentile.

It is perhaps impossible in the nineteenth century of Christendom to realize fully what was the marvel in the first century of the full revelation of an equal welcome for *all nations* to the Messiah's covenant. But the fact that it was then a marvel remains a matter of permanent Divine instruction. Cp. in general on the subject Acts x. ; Rom. ii., iii., ix.— xi. ; Gal. ii.—iv.

in time passed] Lit., **once**.

Gentiles] Lit., **the Nations** ; Heb., *haggôyîm;* the races outside Israel. Rabbinic Judaism regarded them with feelings akin to those with which an old-fashioned high-caste Hindoo regards a European. Some precepts of the Talmud (though much later, in their collected form, than St Paul's day,) are fair illustrations : "It is forbidden to give good advice to a Gentile ;" "it is forbidden to cure idolaters, even for pay ; except on account of fear ;" "he that steals from a Gentile is only to pay the principal; for it is said, He shall pay double unto *his neighbour*" (McCaul's *Old Paths*, p. 17, &c.).

Meanwhile, these gross distortions had behind them the spiritual fact here given by St Paul, that "the Gentiles," before the Gospel, were on a really different level from Israel as to covenant with God in Christ. Pharisaism took a totally wrong line, but started from a point of truth.

in the flesh] Does this mean, *"physically,"* or (Rom. viii. 8; and often) *"in the unregenerate state"*? Surely the former, for the same phrase immediately below clearly refers to a physical thing, literal circumcision. Here probably the special reference is to the *absence* of the bodily mark of covenant. They were uncircumcised Gentiles, at a time when no way was yet revealed, other than that of circumcision, by which to enter into explicit covenant with God.

called Uncircumcision] Or, regarding English usage of the article, **the Uncircumcision** ; this was their *sobriquet* with the Pharisee ; often used, no doubt, by the Pharisee Saul. The lack of the bodily mark was the condemning, and characteristic, thing, supplying a short expression for a state of entire difference and alienation.

called the Circumcision] The race of the circumcised, the Jews. The point of this clause is best given by paraphrase : "So you were called by the bearers of the mark of the Abrahamic covenant, a mark divinely ordained, but spiritually valueless where there is no spiritual contact with God, and therefore, when vaunted as a title ('*called* the Circumcision') by the unspiritual Pharisee, no better than a mere

at that time ye were without Christ, being aliens from the commonwealth of Israel, and strangers from the covenants

bodily operation, ('circumcision in the flesh, wrought by hand')." The best illustration is the close of Rom. ii., where the theme is the uselessness, for spiritual purposes, of the sacramental mark in unspiritual persons. This short clause is, as it were, a condensed statement of the truths fully stated in Rom. ii. But it is quite passing here; the main point here being, not the harsh estimate of Gentiles by Pharisees, but the real difference in covenant-position which that estimate exaggerated.

made by hands] Better, **wrought by hand**. Cp. Col. ii. 11 for the antithesis, "the circumcision wrought without hands;" a thing spiritual, invisible, the covenant mark from the *Divine* point of view—regeneration of nature.—The Pharisees "called" themselves "The Circumcision;" St Paul vitiates the word of privilege, or rather their use of it, by the added words, "hand-wrought, in the flesh."

12. *at that time*] Strictly, **at that occasion**. The Gr. word habitually marks *limited* periods; though this must not always be pressed. Here possibly there is a suggestion of the *transient* period of exclusion, opposed to the long eternity of acceptance.

without Christ] **Apart from Christ**; out of connexion with the MESSIAH. Here no Pharisaic prejudice is in view, but the mysterious fact that *only* through the great prophesied Redeemer is there life and acceptance for man, and that in order to contact with Him there needs "preaching," "hearing," "believing" (Rom. x. 13, 15). Scripture does not present this fact without any relief; but all relief leaves it a phenomenon of Revelation as mysterious as it is solid.

being aliens] Lit., **having been alienated** (the same word as iv. 18; Col. i. 21); as if they had once been otherwise. So, in idea, they had been. Every human soul is (occasionally) viewed in Scripture as having been originally unfallen, and, if unfallen, then in a covenant of peace with God of which the covenant of Israel was but a type. Such a view is wholly ideal, referring not to the actual history of the individual soul, but to the Nature of which the individual is a specimen. Such popular phrases as, "we are *fallen* creatures," have this truth below them. Historically, we *begin prostrate;* ideally, we *began upright*, and have fallen.

the commonwealth of Israel] Perhaps, "*the citizenship.*" The Gr. word occurs elsewhere, in N. T., Acts xxii. 28 only (A. V., "this *freedom;*" the Roman citizenship). But the A. V. here (and so R. V.) is favoured by the word "*alienated.*" It is rather more natural to say "made aliens from a *state*," than "made aliens from *state rights.*" The two interpretations, however, perfectly coincide practically. "*Israel,*" (the Covenant-People with its special name of sacred dignity; see Trench, *N. T. Synonyms*, § XXXIX;) is viewed as an ordered commonwealth or empire under its Divine King; and to be free of its rights is the one way to have connexion with Him.—By "Israel" the Apostle here doubtless means the inner Israel, of which the outer was as it were

of promise, having no hope, and without God in the world :

the husk; see Rom. ix. 6. But he does not emphasize a distinction. Under the Old Covenant, it was generally necessary to belong, in some sense, to the outer Israel in order to be one of the inner.

strangers] The Gr. is a word familiar in *civic* connexions; non-members of a state or city.

the covenants of promise] Lit., and better, **of the Promise**, the great Promise of Messiah, according to which those who "are of the Messiah, are Abraham's seed, and heirs by promise" (Gal. iii. 29). In the light of Gal. iii. 18, we may say that the Promise is more specially of Justi-fication, Acceptance, (as in Abraham's case,) through faith, securing vital connexion with the Messiah.

"*Covenants:*"—for the plural cp. Rom. ix. 4. The reference is to the *many* Compacts, as with Abraham, Moses, Levi, David, Joshua; and *perhaps* to the New Covenant itself, as of course "connected with" the Promise.—The Promise indicated, from the first, blessings for the world, "all the families of the earth"; but these blessings were to be found only "in Abraham and his seed" (Gen. xii. 3, xxii. 18); and thus to those not yet connected with Abraham and the Messiah there was no actual portion yet in the "covenants."

having no hope] The Gr. just indicates (by its special negative particle) that this was not only so, but felt by the Gentiles to be so; "having, *as you knew*, no hope." (So, precisely, 1 Thess. iv. 13.) The deep truth of this is fully attested by classical and other heathen literature, old or modern. Aspiration and conjecture there often was, but *no hope*, in the Scripture sense; no expectation on a firm basis. A profound uncertainty about the unseen and eternal underlies many of the strongest expressions of the classical poets and philosophers. And in the special reference of "hope" here, hope of a Redeemer and a redeemed inheritance, there was (and is) a total blank, apart from revelation.—"In Hellas, at the epoch of Alexander the Great, it was a current saying, and one profoundly felt by all the best men, that the best thing of all was not to be born, and the next best to die." (Mommsen, *Hist. of Rome*, Eng. transl. Vol. iv. pt. ii. p. 586). See the thought still earlier, Sophocles, *Œd. Col.* 1224 (Dindorf).

without God] Lit., **Godless**; without true knowledge of the true God. "Gods many" were indeed, in some sense, popularly believed in ; and large schools of thought recognized a One Supreme, though often with the very faintest views of personality. But this recognition, at its best and highest, lacked some *essentials* in the Idea of the True God, above all, the union in Him of supreme Love and awful Purity. And for the average mind of ancient heathenism He "was not, in all the thoughts," as truly as the impersonal Brahm "is not" in the average Hindoo mind. See further, Appendix D.

in the world] Words which complete the dark picture. "In the world" of fallen humanity, with its dreadful realities of evil, they did not "know the only true God, and Jesus Christ Whom He had sent" (Joh. xvii. 3), and so lacked the one possible preservative and spiritual life-power.

¹³ but now in Christ Jesus ye who sometimes were far off are
¹⁴ made nigh by the blood of Christ. For he is our peace,

13. *but now*] under the changed conditions of actual and accepted
Redemption.

in Christ Jesus] In living union with the true Messiah. Just before,
ver. 12, we have "without *Christ*" merely; here, "in Christ *Jesus*."
The Messiah of Prophecy is now known as also the *Jesus* of the
Gospel.

sometimes] **Once,** as R. V. The A. V. uses a word now antiquated
in this sense, or appearing only as "sometime"—the word used here in
Wiclif's Version (1382), in "The Great Bible" (1539), and the Rhemish
Version (1582).

far off...nigh] That is, from and to the Citizenship of Israel and the
Covenants of promise; the realm, in fact, of Messiah. Cp. Acts ii. 39,
and see Isai. lvii. 19.—The thought of remoteness and nearness in
respect of *God* is of course implied, and comes out clearly in ver. 18;
but it is not the immediate thought of this passage, which rather speaks
of the incorporation of once heathen souls into the true *Israel*. But the
two views cannot be quite separated.—"Nigh" and "far" were familiar
terms with the Rabbis in the sense of having or not having part in the
covenant. Wetstein on this verse quotes, *inter alia*, the following from
the Talmud: "A woman came to R. Eliezer, to be made a proselyte;
saying to him, *Rabbi, make me nigh*. He refused her, and she went to
R. Joshua, who received her. The scholars of R. Joshua therefore said,
Did R. Eliezer put her far off, and dost thou make her nigh?"

by the blood of Christ] Lit. and better, **in the blood,** &c. To
illustrate the phrase cp. Heb. ix. 22, 25; "almost all things according
to the law are purged *in blood;*" "the High Priest entereth the Holy
Place...*in blood* not his own." Whatever the first use of the phrase, it
had thus become an almost technicality of sacrificial language, nearly
equalling *"with* (shed) blood" as the accompanying condition of
acceptable approach. It is not necessary to import into the idea here
the other, though kindred, idea of washing in blood, or even of
surrounding with a circle of sprinkled blood. The *"in"* is, by usage,
as nearly *instrumental* as possible. The sacred bloodshedding of the
Messiah's sacrificial death for His true Israel was the necessary condition to, and so instrument of, the admission of the new Gentile
members. It is the "blood *of the covenant*" (Exod. xxiv. 8; quoted
Heb. ix. 20); and cp. the all-important words of the Lord Himself
(Matt. xxvi. 28), "This is My blood *of the new Covenant*, which is shed
for many for the remission of sins."

14. *he is our peace*] *"He:"*—the glorious living Person gives its
essence to the sacrificial Work.

"Our peace:"—i.e., as the connexion indicates, the "peace" between
the Tribes of the New Israel, the Gentile and Jewish believers; such
peace that now, within the covenant, "there is neither Jew nor Greek "
(Gal. iii. 28; Col. iii. 11). The special aspect of this truth here is the
admission of the non-Jewish believer to the inmost fulness of spiritual

who hath made both one, and hath broken down the middle
wall of partition *between us;* having abolished in his flesh 15

privilege; but this is so stated as to imply the tender companion truth
that he comes in not as a conquering intruder but as a brother, side by
side with the Jewish believer, in equal and harmonious peace with
God.

who hath made both one] Lit., **Who made both things one thing.**
"Both" and "one" are neuters in the Gr. The idea is rather of positions and relations than of persons (Monod).—"*One:*"—"one thing,"
one community, or rather, one organism. (By the same word is expressed the Unity of the Father and the Son, Joh. x. 30.) In Gal. iii.
28 ("ye are all one") the Gr. has the masculine, "one [person]," "one
[*man*]," as expressly in the next verse here.

hath broken down...partition] Lit., **did undo the mid-wall of the
fence**, or **hedge.** The next verse makes it clear that this means the Law.
In Divine intention the Law was a "hedge" (Isai. v. 2) round the Old
Israel, so long as their chief function was to maintain a position of seclusion. And it thus formed a "partition" between the Old Israel and
the outer world, not only hindering but, for the time, forbidding such
fusion as the new order brought in.

It is possible that the phrase was immediately suggested by the demarcation between the Court of the Gentiles and the inner area of the
Temple.

15. *having abolished*, &c.] Lit., **The enmity, in His flesh, the law
of the commandments in decrees, annulling.** In this difficult verse
our best guide is the Ep. to the Romans, esp. vii. 1–6, viii. 2, 3,
passages very possibly in mind when this was written. See also the
closely parallel passage, Col. i. 21, 22. With these in view we may
interpret this to teach that the Lord, by His death (Col. i. 22), "in the
likeness of the flesh of sin" (Rom. viii. 3), broke ("annulled") for all
believers their condemning relations with the Law (in the highest sense
of the word Law), as a preceptive code, prescribing but not enabling,—
a code imposing absolute decrees as the absolute condition of acceptance; and thereby, *ipso facto*, brought to an end the Mosaic ordinances
with their exclusions, which existed mainly to prefigure this Work, and
to enforce the fact of its necessity, and incidentally to "fence in" the
race through whom the Messiah, as the Worker, was to come.

The passage thus teaches that Christ has "annulled" the old antipathy between Jew and Gentile, by what He did in dying. But it
cannot teach this without teaching also the deep underlying truth that
He did it by effecting relations of acceptance and peace between Man
and God; not putting aside the Preceptive Law as a thing obsolete, but
so "going behind it" in his Atonement as to put believing man in a
different relation to it, and so, and only so, removing the external hedges
of privilege and exclusion. Comparing Col. i. 21, 22, it is plain that
this greater reconciliation lies, in the Apostle's thought, behind the
lesser, though the lesser is more immediately in point.

"*The commandments in decrees*" are, doubtless, in part, the "touch

the enmity, *even* the law of commandments *contained* in
ordinances; for to make in himself of twain one new man,
16 *so* making peace; and *that* he might reconcile both unto

not, taste not," of ceremonial restrictions; but not these only.   They
are the whole system of positive edict, moral as well as ceremonial,
*taken apart from enabling motive, and viewed as the conditions of peace
with God.*
   "*The enmity, even the law* &c.," may be fairly paraphrased, "the
enmity, expressed and emphasized (under the circumstances of the Fall)
by the Law, by its existence and claims as preceptive Law."
   for to make]   **In order to create.**   "It is a new creation," 2 Cor. v.
17; where the reference is to the regenerate individual, as here to the
community of the regenerate.
   in himself]   Perhaps, **in Him.**   But the reference is in either case to
Christ, the subject of the whole context. Cp. Col. i. 16, where "*In Him
were created*" is used of the First Creation.   In both Creations, Old and
New, Christ is the Cause and Bond of being. The New Man, like
the Universe, exists and consists by vital union with Him.
   one new man]   The phrase "new man" occurs only here and iv. 24,
where see note. Here the great organism of the saints, Jew and Gentile,
is viewed as, so to speak, one Person; a view closely akin to that of the
"One Body" of Christ; 1 Cor. xii., &c.   "We are all in God's sight
but one in Christ, as we are all one in Adam" (Alford).
   The Old Race is *solidaire* with its Head, Adam, by solidarity of Nature
in itself and of standing towards God. So the New Race is *solidaire*
with its Head, Christ, in Whom, and at once, it both receives the
standing of justified acceptance for His Merits, and derives "Divine
Nature" by His Spirit.   And solidarity with the Head seals the mutual
solidarity of the members. As the Old Race is not only men, but Man,
so the New Race is not only new men, but New Man.
   so making peace]   Here, as just above, the immediate thought is of
the reconciliation of Jew and Gentile in Christ, but behind it lies the
thought of that greater reconciliation which is expressed fully ver. 18;
"access through Christ, for both, in one Spirit unto the Father;" and
just below.
   16.   *reconcile both unto God*]   The Gr. verb here rendered "reconcile"
occurs elsewhere (in exactly the same form) only Col. i. 20, 21; but a form
nearly identical occurs *e.g.* Rom. v. 10; 1 Cor. vii. 11; 2 Cor. v. 18,
19, 20.   The idea of the verb is on the whole that of the propitiation of
an alienated superior, to whom offending inferiors are, with his consent,
led back as accepted suppliants.   God (2 Cor. v. 19) "reconciled the
world unto Himself" by providing, in His Son, the Divine pacification
of the Divine displeasure against the world.   Christ "reconciles us to
God" by being and effecting that pacification.   Hence Reconciliation,
in practice, nearly approaches to both the ideas, Atonement and Justification.   The Lord, here, "*by the cross*," reconciles the Church to God;
effects its acceptance; secures the "non-imputation of trespasses" (2 Cor.
v. 19).

God in one body by the cross, having slain the enmity
thereby: and came and preached peace to you which 17
were afar off, and to them that were nigh; for through 18

"*Both*":— here in the masculine plural; both great *groups*, Jewish
and Gentile believers.

in one body] A phrase in contrast (see last note) to "both;" the two
groups become the One Body, the One Man, of ver. 15.

by the cross] The only mention of it in this Epistle. Observe here,
as consistently in the N. T., the isolation of the Lord's Death from His
Life-work, where ideas of atonement are in view; a fact most suggestive
of the doctrine that that Death was a true and proper propitiatory Sacrifice, an altar-work, and not only a supreme act of self-sacrificing sympathy
with man's need and God's holiness. For on the latter view there is no
clear line of demarcation between the Death and the self-sacrificing
Life.—Cp. the parallel, Col. i. 20 ("the blood of the Cross"), and see
above on i. 7.

having slain the enmity thereby] I.e. by the Cross, the Atoning
Death.—" *The enmity:*"—that spoken of ver. 15; immediately, that
between Jew and Gentile; ultimately (for this underlies the conditions of
the existence of that other) that between man and God (Rom. viii. 7).—
"*Slain:*"—a word chosen, instead of *e.g.* "cancelled," "abolished,"
because the work was done *through death*. What was really, in final
effect, *executed* at Calvary was the obstacle to peace; whether peace in
the sense of the harmony of redeemed souls, or peace in the sense of
reconciliation to God, the basis of the other. Cp. Col. ii. 14.

17. *and came*] from the work of the Cross, from the Grave.
"Peace" was His first word in Resurrection-life to His gathered Church
(Joh. xx. 19); and that Church was then, and not till then, sent to the
world, "far off" as well as "nigh," to be an "ambassador on behalf of
Christ" (2 Cor. v. 20), representing Him in His preaching ministry of
peace. Thus vicariously, but really, had He "come" to the Ephesians
among others.—Cp. Acts iii. 26; "God, having raised up His Son Jesus,
sent Him to bless *you;*" and, for the phrase "*preaching* peace," Acts
x. 36.

peace] The word and thought still, as before, refer immediately to
the inner harmony of the New Israel, ultimately to that Israel's "peace
with God." The next verse suggests this double reference; (1) "we
both have access &c.;" (2) "we have access *unto the Father.*"

to you...nigh] See on ver. 13. The whole phrase is from Isai. lvii.
19, "Peace, peace, to him that is far off and to him that is near, saith
the LORD" (LXX., "to *them* that are far off &c."). The Apostle im-
plicitly claims the Prophet as foretelling (whether he knew it or not)
peace in and to the New Israel.—The best reading here repeats "peace;"
"and **peace** to them that were nigh."

18. *for*] It is possible to render "*that,*" and so to make this the
substance of the message of "peace." The difference is not important.
But it is grammatically better to retain A.V. (and R.V.).

him we both have access by one Spirit unto the Father.
¹⁹ Now therefore ye are no more strangers and foreigners, but

both] Masculine plural, as ver. 16, where see note. Both the great *groups*, in all their *individual members*, have this access.

access] Better, **our introduction**; the proper meaning of the original word, reminding the accepted Christian that he owes his freedom of entrance to Another. True, the freedom is present, perpetual, and assured; but it not only was first secured by the Redeemer's work, but rests every moment on that work for its permanence. We are, thanks be to God, evermore free to and in His presence-chamber, but we are also evermore free there "*through* His Son," Who "*ever liveth to make intercession* for us."—The word occurs elsewhere Rom. v. 2; and below, iii. 12.

by one Spirit] Lit. and better, **in one Spirit**; surrounded, animated, penetrated, by the Spirit. This is undoubtedly the Holy Spirit, the Paraclete, so largely in view in this Epistle. Cp. 2 Cor. xiii. 14; 1 Pet. i. 2; Jude 20, 21; among other passages, for a similar implicit recognition of the Persons of the Holy Trinity in the Divine harmony of their actions for and relations to the saints.

"*One:*"—in contrast to the "*both.*" See Acts x. for the fact that even to Apostles after Pentecost it was still a discovery that the Holy Ghost should visit and bless Gentiles with the same freedom and fulness as Jews.

the Father] "His Father and our Father;" Joh. xx. 17. This profound word, rich in life, love, and joy, was indeed a new treasure, in its Christian sense, to "them that were afar off." No pagan mythology, or philosophy, though the *word* was not unknown to them, knew the *thing;* the Divine reality of an eternal and paternal Holy Love. To the Israelite the LORD was indeed known as "like unto a Father pitying his children" (Psal. ciii. 13); "doubtless our Father" (Isai. lxiii. 16); but even to him the word would develope into inexhaustible riches when read in the light of the Sonship of the true Messiah.

Observe that the approach of the soul is here, as always, *ultimately* to the Father. Not that the Son, and the Spirit, are not eternal and Divine; but He is—the FATHER.

19. *Now therefore ye*] He now turns direct to the Gentile believers, and rejoicingly recounts to them the actual grandeur of their privileges in grace.

no more] as you once were. See on ver. 12 above. The finished work of Christ, realized by accepting faith, has entirely broken for them the old *régime*.

strangers] "to the covenants of the Promise;" ver. 12.

foreigners] In secular matters, the word would mean a resident alien, a non-naturalized foreigner; liable to legal removal at any moment, *e.g.* on outbreak of war. If such a word were true of Gentile Christians, they would be merely *tolerated* sojourners, as it were, in the "city" of Messianic light and mercy, without any claim to abide. The glorious contrary was the case. "If they were Christ's, they were *Abraham's*

fellowcitizens with the saints, and of the household of God; and are built upon the foundation of the apostles and 20

seed, and *heirs* [of the Gospel Canaan] *according to Promise*" (Gal. iii. 29).

but] Insert, with MSS., **ye are**, after this word; an additional emphasis of assertion.

fellowcitizens] Cp. Gal. iv. 26; Phil. iii. 20 (Greek); Heb. xi. 10, 16; Rev. iii. 12, &c.

the saints] "Not *angels*, nor *Jews*, nor *Christians then alive* merely, but the saints of God in the widest sense—all members of the mystical body of Christ" (Alford). See further on the word, note on i. 1.

of the household] Members of the family, kinsfolk. So the word always means in N. T. (Gal. vi. 10; 1 Tim. v. 8; here;) and LXX. The idea is not of domestic *service*, but of the "child at home." In the deepest sense the Gentile believer, once "far off" in both position and condition, is now *at home* with his Living Father in Christ.

20. *and are built*] Better, **Having been built**; once built (aorist), by your Redeemer. The metaphor here boldly changes, from the inmates of city and house, to the structure. Possibly the element "*house*" in "household" suggested this. For similar imagery, cp. 1 Cor. iii. 9, 10; 1 Pet. ii. 4—8; Jude 20; and see Matt. vii. 24, 25. And for curious developments of the imagery here, in very early Christian literature, see St Ignatius *Ep. to the Eph.*, ch. IX, and the *Shepherd of Hermas*, 'Vision' iii. And for an application of the imagery in ancient hymnology, the hymn (cent. 8 or 9) *Urbs beata Hirusalem* (Trench, *Sacr. Lat. Poetry*, p. 311).

the foundation of the apostles and prophets] The foundation which consists of them; in the sense that their doctrine is the basis of the faith, and so of the unity, of the saints. Cp. Rev. xxi. 14; and the words spoken (Matt. xvi. 18) to Peter, "upon this rock I will build My Church." Not to enter into the details there, it is plain that the personal address to Peter is deeply connected with the revelation to and confession by Peter of the Truth of Christ. The Collect for the day of SS. Simon and Jude, constructed from this passage, is a true comment on it.

"*The apostles and prophets:*"—Who are the Prophets here? Those of the O. T. or those of the Gospel, (for whom cp. *e.g.* iii. 5, iv. 11; Acts xv. 32; and often)? For the first alternative, it is a strong plea that the O. T. prophets are always regarded in the N. T. as Evangelists before the time; cp. *e.g.* Luke xxiv. 25; Acts iii. 18, 21, 24, x. 43; Rom. xvi. 26. The last passage regards the "prophetic scriptures" as the great instrument of apostolic preaching. But on the other hand we should thus have expected "prophets and apostles" to be the order of mention. And iii. 5, giving the same phrase with distinct reference to the "prophets" *of the Gospel*, is a parallel nearly conclusive in itself in favour of that reference here. In iv. 11, again, we have the "prophet" named *next to the "Apostle"* among the gifts of the glorified Saviour to this Church; a suggestion of the great prominence and

prophets, Jesus Christ himself being the chief corner
21 *stone;* in whom all the building fitly framed together grow-

importance of the function. We take the word here, then, to mean
such "prophets" as Judas and Silas (Acts xv. 32); men, we gather,
who, though not of one office with the Apostles, shared some of their
functions; were directly inspired, on occasion, with knowledge of the
future (Acts xi. 28), and with truth of spiritual doctrine (iii. 5, and
1 Cor. xiv); and were specially commissioned to preach and teach such
things revealed. May we not probably class the non-apostolic writers
of the N. T. among these "prophets"? See further, Appendix F.

The mention of them here is in special point, because public faith
and doctrine is in question. The work of the "prophets" had,
doubtless, greatly contributed to the wide spread and settlement of the
truth of the free acceptance in Christ of *all* believers, Gentiles with
Jews. Observe that in Acts xv. 32 it is two *"prophets"* who "exhort
and *confirm"* (the Gr. word suggests precisely *settlement on a foundation*)
the Gentile believers at Antioch, in the very crisis of the conflict between
Pharisaic limits and the universality of the Gospel.

Jesus Christ himself being the chief corner stone] It is possible to
render "the chief corner stone *of it* (the foundation) being Christ Jesus;"
but far less probable. The "Himself" is almost demanded by the
separation and contrast of the supreme position of the Lord. So R. V.
—There is a slight emphasis, by position, on "*being.*"

"*The chief corner stone:*"—one word in the Gr.; found also 1 Pet.
ii. 6; where Isai. xxviii. 16 (LXX.) is quoted nearly verbatim.
Precisely, the LXX. there runs, "I lay *among the foundations* of Sion a
stone costly, chosen, chief of the corner, precious;" words which
indicate that the idea, to the Greek translators, was that of a stone
essential to the *foundation*, not in the *higher structure;* and this is
confirmed by St Peter's use of the quotation. Thus on the whole we
take the image to be that of a vast stone at an angle of the substructure,
into which the converging sides are imbedded, "in which" they
"consist;" and the spiritual reality to be, that Jesus Christ Himself is
that which gives coherence and fixity to the foundation doctrines of His
Church; with the implied idea that He is the essential to the foundation,
being the ultimate Foundation (1 Cor. iii. 11). Apostles and Prophets
reveal and enforce a basis of truths for the rest and settlement of the
saints' faith; those truths, at every point of juncture and prominence,
are seen to be wholly dependent on Jesus Christ for significance, harmony and permanence.

In the Heb. of Isai. xxviii. 16 (and so, or nearly, Job xxxviii. 6;
Psal. cxviii. 22 (Messianic); Jer. li. 26) the phrase is "stone," or
"head," of "corner," or of "prominence." See too Zech. x. 4, where
the solitary word "corner" appears to convey the same image.

21. *in whom*] In close and vital connexion with Whom. See last
note.

all the building] R. V., "*each several building;*" as if the great
Temple were viewed for the moment in its multiplicity of porches,

eth unto a holy temple in the Lord : in whom you also are 22

courts, and towers; each connected with the great bond of the sub-structure, in and on which the whole architecture was rising.—An interesting grammatical question arises over the reading here and this rendering, and will occur again iii. 15 :—does the Greek phrase, in the best attested reading, *demand* the rendering of the R. V. as against that of the A. V.? We incline to the reply that it does not. The law of the definite article (the absence of which here occasions the question) is undoubtedly somewhat less exact in the Greek of the Scriptures than in that of the classics. And this leaves us free to use (with caution) *the* context to decide problems which in the classics would be decided by pure grammar. Such a case we take this to be; and the question to ask is, does the context favour the imagery of *detail* or that of *total?* Surely the latter. The idea points to one great building, getting completed within itself, rising to its ideal. We retain accordingly the A. V. See further, next note.

fitly framed together] One word, a present participle, in the Greek. The same occurs below, iv. 16 ("fitly *joined* together"), and nowhere else in N. T. The idea is not of a completed but of a progressive work, a "framing together" of the structure ever more closely and firmly. The building shrinks into greater solidity, binds itself into more intense coherence, as it grows. The spiritual union of the saints needs but to be more believed and realized to tell more on their actual closeness of connexion.—The idea conveyed by this word, which is of course in the singular number, is (see last note) far rather that of one great building growing in internal solidity than of many buildings growing in contact.

groweth] with the perpetual addition of new "living stones" (1 Pet. ii. 5) and the resulting new connexions. Observe two distinct ideas in harmony; growth in compactness, growth in extension.

unto a holy temple] R. V., margin, "into an holy **sanctuary**." The Greek (*nâos*) is not the temple-*area* with its courts and porches (*hiëron*), but the temple-*house;* the place of the Presence.—The phrase, "unto," "into," suggests (like that in the next verse) a sanctuary not yet complete and ready for the Presence. The true Church, indeed, *is already* (1 Cor. iii. 16; 2 Cor. vi. 16; and cp. 1 Cor. vi. 19 of its individual members) "the sanctuary of the living God." But it is this as a still imperfect thing, and still imperfectly; the absolute and final in the matter is yet to come; and this will so transcend the partial and actual that it is spoken of *as if* the Indwelling were not yet. We may faintly illustrate by an unfinished cathedral, used already for Divine worship, but not yet ideally prepared for it.—See Rev. xxi. 22 for another side of truth in temple-imagery. There, in the final state, there is "no sanctuary," for God and the Lamb "are the sanctuary of" the holy City. All, absolutely all, is hallowed by Their Presence indwelling; Sanctuary and Shechinah are, *as it were,* one; and nothing is there that is not Sanctuary.

Great indeed is the conception in this passage. The saints, in their community "in the Lord," are preparing, through an Indwelling partial

builded together for a habitation of God through the Spirit.

though real, for an Indwelling complete and eternal; the two being, in continuity, one. In no mere figure of speech, their GOD already "dwells" in their bodies, and in their community; dwells there as in a Sanctuary—in manifested Light, in Peace of covenant and propitiation, in Oracle-speech of "the Spirit's witness," in eternal Life. And this precious present fact is germinating to the future result of a heavenly and everlasting Indwelling (likewise in individuals and in community), when the Sanctuary shall reflect without a flaw its Indweller's glory; when our union and communion with Him, in other words, shall be perfect, absolute, ideal. "We shall be like Him; for we shall see Him as He is."

in the Lord] The Lord Christ. We have "God" in the next verse, in a way which indicates this distinctive reference here. The imagery leaves the precise idea of the Corner Stone, to present the Lord as the living bond and principle, the secret both of growth and sanctity.

22. *you also*] He reminds them of the joyful fact that they are special examples of the general truth that "the Gentiles are fellow-heirs."

are builded] A present tense in the Greek; **are building, being builded**. It is a process; carried on in new accessions of regenerate souls, and new and deeper "framing together" of the already regenerate.

for a habitation] For the significance of "for," see remarks on "unto" in ver. 21.—The word rendered "habitation" (elsewhere Rev. xviii. 2 only) means, by its form, emphatically a permanent abode. The true idea is of the eternal Indwelling of God in the glorified Church. But this is reached through the lasting, though partial, Indwelling now. See notes above; and below, on iii. 17.

God] Not here specially Christ. The prospect is of the world where "God shall be all in all" (1 Cor. xv. 28), words which foretell no removal (God forbid) of "the Lamb" from "the Throne," but a manifestation of the Father supreme and unimaginable. Meanwhile, again, the present is the germ of that Future; "My FATHER will love him, and We will come unto him, and make Our abode with him" (Joh. xiv. 23[1]); and "ye are the temple of the living God" (2 Cor. vi. 16).

through the Spirit] Lit. and better, **in (the) Spirit**. The living Temple, in its every stone, is what it is by the immediate action of the Holy Spirit, "Who sanctifieth the elect people of God." They are thus "*in* the Spirit" (Rom. viii. 9), surrounded, as it were, by His presence and power. And so it will be, as this passage indicates, in the final state where the "pure River" will still "proceed from the Throne of" the Father and the Son. Will not the Holy Spirit's work, far from ceasing, be supremely effectual, in the world of "*spiritual bodies*" (1 Cor. xv. 44)?

We undoubtingly explain "in spirit" here to mean "in the Spirit"

---

[1] The one passage where the coming of the Father is spoken of. What awful grandeur is bestowed by this 'We' on the believer! (Note by the Dean of Peterborough).

For this cause I Paul, the prisoner of Jesus Christ for you **3**

(with A. V. and R. V.), remembering the prominence in the whole
Epistle, and not least in this part, of the subject of the Holy Spirit's
work.

Thus closes the special revelation of the plan and nature of the great
Living Sanctuary, built on the Son, by the Spirit, for the Father, to be
the scene of the manifestation of His Glory to whatsoever spectators
Eternity shall bring to see it.

Ch. III. **1—13** He would pursue the subject of the Temple,
but digresses to say more of the world-wide scope of
the Gospel

For this cause] With such a present and such a future for my reason,
motive, hope. Here begins a sentence broken immediately by a great
digression. Where is it resumed? At ver. 8, or at ver. 13, or at ver.
14? On the whole we decide for the latter, not only because the identical phrase "for this cause" recurs there, but because the thought of the
Indweller, and the Foundation (*"grounded,"* ver. 17), recurs there also.
It is thus as if the Apostle had been just about to pray that the great
Lord of the Temple might take a new (an ever new) possession of the
Edifice preparing for Him; but had been diverted, by the designation he
gives himself, to speak at large of his Gentile commission. For a
parenthesis on the like scale see the latter half of Rom. v. Such
deviations into side-fields of pregnant thought are characteristic of
some minds of high calibre; and we are never to forget that while it is
everywhere the Inspirer who speaks through the Apostle, He as truly
uses the Apostle's type of mind as He uses the Greek type of language
to be His perfect vehicle of expression.

I Paul] For a similar emphatic *Ego*, cp. 2 Cor. x. 1; Gal. v. 2;
Col. i. 23; Philem. 19. (1 Thess. ii. 18 is not quite in point, nor the
passages, Col. iv. 18; 2 Thess. iii. 17; where he speaks of his *autograph*
name.) The motive here seems to be the profound personal interest of
the Apostle in his great commission, brought to the surface by the
statement he has just made of the grandeur of its issue in the completion
of the Temple of the Universal Church. "It is I, positively I, who
am, wonderful to say, chief minister in the process." And there may
also be the emphasis of intense personal interest in the Ephesian
converts; a loving pressure, so to speak, of his personality upon theirs.—
On the *"self-consciousness"* of St Paul, see Howson, *Character of St
Paul*, Lect. II.

the prisoner of Jesus Christ] So Philem. 1, 9; 2 Tim. i. 8; and
below, iv. 1, with an interesting difference, which see. Our Epistle thus
stands grouped with Philippians, Colossians, Philemon, 2 Timothy, as an
Epistle written from prison.—*"Of Jesus Christ"*:—under all aspects
of life Paul belongs to Christ. Whatever he is, does, or suffers, it is
as *Christ's property*. There is also an obvious reference to the fact that
his imprisonment was *for Christ's cause;* but this is not all.

for you] **On behalf of you.** See Acts xxii. 21 for illustration. His

2 Gentiles, if ye have heard of the dispensation of the grace
3 of God which is given me to you-ward: how that by revelation he made known unto me the mystery; (as I wrote afore

imprisonment, due to Jewish hostility, was thus ultimately due to his
assertion of the free welcome of the Gentiles to Messiah's covenant.
Acts xv. records the crisis within the Church which corresponded to this
assault from without.

2. *If ye have heard of*] Lit. **if so be that ye heard of.** This phrase
occasions the question, Could this Epistle have been addressed to a
Church familiar with St Paul? And it has thus seemed, to some
extreme critics, an argument against the genuineness of the Epistle, a
lapsus plumæ on the part of a fabricator; and, in very different
quarters, an argument against the special destination to Ephesus
(see *Introduction*, ch. iii). Not here to notice the *anti-Pauline* inference
it is enough to say of the *anti-Ephesian* that it proves too much.
What was known of Paul in the Ephesian Church would practically be
known of him throughout the missions of Asia (see Acts xix. 10, 26),
so that the phrase remains as difficult as before. The true account
of it, surely, is that it is a phrase of almost irony, an allusion to
well-known fact under the disguise of hypothesis. His Gentile commission was no new thing, and was widely known, when this clause was
written; but a natural and beautiful rhetoric prefers to treat it as if
possibly obscure or forgotten.—That St Paul had never been silent at
Ephesus on the subject appears from Acts xix. 8, 9, where we see him
withdrawing the converts from the synagogue.

the dispensation] **The stewardship.** For the figure, cp. 1 Cor. iv. 1,
2, ix. 17; Col. i. 25; 1 Pet. iv. 10.

the grace of God which is given me] Such is the grammatical connexion; not the "stewardship" but the "grace" is the thing given.
And the "grace" is explained by Rom. i. 5 ("grace and apostleship")
and below, ver. 7, 8. It was the loving gift of commission and inspiration to preach Christ among the Gentiles.—For similar allusions to his
life-work cp. Acts xxii. 21, xxvi. 17, 18; Rom. i. 5, xi. 13; Gal. ii. 2, 9.

3. *by revelation*] Probably at or about the time of his conversion.
Acts xxvi. 17, 18, indicates that the Lord then and there gave him the
special commission, and it is likely that a period of special and direct Divine
instruction followed, perhaps in "Arabia" (Gal. i. 17). See Gal. i. 11,
&c. for the positive assertion that "his gospel" was a direct revelation,
and the connexion of this with events at and just after the conversion.
Perhaps visions such as St Peter's (Acts x.) entered into the process. It
is a wonderful paradox, yet deeply truth-like, that the great champion
of Pharisaism should have been chosen to be *the* Apostle of the heathen.
—For the phrase, "by revelation," cp. Rom. xvi. 25 (Greek); Gal. ii. 2;
and for St Paul's claim to be a recipient of revelations, 2 Cor. xii. 1, 7;
Gal. i. 16.

he made known] Better, **was made known.**

the mystery] Explained below, ver. 5, 6, as being the long-kept

in few *words*, whereby, when ye read, ye may understand 4
my knowledge in the mystery of Christ) which in other ages 5
was not made known unto the sons of men, as it is now revealed unto his holy apostles and prophets by the Spirit;
that the Gentiles should be fellowheirs, and of the same 6

secret of the absolutely equal welcome to Christ of the Gentile with the
Jew.—On the word " *mystery*," see note on i. 9.

as I wrote afore] The reference is to previous passages in this Epistle;
i. 9, &c., ii. 11, &c. English idiom would say, **as I have written
afore.**

4. *may understand*] R.V., **can perceive**; and so better.

my knowledge] Better, **intelligence, understanding** (R.V.). The
thought is, not any laudation of the Apostle's intellect, but substantia-
tion of his God-granted insight, verified by the spiritual reader, and resulting in further confidence on the reader's part.

of Christ] The great Secret was bound up with His work (ii. 14) and
His glory (i. 10). As to experience, its essence was "Christ in you,
the hope of glory" (Col. i. 27). See also Col. i. 27; where, probably,
read "the mystery of God, [which mystery is] Christ."

5. *ages*] Better, **generations**. The reference (see next words) is to
human time, and the periods before the Gospel.

unto the sons of men] A designedly large phrase; mankind in general,
both inside and outside the Jewish pale. Outside, the secret was wholly
unknown; inside, it was only dimly and sparingly intimated, though
certainly intimated (cp. Acts xiii. 47; Rom. xv. 8—12). That it was
in *some measure* revealed is suggested by the phrase here, "*As* it is *now*
&c." On the present scale, in the present mode, it was not then revealed; but not therefore quite concealed. But the O.T. hints were
after all little more than prepared materials for N.T. revelation.

his holy apostles and prophets] On the "prophets," see note on ii. 20.
—The recipients are called "holy" to mark their special nearness to, and
knowledge of, the revealing God, and so the absolute truth of their
report.

by the Spirit] Lit., and better, **in [the] Spirit.** They were "in the
Spirit" (Rev. i. 10) while receiving the knowledge of the great mystery.
The Holy Ghost possessed them, that He might inform them.

6. *That the Gentiles*, &c.] It is well to pause over a passage like
this, and reflect that what seems now to be an axiom of religious thought,
the equality of mankind in view of the offer of salvation, was once an
immense and long-withheld discovery. See above, on ii. 11.

should be] Better, **are**; in the plan of God, now disclosed.

fellowheirs] Cp. Rom. viii. 17; Gal. iii. 29, iv. 7. They are the
children of God and brethren of Christ, equally with Jewish believers,
and so equally *heirs* of their Father's kingdom; "joint-heirs with
Christ" of "the better country, that is the heavenly" (Heb. xi. 16).

of the same body] Better, **fellow-members**, a version which preserves
the likeness of the two Greek words represented by this expression
and "fellowheirs" respectively. On "the body," see notes on ii. 16.

body, and partakers of his promise in Christ by the gospel:
7 whereof I was made a minister, according to the gift of the
grace of God given unto me by the effectual working of his
8 power. Unto me, *who am* less than the least of all saints,
is this grace given, that *I* should preach among the Gentiles
9 the unsearchable riches of Christ; and to make all *men* see

partakers] **Fellow-partakers**, R.V., still preserving the similarities
of the Greek.
his promise] See on ii. 12. Read, **the promise**.
in Christ] Only in vital union with Christ was the promise to be
inherited. It was inextricably involved in Him.
by the gospel] Better, **by means of the Gospel**; the instrument by
which the Divine Plan of Gentile incorporation is to be made actual.
Cp. 1 Cor. iv. 15, "I begot you by means of the Gospel." See also
Rom. x. 8—15, xvi. 25, 26.
7. *a minister*] *Diāconos*, a worker, helper. Cp. Col. i. 23. The
word implies activity and subordination.—"I" here is not emphatic.
according to the gift, &c.] See above on ver. 2. The "gift" includes
the commission and the inspiration. His "ministry," both in field and
in effect, was "according to" this great gift.
given] I.e. (by the best attested reading) the *grace* which was given.
So R.V. "the gift of **that grace which** was given."
by the effectual working &c.] Read certainly, **according to the working**, &c. For similar phrases cp. i. 19; Phil. iii. 21; and esp. Col. i. 29,
where, as here, he speaks of working "according to" a power experienced by himself.—A comma should be read before this second "according to." The statement is that he "became a minister, according
to," in a way explained by, two things, a Divine Gift, and a Divine
working Power. Observe the recognition, at once restful and energizing,
that the actual movements of the power of God were the force behind
all his apostolic activity. "By Him he moves, in Him he lives." Cp.
besides Col. i. 29 just cited, 1 Cor. xv. 10; 2 Cor. iii. 5, iv. 7, xii. 9, 10;
Gal. ii. 20; Phil. iv. 13; Col. i. 11.
8. *Unto me*] A slight pause and new start here occurs in the long
parenthesis. The thought of his commission, and of the Divine power
which enabled him, leads by contrast to the thought of the personal in-
significance and unworthiness of the subject of that power, in view of the
field and of the message.
less than the least] One Greek word, and that a unique one. It is a
comparative-superlative; "more least," "leaster," where "lesser" would
be the regular form. The holy intensity of thought breaks the bounds
of accidence. For the sentiment—no flight of rhetoric, but the strong
and true result of a profound view of the glory and mercy of Christ—cp.
1 Cor. xv. 9; 1 Tim. i. 15, 16.
this grace] See on ver. 2 above.
among] Better, **unto**.
unsearchable] Lit., "*not to be tracked by footprints*," a deeply sug-

what *is* the fellowship of the mystery, which from the beginning of the world hath been hid in God, who created all

gestive word. In N.T. the word occurs only here and Rom. xi. 33 (A.V., "*past finding out*"). In the LXX. it appears thrice, in the Book of Job; v. 9, ix. 10, xxxiv. 24.

riches] See on i. 7 for St Paul's love of this and kindred words.

The whole phrase here before us is one of the greatest in holy Scripture. It presents the truths, harmonized into one truth, of the simplicity and the infinity of the Gospel. All is centralized in Christ, the Christ of Pauline, of New Testament, theology, the Incarnate Son slain, risen, and glorified; and from that Centre diverge countless lines of application to every need of the human soul. A Gospel thus described is totally different from an ethical code, or system; and equally different from a mere growth, however sublime, of human sentiment and aspiration. It claims to be nothing less than a direct unfolding of Divine resources of love and power.—See Appendix E for a remarkable incident in Christian biography, connected with this clause.

9. *and to make all* men *see*] Lit., "*to illuminate all men.*" The Latin versions have *illuminare omnes.*—Some ancient MSS. (including the great MS. of the British Museum, and the Sinaitic), and other authorities, omit "all men." But the external and internal evidence for retention greatly preponderates.—The idea is of the Apostle as "casting bright light" on the universal scope of the Gospel, in the eyes of "all men," no longer only of Jews.—The verb is the same as that in 2 Tim. i. 10; where lit., "hath thrown light upon, hath *illuminated,* life and immortality." Truths once in shadow are by the Gospel brought out into the sun.

the fellowship] The true reading is undoubtedly **dispensation, or stewardship**. The reading represented by A.V. is probably an explanation, which crept into the text; representing very nearly the meaning of the true word. "*The dispensation* of the secret" is, in effect, the *world-wide distribution*, through the stewards of God, of the news and the blessings of the full Gospel, so long held in reserve.

See notes above on vv. 2—6.

from the beginning of the world] Lit., "*from the ages;*" R.V., **from all ages**. To define somewhat the meaning of the phrase; the great Truth in question was hidden in comparative secrecy, from the starting point of the progress of the developments ("ages") of the Divine dealings for man, up to the actual Advent of the Messiah. We gather here that this was so not only at and after the call of Israel, but in the patriarchal age, and even in the angelic age, or ages. See below on ver. 10.

hid in God] the great Treasury of unknown blessings.

who created all things] Omit "*by Jesus Christ,*" with the preponderance of ancient authority.—The truth of the *One* Creator appears here as in deep harmony with the *universal* scope of His Redemption. All through Scripture, in very different contexts, the truths of Creation and Redemption are seen in connexion. See a vivid illustration in Col. i.,

10 *things* by Jesus Christ: to the intent that now unto the
principalities and powers in heavenly *places* might be known
11 by the church the manifold wisdom of God, according to
the eternal purpose which he purposed in Christ Jesus our

where the Father, in and through the Son, both "creates all things,"
and "reconciles all things."

10. *now*] In the great "fulness of the times;" the age of the
Gospel.

the principalities and powers] See on i. 21. Here, as there, the
reference is to "governments and authorities" in the world of holy
Angels. "These things angels covet to look into" (1 Pet. i. 12); as
we find them doing, for example, in the closing visions of Daniel. To
their pure and powerful but still finite intelligences the work of man's
Redemption is not only a touching interest, an object of benevolent attention; it is indescribably important, as a totally new and unique
revelation of the Mind and Ways of their Lord, and perhaps (though
here the hints of Scripture are few and dark) as indicating how their
own bliss stands secure.—See some excellent pages on this last subject
in *The Incarnation of the Eternal Word*, by the Rev. Marcus Dods,
(1835) pp. 7—25.

in heavenly places] See on i. 3.

might be known] The verb implies the gift of information *ab extra*.
The angelic mind, like the human, needs and is capable of such information.

by the church] Better, **through**. The means of information to these
exalted students is God's way of redemption and glorification for His
saints of our race; His action for and in "the blessed company of
all faithful people." The thought is one to stimulate the feeblest and
most solitary Christian; while yet its chief concern is with the aggregate,
the community, in which the grace which works freely and primarily in
the individual attains its perfect harmony and speaks to the heavenly
"watchers" (Dan. iv. 13, &c.) with its full significance.

the manifold wisdom] Lit., "*the much variegated* wisdom." The
adjective is stronger (by the element "*much*,") than that in 1 Pet. iv. 10
("manifold *grace*"). It occurs only here in N.T. The reference
probably is to the *complicated problem* of man's redemption, met and
solved by the "unsearchable riches" of the work of Christ. Alike as a
race and as individuals, man presented difficulties innumerable to the
question, how shall God be just, and the justifier, and sanctifier, of
this race? But *every* difficulty was, and is, met in "Christ, the Wisdom
of God" (1 Cor. i. 24, 30).

11. *according to the eternal purpose*] Lit., and better, **according
to the purpose of the ages**. I.e. the Church, as watched by the angels,
presents to them the final result (final *in kind*) of the great Plan of
Divine developments by which the glory of God was to be displayed in
His dealings with Sin. The redeemed Church *corresponds to* this Plan;
it is (in kind, in essence,) the realization of the Divine Idea. No other

Lord: in whom we have boldness and access with confidence 12
by the faith of him. Wherefore I desire that *ye* faint not at 13

and better thing in that kind is to succeed it. The past "ages," angelic,
paradisaic, patriarchal, Mosaic, prophetic, have led up to the Universal
Church, in its spiritual reality, as their goal.

in Christ Jesus our Lord] Lit., **in the Christ, Jesus our Lord.**—The
" Purpose" was "purposed" (lit. "made ") "*in* Him," inasmuch as
both Idea and Working were altogether bound up with Him. "In
Christ" God was to "reconcile the world"; "in Christ" the saints
were to "have redemption in His blood"; "in Him" to be "rooted
and built up"; "complete in Him"; "abiding in Him"; "walking in
Him"; "dying in Him" (Rev. xiv. 13); "made alive in Him"
(1 Cor. xv. 22). Thus "in the Christ," the Eternal and Anointed Son
and Word, the Idea stood forth formed ; and in that Christ, as "Jesus
our Lord," incarnate, sacrificed, glorified, the Idea is carried into
realization.

12. *in whom we have*] Here (see last note) *is* the realization. It
was "purposed in Him" that we His saints should be unspeakably
near to the Father; and so we now *are*, and angels see it.

boldness] Lit., **the** (or **our**) **freedom of speech,** the boldness of
intimate *intercourse*. Here and there (perhaps Col. ii. 15, where
A. V. "openly"; Heb. x. 35; 1 Joh. ii. 28; where A. V. "confidence") the original word seems to lose its special reference to
speech; but certainly not here. The saint (Heb. iv. 16) "comes with
free utterance to the throne of grace "; to *speak* a child's every thought,
desire, and fear.—On the definite article here ("*the* boldness") Monod
remarks that it indicates "une hardiesse *bien connue*", a familiar
characteristic of experience.

access] Better, **introduction**; see on ii. 18.

with confidence] Lit., and better, **in.** This holy confidence with
God is illustrated often in the Acts, and in the Epistles. Meyer
refers to Rom. viii. 38 &c. Still more in point is the passage just
following this, and St Paul's other prayers for his converts.

by the faith of him] So lit., but the better English equivalent for
the Greek is (R.V.) **through our faith in Him**. The same construction with the same meaning occurs Mar. xi. 22 ("have faith *of*
God"); Rom. iii. 22; Gal. ii. 16, 20; Phil. iii. 9. See too Col. ii. 12
("faith *of* the operation of God").

Observe the persistent recurrence of the idea of faith. The entrance
into one-ness with Christ, on our side, by faith (ii. 8), and (here) into the
life lived in that sacred one-ness is realized in the exercise of faith.

13. *Wherefore*] In view of the facts just recited; the welcome
of Gentile believers into the true Israel, the Body of Christ, "according to the purpose of the ages," for the instruction of holy angels,
and for the saints' own joy in intimacy with the Father. In the
propagation of such a Gospel the messenger might well be willing
to suffer for the sake of the converts ; and they in their turn might well
not be discouraged when they saw him suffer for them. These suffer-

14 my tribulations for you, which is your glory. For this cause I bow my knees unto the Father of our Lord Jesus Christ,

ings, far from indicating defeat or failure, were "their glory," proofs that their Lord thought their incorporation into Himself *worth* the severest conflicts and sorrows of an Apostle. Yet the intense community of love between converts and Apostle might still tempt them to depression; and hence this request, so generous and tender.

I desire] I. e. probably, "I desire *you; I* ask as a boon from *you.*" It is possible to explain the words of a *prayer to God;* but the Gr. construction does not favour this, and the much stronger phrase for prayer *in the next verse* is also against it. See further just below.

faint] The same word as that *e.g.* Luke xviii. 1; 2 Cor. iv. 16. The idea is relaxation and cessation of effort under weariness or pain.

It is possible to explain this clause (as R. V. margin) "that *I* faint not"; for the pronoun is not expressed. (In that case we should also, of course, explain "I desire," just above, of prayer to God.) But against this view lie the thoughts that the words, "which is *your* glory," would thus lose point, and, even more, that such a prayer would be a discord in a passage so full of exultation and love, while the received explanation forms on the contrary a rich and true concord in it.

your glory] See last note but two.

14—19 THE MAIN THEME RESUMED: PRAYER FOR THE IN-DWELLING OF CHRIST

14. *For this cause*] The same phrase as that of ver. 1. See note there. Here the broken connexion is resumed. The "permanent habitation of God" (ii. 22) is still in the Apostle's mind, but in another aspect. The thought of the eternal totality, the Church glorified, gives place in a measure to that of the present individuality, the saint's experience now and here of the consciously welcomed "permanent habitation of Christ in the heart," with all its spiritual concomitants. The two aspects are complements of each other. Each "living Stone" (1 Pet. ii. 5) is, as it were, a miniature of the living Temple. In each of them, as if it were an integral microcosm, yet with a view not to itself only but to the final harmony of the whole, Christ works, manifests Himself, and dwells. So, as by the primary and most vital condition, is approached that "far-off divine Event, to which the whole creation moves,"[1] (and the *New* Creation most directly of all,) and with which the close of ch. ii. has dealt. Meanwhile this prospect, and the present *community* of the saints, is not absent from this passage, in which we have the great "*Family*" (ver. 15), and "*all* the saints" (ver. 18); in which great plurals are used throughout; and in which the closing sentences (vv. 20, 21) point by the vastness of their language to a more than individual sphere of realization.

I bow my knees] The attitude of prayer, Luke xxii. 41; Acts vii. 60, ix. 40, xx. 36, xxi. 5. See too Rom. xiv. 11; Phil. ii. 10. The words, doubtless, do not impose a special bodily posture as a necessity in spiritual worship; physical conditions may make kneeling impossible,

[1] *In Memoriam*, at the end.

of whom the whole family in heaven and earth is named, ¹³

or undesirable, on occasion. But they do impose the spiritual attitude of which the bodily is type and expression; profound and submissive reverence, perfectly harmonious with the "boldness" and "confidence" of ver. 12. And so far as body and spirit work in concord, this *recommends* the corresponding bodily attitude where there is no distinct reason against it.

the Father] The words, "*of our Lord Jesus Christ*," are to be omitted. They appear in very ancient documents, including the Syriac and Latin versions. But the great Latin Father and critic, St Jerome (cent. 4—5), in his comment on this verse, expressly says that the "Latin copies" are in error; and the evidence of both Greek MSS. and patristic quotations preponderates for the omission.

15. *of whom...is named*] Lit., "*out of Whom*, &c." The *derivation* of the "name" is from His Fatherhood.

the whole family] Gr., *patria*. It is difficult to preserve in English the point of the Gr. here. "Father" and "family" have no verbal kinship, while *patêr* and *patria* have. "The whole fatherhood," or "every fatherhood," would scarcely convey a clear idea.

An interesting question of interpretation arises here. The Revisers render "*every family*," or (margin) "*every fatherhood*"; and in this they have the concurrence of many commentators, modern and ancient. Indeed, there could be no doubt of their rendering were the usages of Greek in the N. T. and in the classics the same; the absence here of the article before *patria* would be decisive in Xenophon, for example. But the law of the Gr. article is in some respects less precise in the N. T., as was observed on ii. 21 (where see note); and we are at liberty here, as there, though of course with caution, to take the context into account, before surrendering the A. V.

The alternatives then are, (1) to understand the Apostle to diverge to the thought that God's spiritual Fatherhood is the Archetype of all family unions, in earth and heaven; the source from which every other "father" draws his "name," his title and idea; (2) to understand the Apostle to dwell on the thought of the oneness of the family union of saints and angels under the Eternal Father of Spirits Who gives "name," designation as His children, to the whole company.

We feel the difficulty of the question. And we are willing to own that there *may* be communities in the heavenly world to which the idea of family may attach. But if so this is the solitary hint of it in Scripture. And meanwhile the context as a whole seems to us to plead strongly for the idea of oneness as against particularity. And the phrase "in heaven and earth," compared with i. 10 (where carefully observe the connexion), suggests to us far rather the idea of the Great Family "gathered up" in Christ than the extraneous and new idea of many families, connected or not connected with Him. We plead accordingly for the A. V.

And we thus see presented in the passage the great truth, so characteristic of the whole Epistle—the spiritual oneness of the holy Community.

16 that he would grant you, according to the riches of his glory,
to be strengthened with might by his Spirit in the inner

It is worth observing that the word "family" was used by the Rabbis
in a sense somewhat akin to the sense (thus explained) of this passage.
With them "the upper family" and "the lower family" meant, respectively, the Angels and Israel. Wetstein here quotes a Rabbinic comment
on Jer. xxx. 6:—"*All faces;* even the faces of the upper and lower
family; of the angels and of Israel." And again; "God does nothing
without counsel taken with His upper family." This is not a perfect
parallel here, where, as we take it, the idea is strictly of one united
brotherhood; but it is near enough to have had, possibly, a share in
moulding the phrase here.—The suggestion to translate the Greek, "the
whole family in heaven, and that on earth," oversteps, we think, the
limits of the grammar.

16. *according to the riches of his glory*] I. e., as He can do Who
is Lord of the resources of an Eternal Nature and Heavenly Kingdom.
(See on i. 18 for the phrase "riches of glory" in another reference.)
The glory of God is, in brief, Himself, as the Infinite and Holy One,
with all results, for Himself and His creatures, of His being such.

to be strengthened] The Gr. verb is elsewhere used with ideas of
spiritual firmness and vigour (Luke i. 80, ii. 40; 1 Cor. xvi. 13). So it
is here. The saints are to be so strengthened as *not to fear* things
of which nature is afraid; even the felt indwelling of the Holy One, and
His absolute dominion in the inmost heart.

with might] The power of God.

by his Spirit] The Holy Ghost; everywhere present in the doctrine
of this Epistle. He is so to deal with "the inner man" as that the
presence of Christ shall be permanent in the heart. Cp. Rom. viii. 9,
10, where observe the transition from, "the Spirit of God dwelleth in
you", to, "Christ is in you." And see, too, the Lord's words, Joh. xiv.
16, 18, 21, 23, xvi. 7, xvii. 11. There we find that while He is "no
more in the world," and it is "expedient that He go away," yet "the
Spirit of Truth" shall not only come, but so come that the disciples
shall not be "left orphans"; their Lord shall "come to them"; His
Father and He will "make Their abode" with each faithful believer.
We thus get fragments of a Divine comment on the glorious passage now
before us; to the effect that this Presence, this permanent Indwelling, of
the Saviour, is essentially a Presence in and by the Spirit, mediated by
the Spirit; not physical, or quasi-physical, or under any mode other
than, and different from, a Presence through the Spirit's agency upon
the "inner man." Where the Spirit "permanently abides," there, and
therefore, does the Saviour so abide; with just this difference, or condition, that we are to think, in the passage before us, of the indwelling
Spirit as *directing His agency expressly and specially* in the direction of
making the Saviour's Presence a permanent reality to the "heart."

Compare further the Seven Epistles of the Revelation, where the
voice of the glorified Saviour is identified, in every instance, with that of
the Spirit.

man; that Christ may dwell in your hearts by faith; that 17

in the inner man] Lit., "*into* the inner man"; as if to say, "*deep in*
it"; "penetrating *far into* it."—"*The inner man*":—see for the same
phrase, Rom. vii. 22; 2 Cor. iv. 16. Here it means, practically, the
regenerate human spirit. In itself, the phrase may mean no more
than the invisible as against the material in man; but the three N. T.
passages thus before us indicate its actual reference, in St Paul's voca-
bulary, to the regenerate self.

17. *that Christ may dwell*] This clause is in close connexion with
the preceding. The "strengthening" is the requisite to the "dwelling";
the "dwelling" the sure sequel to the "strengthening." See last note
but one.

"*Christ*":—lit."*the Christ*," as so often in this Epistle (i. 10, 12,
20, ii. 5, 13, iii. 4, 8, 11, iv. 7, 12, 13, 20, v. 2, 5, 14, 23, 25, vi. 5;
besides uncertain readings).—Not to press distinctions too far, we may
yet point out that the Lord is here presented not specially as Jesus, but
as the MESSIAH, in His anointed majesty as the Prophet, Priest, and King
of His saints. The thought of His Presence includes that of our ten-
derest affections towards Him, but rises also above it. It is the Presence
of the Supreme Teacher, Redeemer, and Possessor.

"*dwell*":—the Gr. verb indicates *permanent abode.* It is akin to
the noun, ii. 22; where see note. See it used 2 Pet. iii. 13, of the
eternal presence of Righteousness in the New Universe. It marks a
residence quite different from transient or casual lodgment.

The tense is the aorist (infinitive), and the idea of the aorist is singleness of act. Accordingly, the Lord is viewed here as not merely
"dwelling," but, in a definite act, "*coming to dwell*," "taking up
abode." The question arises, did the Apostle contemplate the Ephesians as all alike devoid of the Indwelling in question, and needing
it to begin? It is difficult to grant this, in an Epistle addressed to a
large community, and one evidently rich in life and love. Well-nigh
every stage of spiritual development must have been represented there.
Yet the aorist must have its meaning. And surely the account of it is this,
that the Apostle views them each and all as ever needing, at whatever
stage of spiritual life, such an access of realization and reception as
should be, to what had preceded, a new Arrival and Entrance of Christ
in the heart. Local images are always elastic in the spiritual sphere;
and there is no contradiction thus in the thought of the permanent
presence of One who is yet needed to arrive.

On the other hand there are possible stages of Christian experience
in which, practically, the Lord's "coming in to dwell," as here, would
be a thing wholly new; and many such cases, doubtless, were found
at Ephesus. Not only here but throughout the N.T. the saint is viewed
as meant to enjoy a prevailing, not an intermittent, intercourse with
his Lord in faith and love; an *habitual* "access," "confidence," "peace
and joy in believing," and "fruit-bearing" power. Where such enjoyment does not as yet exist there is still lacking that which is in view
here. True, it will be only a crude analysis that will claim to discern

18 ye, being rooted and grounded in love, may be able to

and decide peremptorily in such spiritual problems.   But this does not
alter the facts and principles of the matter in themselves.

in your hearts]   A phrase important for the interpretation of the
clause.   It shews that the Indwelling here is subjective rather than
objective ; an Indwelling conditioned by the saint's realization.   "Christ"
is " in" every genuine disciple (2 Cor. xiii. 5), in the sense of the disciple's
covenant and vital union with Him (1 Cor. vi. 15, 17).   But this was
certainly the case already with the Ephesian saints.   Here then we
have to do not so much with fact as with grasp on fact ; the reception
of the (already vitally present) Lord in habitual realization by the conscience, understanding, imagination, affections, and will.   For the
"*heart*" in Scripture is the "seat" of all these: see *e.g.* Gen. xx. 5;
Deut. iv. 39; Isa. vi. 10; Mar. xi. 23; Luke xxi. 14; Acts xi. 23; Rom.
v. 5; 1 Cor. ii. 9; Jas. i. 26; 1 Joh. iii. 20.   See on i. 18.—"Though all
of us is a temple for Him, yet the heart is the choir, where He properly
sitteth" (Bayne (cent. 17), *On the Ephesians*).

by faith]   That is, trustful acceptance; holy and humble reliance
upon Divine promises, such promises as those of Joh. xiv. 21, 23; Rev.
iii. 20.   Observe that the Indwelling here in view is to be effectuated
by means of spiritual action (God-given, as this passage has shewn, but
not the less personal) on the saint's part.   And observe that it is not *aspiration*, but *faith*, that is the action.   Aspiration will certainly be present,
as an essential condition; there must be conscious desire.   But it is
faith, submissive trust in the Promiser, which is alone the effectuating
and maintaining act.

Lit., "through *the* faith":—i.e., perhaps, "by means of *your* faith,"
faith as exercised by you; but the article must not be *pressed* in
translation, where an abstract principle is the noun.—"The faith" in the
sense of the *Christian creed* is manifestly not in place here, where the
context is full of the idea of the actions of grace in the soul.

that ye]   Here appears the holy *purpose* of the experience just
described.   The Indwelling is to be specially *in order to* the attitude
and the knowledge now to follow.

being rooted and grounded in love]   "*In love*" is highly emphatic by
position in the Gr.—Does it mean the love of God for us, or ours
for God?   Perhaps it is needless to seek a precise answer.   "Love,
generally " (Alford), is to be the region of this great experience of
the soul; a sphere of which the Divine Love and the regenerate
spirit's response are, as it were, the hemispheres.   But we may at least
suggest, with i. 4 in mind (see note there), that the Divine Love is
mainly in view.   Is it quite intelligible to regard the saint's love as the
soil and basis of his saintship?   For observe it is the saints themselves,
not this or that *in* them ("*ye* being rooted, &c."), that the Love in
question thus sustains and feeds.

The chain of thought will thus be : " I pray that your hearts may so
receive Christ as their perpetual Indweller, that you may, in this
profound intimacy with HIM, see and grasp your acceptance and life
in the Eternal Love, manifested through Him."

comprehend with all saints what *is* the breadth, and length,

"*rooted and grounded*":—perfect participles. The second, lit. **founded**, recurs to the imagery of the Temple and its basis; ch. ii. The first, giving a metaphor much rarer with St Paul (Col. ii. 7 is the only close parallel), suggests the additional idea of derived life and its development. The saints are viewed both as "trees of the Lord, full of sap," deep in the rich soil of the Love of God (cp. Psal. i. 3, xcii. 12, 13; Jer. xvii. 8), and as constituent stones of the great Temple which rests ultimately on the same Love.—Col. ii. 7, just quoted, gives the same collocation of ideas, but with differences. The participle there rendered "built up" is present; "*being builded* upon." And "in *Him*" takes the place of "in love." This latter difference is no discrepancy; "the love of God is in Jesus Christ our Lord" (Rom. viii. 39).

Such, as to root and basis, *is* the true saint's position. It is not created, but realized, when the experience of ver. 17 takes place in him. And the following clauses dilate on the spiritual use which he is to make of it.

18. *may be able*] R. V., **may be strong**; more lit. still, **may get strength**; the verb being aorist, pointing to a new crisis. The idea is of a wide grasp, a mighty stretch of thought and faith, only to be made by spirits perfectly *assured* (ver. 17) *of their footing.*

to comprehend] R. V., "*apprehend*"; a minute and over-careful change.—The Gr. is used (*e.g.* Acts iv. 13, x. 34, xxv. 25) of mental perception, or ascertainment.

with all saints] Lit., **with all the saints.** For the phrase cp. i. 15, vi. 18; Col. i. 4; 1 Thess. iii. 13; Philem. 5; Rev. viii. 3, and perhaps xxii. 21. On the word "saint" see note on i. 1.—The thought emphasized here is that of the great Community. The Apostle has spoken of experiences possible only in the *sanctum* of the individual regenerate "heart," but he reminds the reader here that these are never to terminate in themselves. The individual, as he is never other than a "member" of Christ, is never other than a "member" of his brethren (see Rom. xii. 5). His grace and light are to be, as it were, contributions to the combined experience of the true Church, as the grace and light of the true Church are to enhance his own.

what is *the breadth*, &c.] The Object is left unnamed. What is it? We explain it, with Monod, as the Divine Love, which has just been named (see last on ver. 17), and is to be named (as the Love of Christ) immediately again. At least, it is that Work, Purpose, Covenant, of God in Christ which is ultimately resolved into the Eternal and Sovereign Love.

The imagery is perhaps suggested by a vastly spacious building, with its high towers and deep foundations. But may it not rather be suggested by the visible Universe itself, as if a spectator gazed from horizon to horizon, and at the boundless air above, and thought of the depths beneath his feet? We may partially illustrate the language, in any case, by such passages as Psalm ciii. 11, 12.

19 and depth, and height; and to know the love of Christ, which passeth knowledge, that ye might be filled with all

Some curiosities of interpretation attach to this verse. Severianus (cent. 4, 5), quoted by Alford, finds here an allusion to the shape of the Cross, and in it to the Lord's Godhead ("*height*") and Manhood ("*depth*"), and to the extent of the apostolic missions ("*length and breadth*"). St Jerome (cent. 4, 5) in his Commentary here interprets the words at some length, and finds in the "*height*" the holy angels, in the "*depth*" the evil spirits, in the "*length*" those of mankind who are on the upward path, and in the "*breadth*" those who are "sinking towards vices. For *broad and ample is the way which leadeth to death.*" The Calvinist Zanchius (cent. 16) adopts from Photius (cent. 9) the explanation that the reference is to "the mystery of the free salvation through Christ of the Gentiles and the whole human race"; called *long*, because decreed from eternity; *broad*, because extended to all; *deep*, because of the descent of Christ to Hades, and because of the resurrection of the dead; *high*, because Christ ascended above all heavens. (Quoted in Poole's *Synopsis Criticorum*.)

19. *And to know*] An aorist verb, expressing a new and decisive development of knowledge, knowledge of the spiritual kind, the intuition of the regenerate spirit, realized in its own responsive adoring love.

the love of Christ] Who "loved the Church, and gave Himself for it" (v. 25); "Who loved me, and gave Himself for me" (Gal. ii. 20). See further Rom. viii. 35, with 39; 2 Cor. v. 14; Rev. i. 5.—The context favours the chief reference here of these sacred words to the Lord's love for the true Church, without excluding, what cannot be excluded in the matter, His love, and the sense of it, for the individual saint.

which passeth knowledge] knowledge of every sort, spiritual as much as intellectual. Here is an Object eternally transcending, while it eternally invites, the effort after a complete cognition. For ever, there is more to know.—To find a reference here to heretical or unspiritual *gnôsis* is frigid and out of place, in a passage glowing with the highest truths in their loveliest aspects.—For a similar phrase, cp. Phil. iv. 7.

The testimony of such words as these to the Nature of Christ is strong indeed, none the less so because not on the surface. No created Person, however exalted, could either be, or be commended as being, to the human spirit, an infinite object of knowledge in any aspect.—"None fully knoweth the SON save the FATHER" (Matt. xi. 27).

that ye might be filled] An aorist again; indicating a crisis and new attainment. For the thought, cp. Col. i. 9; "that ye may be filled with the knowledge of His will"; such knowledge as to lead to "walking worthy of the Lord unto all pleasing." See too, for kindred language, Rom. xv. 13, 14. The idea is of a vessel connected with an abundant source external to itself, and which will be filled, up to its capacity, if the connexion is complete. The vessel is the Church, and also the saint. It may be only partially filled; it may be full—every faculty of the individual, every part of life and circumstances, every member of the community, "*ful*-filled with grace and heavenly

the fulness of God. Now unto him that is able to do ex- 20
ceeding abundantly above all that we ask or think, according to the power that worketh in us, unto him *be* glory in 21

benediction." And this latter state is what the Apostle looks for.
See further, on ver. 18.

with] Lit., and better, **unto**, "up to." The "fulfilling" is to be
limited only by the Divine resources. Not, of course, that either Church
or soul can contain the Infinite; but they can receive the whole,
the plenitude, of those blessings which the Infinite One is willing and
able at each moment to bestow on the finite recipient.

all the fulness of God] I.e., as in Col. ii. 9 (and see note on
i. 23), the totality of the Divine riches, whether viewed as Attributes
as in God, or Graces as in us; whatever, being in Him, is spiritually
communicable to the saints, the "partakers of Divine nature" (2 Pet.
i. 4). The believing reader will find inexhaustible matter in such a
phrase for thought, prayer, and faith[1].

20, 21 ASCRIPTION OF PRAISE, CLOSING A MAIN SECTION OF THE
EPISTLE

20. *Now unto him*] The Father, in Whose "glory" all things terminate. As it is of His essence to demand praise, so it is of the
essence of regenerate life to yield it to Him.

that is able] For this phrase in doxology cp. Acts xx. 32; Rom. xvi.
25; Jude 24. Faith both rests and is reinvigorated in the assurance,
and re-assurance, of the Divine *Ability*, wholly objective to the believer.
Cp. Matt. xix. 26; Rom. iv. 21, xi. 23, xiv. 4; 2 Cor. ix. 8 (a good
parallel here); Phil. iii. 21; 2 Tim. i. 2; Heb. vii. 25. (In the three
last passages the reference is to the Saviour.)

exceeding abundantly] One compound word in the Greek; elsewhere, 1 Thess. iii. 10, and (nearly identical) v. 13. Strong expressions
of largeness, excess, abundance, are deeply characteristic of St Paul.

all that we ask or think] The word rendered "think" means more
specially **understand**. Cp. *e.g.* Matt. xv. 17 and above, ver. 4. So the
Latin versions here; *intelligimus*. No narrow logic will be applied
to such a clause, if we seek its true meaning. To be sure we can,
if we please, "ask for," and in a certain sense "conceive of," *infinite* gifts of grace; though it is to be observed that the phrase is, not
"all that we *can ask*" but "all that we *ask*." But the reader who
studies the words in their own spirit will not perplex himself thus. He
will see in them the assurance that his actual petitions and perceptions,
guided and animated by Scripture and by grace, yet always fail to
include all that HE is able to do, in the range and depth of His working.

according to the power, &c.] The power of the indwelling Spirit.
See for a remarkable parallel Col. i. 29, where the Apostle speaks of
his own toils and wrestlings as "*according to* that working of His which

---

[1] Observe the silent testimony of this whole paragraph against disproportioned
theories of the true use of the holy Sacraments. The theme is the mode of development of Divine Life in the saint, and yet no allusion is made (here or elsewhere
in the Epistle) to the Holy Communion.

the church by Christ Jesus throughout all ages, world without end.   Amen.

worketh in me in power."   There he speaks of the present and actual, here of the possible. In the saint and in the true Church resides already a Divine force capable in itself of the mightiest developments.   To attain these, not a new force, but a fuller application of *this* force, is required.

21. *glory*] Lit., and better, **the glory**; the glory due to the Father of the Saviour, and of the saints in Him.

in the church by Christ Jesus] Lit., **in Christ Jesus.**   "The glory" is ascribed "*in* Him" as the Father is manifested in Him, and "in Him reconciled the world to Himself."—But very strong evidence favours the reading **in the Church and in Christ Jesus.** If this is adopted, and it is *nearly* certain, the meaning is that the reasons of eternal praise to the Father lie both in the Church and in the Saviour; in the Church, as chosen and glorified by Him, in the Saviour as His supreme and all-including Gift.

throughout all ages, &c.] Lit., **unto all the generations of the age of the ages.**   Such is the length of prospect revealed for the Church of Christ, as the "habitation of God" (ii. 22). The meaning manifestly is, "to all eternity," whatever manifestations the eternal Future may bring. This is viewed as one vast "age" (*aiōn*), the sum and circumference of ages, which ages again contain developments faintly imaged by the "generations" which make up the centuries of Time.—The phrases "for ever," or "for ever and ever," of our A. V., usually represent the "unto the age," or "unto the ages," or "unto the ages of the ages," of the Greek. The first Gr. phrase is almost confined to St John's Gospel and Epistles; the last is distinctive of the Revelation, but it occurs also in St Paul and St Peter.   St Peter (2 iii. 18) writes "*unto the day of* the age," the "Day" which shall usher in the Eternal State.—On the word *aiōn* see further, last note on i. 21.

Amen] The word is properly a Hebrew adverb ("surely"), repeatedly used as here in O. T. See Psal. lxxxix. 52; Jer. xi. 5 (marg. A. V.) ; &c.

On the great passage thus closed Monod remarks: "This doxology, which concludes at once the Apostle's prayer and the first part of his epistle, would be remarkable anywhere, but it is doubly so here...After the grandest promises which human language can express, the Holy Spirit here closes by declaring that all which can be expressed is infinitely below the reality which is in God....But nothing less could answer the vast and undefined need of the heart. All that the mind can clearly grasp and the mouth articulately utter is incapable of satisfying us.   And thus this close, so astonishing and unexpected, is just what we needed...But alas, if this language which is infinitely below the reality which is in God is infinitely above the reality which is in us!...To pass from Scripture to our experience, seems like a fall from heaven to earth. ...The Lord teach us how to bring our experience into harmony with His promises."

I therefore, the prisoner of the Lord, beseech you that *ye* **4**
walk worthy of the vocation wherewith ye are called, with **2**
all lowliness and meekness, with longsuffering, forbearing

CH. IV **1—16** PRACTICAL RESULTS: SPIRITUAL UNITY IN
DIVERSITY OF GIFTS

1. *I therefore*] Here begins what may be called the Second Part of
the Epistle. Hitherto the Apostle has dealt with the eternal and
spiritual aspects of Redemption. He now comes to their sequel and
manifestation in conduct and life. Not that he leaves behind, for a
moment, the eternal facts and spiritual principles. Scripture always
brings the doctrinal into the practical, as reason and mainspring; and
nowhere more than in this Epistle. But the main stress of thought is now
on the effects rather than on the causes; it deals with the holy *sequitur*,
the *"therefore,"* of the matter. Compare the Epistles to the Romans
and Colossians for a similar arrangement; and, to some extent, the First
to the Corinthians.

the prisoner of the Lord] Lit., **the prisoner in the Lord.** His bonds
are due to his union with Christ. They are thus a strong Christian
argument with his converts. See further on iii. 2, above.

beseech] Cp. Rom. xii. 1 for the same word in just the same connexion.
The Gr. is a verb more elastic in reference than our "beseech," often
meaning "to exhort," "to encourage," and (without the thought of
entreaty) "to request." But the thought of entreaty is quite in place
here.

walk] See on ii. 2, 10, above. The distinctive notion of the word
is that of the moral action and conduct of life.

worthy of the vocation] Better, **worthily of the calling.** For similar
phrases, cp. Phil. i. 27, "walk worthily of the Gospel of Christ"; Col.
i. 10, "walk worthily of the Lord"; 1 Thess. ii. 12, "walk worthily of
God." Ideally, of course, no human walk is "worthy of" the Gospel,
the Call, or the Divine Caller. But practically it can and should be so,
in the sense of being governed at every step by the Divine motives,
applied by grace, and so presenting a true correspondence to those
motives.

"The vocation":—see on i. 18, "His calling."

are called] Lit., and better, **were called,** when they heard and believed.

2. *with all lowliness*] So, exactly, Acts xx. 19, in St Paul's review
of his own "walk" *at Ephesus*; "serving the Lord *with all lowliness*."—
"With":—the idea is strictly of accompaniment, attendance. But in
view of actual N. T. usage of the preposition this must not be pressed.
Lowliness was to *characterize* them.

Observe the moral lesson here. The first and most characteristic
effect of the heights and depths of Divine privilege and spiritual experience just unfolded is to be the sincerest and most unselfish *humility*.

lowliness] The Gr. word imports an unaffected lowly estimate
of self. See Trench's *Synonyms of the N. T.*, under ταπεινοφροσύνη,

3 one another in love ; endeavouring to keep the unity of the
4 Spirit in the bond of peace.   *There is* one body, and one

πραότης.   It is a distinctively Christian grace, viewed as a thing
always to be sought and cherished.   Pagan ethics, at best, just recognized it as right where necessary, but not as good and happy *per se.*
The Gospel puts its obligation and its blessedness on the same footing
for *all* believers, as all absolutely dependent for all true good upon the
mercy of Another.

The corresponding adjective is used (Matt. xi. 29) by our Lord of
Himself.   Trench remarks that we have Him there recognizing His
entire dependence as Man on the Father.   Not moral defect but "crea-
tureliness," he says, is the thought there.   "In His human nature He
must be the pattern of all…creaturely dependence."

Observe the force of the phrase; "*all* lowliness."   The grace was to
have the most unreserved scope and exercise.

meekness]   See Trench again, as just above.   The Gr. word imports
gentle and entire submission under trial, whatever the trial be, in the
consciousness that no other attitude can be right for self.   Meekness
thus rests "on deeper foundations than its own, namely on those which
lowliness has laid for it, and it can only continue while it continues to
rest on these."   In this respect "it is a grace in advance of lowliness"
(Trench).

longsuffering]   Grouped with "meekness," Gal. v. 22; Col. iii. 12.
It so far differs from it as not necessarily to import the patience or submission due to a sense that a chastisement is right, but rather patience
for whatever good reason; *e.g.* largeness of view of things, or deep
internal peace and joy.—It is used of the Divine patience, Rom. ii. 4;
ix. 22; 1 Tim. i. 16; 1 Pet. iii. 20; 2 Pet. iii. 15.

forbearing one another in love]   Here was to be the special motive to
"longsuffering," the family-affection of fellow-members of Christ.   It is
implied that there were sure to be occasions for such forbearance.   Cp.
Col. iii. 13.

3. *endeavouring*]   R. V., better, **giving diligence.**   The A. V., to
a modern reader, suggests (as the Gr. does not) a certain imperfection
and precariousness of result.

the unity of the Spirit]   The sacred Oneness effected and maintained
by the One Holy Spirit who had, by uniting them to Christ, united
them to each other.   This Oneness has many aspects.   The aspect here
is that of realized community of feeling and purpose, based on the fact
of community of regenerated position and nature in Christ.

in the bond of peace]   Grammatically, this may mean either "in
peace, as the bond"; or "in that which secures peace."   Bengel prefers
the latter; "the *bond*, with which *peace* is bound, is even *love.*"   But
we have recently (ch. ii.) had Christ Himself presented as the "peace"
of His people one with another; and is not the same thought present
here?   To realize their connexion with Him as such was the way to
maintain the sense and exercise of spiritual solidarity.

4. *one body*]   See on i. 23; ii. 15, 16; and below, ver. 15, 16.
Here as always the imagery of the Body suggests not only union but

Spirit, even as ye are called in one hope of your calling;
one Lord, one faith, one baptism, one God and Father of $^5_6$

united energy and operation.—Its frequent recurrence emphasizes its
importance and significance. Vital union with Christ, by the Spirit, is
the one true secret of holy growth and action, alike for the individual
and the community.—The "*one*" is highly emphatic. As regards the
vital Union, there is one Organism, and one only. Let the relations of
practical Christian life and work correspond to that fact, to the utmost
possible.

one Spirit] The same Divine Spirit as above, ver. 3. He, the immediate Agent in regeneration (Joh. iii.), unites each regenerate individual
to the Head, and, as the Sanctifier, maintains that union. He is thus
comparable to the all-pervading spirit energizing and preserving the
human frame.

Bengel remarks on the close sequence, in the "Apostles' Creed," of
the articles of the Holy Ghost and of the Holy Church. Cp. at large
1 Cor. xii.

ye are called] Perhaps a special reference to the work of the
Holy Ghost, the immediate Agent in the "call" of grace. Cp. 1 Cor.
xii. 13.—Lit. and better, **ye were called**.

in one hope of your calling] On the "hope" and the "calling," see
on i. 18. They were called "*in*" the hope; i.e., so as to be in it,
embraced and possessed by it.—On the spiritual power of the "*one*
hope" cp. Col. i. 4, for a real parallel. There, the "love for all the
saints" is (lit.) "*on account of* the hope laid up in heaven." The
community of blissful prospect binds faster the communion of sympathy
and affection.

5. *one Lord*] Jesus Christ; Possessor and Prince of all His people
equally.

one faith] Is "faith" here the "Christian creed," or "trustful
acceptance" of Christ, "saving faith"? Probably the latter, in view
of the great rarity of the former meaning of the word in St Paul
(Gal. i. 23; Phil. i. 27; present perhaps the best cases, and even these
are not quite clear). The words here thus mean, "one and the same
way of access to and union with the One Lord."

one baptism] The one Divine Seal upon the one God-given faith in
the One Lord. This holy Seal is "one" in respect of the Unity of
the Triune Name (Matt. xxviii. 19) "into" which, and which alone,
all partakers of the covenant of Christ are baptized. The "one baptism for the remission of sins" is baptism into that Name, or into
its equivalent (Acts ii. 38), the Name of the Son of the Father and
the Giver of the Spirit.

6. *one God and Father of all*] The ultimate Source of spiritual
unity. Baptism seals faith, faith unites to the Lord Christ, Christ
reveals the Father as "the only true God" (Joh. xvii. 3), with Whom
He, one with His Church, is eternally one.—"*Of all*":—here, obviously, all believers. Other aspects of Divine Fatherhood are not
here in question. See above on i. 2. And cp. on this ver. 1 Cor. viii. 6.

7 all, who *is* above all, and through all, and in you all. But
unto every one of us is given grace according to the
8 measure of the gift of Christ. Wherefore *he* saith, When
he ascended up on high, he led captivity captive,

above all, &c.] The thought in these clauses progresses downwards
and inwards. The Eternal Father, in His Son, supremely presides "*over*
all" His regenerate children, carries out action "*through*" them, and
dwells "*in*" them. On the last word see ii. 22; 2 Cor. vi. 16 – 18; 1 Joh.
iv. 12, 16.—"*In you all*":—there is clear evidence for the omission
of "you"; considerable evidence for the reading "us"; but a preponderance, chiefly of patristic quotations, against any pronoun. The
context however is clear for the special reference to the Church. The
power and immanence of God in the Universe would be only a remote
plea for Christian union.

7. *But unto every one*] A motive to holy union from the opposite
side; that of "diversity of gifts." See Rom. xii. 3—8; 1 Cor. xii.
4, &c.; 1 Pet. iv. 10, 11. Harmony of spiritual life and work should
be promoted by equal remembrance of the oneness of the source of
life and the inevitable diversity of its exercises and applications.

is given] **Was given**, in the great ideal distribution at the Lord's
exaltation, and actually when we were each "sealed" (i. 14).

according to the measure of the gift of Christ] I. e., not indefinitely,
or confusedly, but as the great Master, Christ, adjusted, *measured*,
His mighty *Gift* to His sovereign allotment of each servant's *work*.
All was mere bounty, free gift; but all also profound design, manifold
in detail, one in end.

8. *Wherefore* he *saith*] Or **it**, i.e. the Scripture, **saith**. St Paul's
usage in quotation leaves the subject of the verb undetermined here
and in similar cases (see *e.g.* ch. v. 14). For him, the word of the Scripture and the word of its Author are convertible terms.—"*Wherefore*":—
as if to say, "the Scripture statement *of course* answers to the spiritual
fact just given."

When he ascended, &c.] Psal. lxviii. (LXX. lxvii.) 18. The Heb.
there is lit., "Thou didst ascend on high; Thou didst lead captive a
captivity (a band of captives); Thou didst take gifts amongst men,"
or more lit., "in man." The LXX. renders, "When Thou didst
ascend on high, Thou didst lead captive a captivity; Thou didst take
gifts in man." The Targum, or Chaldee paraphrase, which is little
likely to have been influenced by this passage, renders, "Thou hast *given*
to them gifts, even to the sons of men."

On this quotation, we first examine the discrepancy between "*take*
gifts" and "*give* gifts," and between "*among* men" and "*for*" or "*to*
men," and then briefly remark on the use made of the Psalmist's words
by the Apostle.

a. The first discrepancy is not to be reconciled by an attempt to
make the Heb. verb mean both "give" and "take." But what if
the "taking" was for the purpose of "giving"? The Conqueror,

and gave gifts unto men. (Now that he ascended, what 9 is it but that he also descended first into the lower parts

Divine or human, in Ps. lxviii. may well be conceived as *receiving* grants for *distribution* among his vassals. If so, the Targum (see above) and the Apostle rightly convey the intention of the Psalmist.

"*Among* men"; "*for* men." The great compression of Hebrew poetical diction makes it quite possible to explain, "*so as to be* among men." Thus again "to," or "for," will rightly convey the intention of the Psalmist, whatever were his precise and conscious thought in depicting the Conqueror as making gifts and grants to "*man*."

β. The "first reference" of Psal. lxviii. is a large and difficult question. See Dean Perowne's full statement of problems and theories in his Commentary on the Psalms; see too Dr Kay's notes. It is enough here to say that the Psalm celebrates, apparently, some great sacred triumph, or triumphs, at the Sanctuary of Zion; an occasion on which the supreme Conqueror, JEHOVAH, is represented as "ascending" after battle to His throne. One type of criticism will see in this nothing beyond a national Ode of Victory, and will regard the Apostle's quotation as an "unscientific" accommodation. For ourselves, believing that our Lord taught a very different view of the Ancient Scriptures, we feel free to recognize any "first reference" fairly provable, but also bound to believe that the Divine Author worked through the human author, so as to convey eternal and permanent truth through his imagery and words, and so as to make the whole terminate on CHRIST, whether or no the human author was aware of it. And we believe that the same Divine Author worked here through the memory and thought of the Apostle, so as to secure, in his quotation and exposition, the true development of the Divine intention of the earlier passage.

We thus accept the present verse as reciting a true testimony of the Spirit of Prophecy to the foreseen facts of the Ascension of the Divine Messiah after conflict and conquest, and the distribution of blessings consequent upon it. The "captivity" will denote whatever persons or powers are in any way His conquest; whether as "enemies under His feet" (1 Cor. xv. 25, &c.), or self-surrendered rebels reconciled to His will (2 Cor. x. 3—5, &c.).—For the thought, "He *received* gifts (to *distribute*) amongst men," cp. Acts ii. 33.

9. *Now that he ascended*] More lit., **Now the [word, or thought,] He ascended.**

what is it] As if to say, "What does it imply? It implies a previous descent, from the seat of royalty. And, in the light of the Fulfilment, this implied descent was 'to the lower parts of the earth.'" The Apostle does not mean that the Psalm teaches anything special about the Descent, but that it implies *a* Descent, and that what that Descent was, Christians know. And the interest of the implied reference is, its supernatural correspondence in outline to Gospel facts; its imagery being of One who has *left His throne* and now returns upward.

first] Evidence is divided as to the right of this word to a place in the text. It is obviously, at worst, explanatory of the sense.

10 of the earth ?   He that descended is the same also that
ascended up far above all heavens, that he might fill all

the lower parts of the earth] Does this mean "the lower regions,
even the earth," as distinct from heaven? Or, "the lower regions of
the earth," i.e. the region underground, the grave and its world? Our
great theologian and critical scholar, Bp Pearson (*Exposition of the
Creed*, Art. V.), inclines to the former view, with a reference to the
Incarnation only. The phrase, so taken, may perhaps be illustrated by
Isai. xliv. 23; where, however, "lower parts of the earth" (LXX. "foundations of the earth ") may be contrasted with "mountains." (Cp. also,
perhaps, Psal. cxxxix. 15.) On the other hand Psal. lxiii. 9 is distinctly
in favour of a reference to "the grave." Our judgment is on the whole
for the second view, with a reference to the Death and Burial of the
Incarnate Lord. Such a reference seems better to *balance*, in a sense,
the phrase just below, "*far above all heavens*"; it falls in better with
the amplitude of the words, "that He might fill all things" (cp. Rom. xiv.
9); and it is in the manner of the N. T. to connect the *Resurrection* and
Ascension as parts of one great whole. And the Lord's Death is so
profoundly concerned with the procurement of blessings to His Church
that an allusion to it is *à priori* likely here.—Many of the Fathers (see
Pearson's notes under Art. V. of the Creed) take this passage to refer to
a definite work done by the Lord in the under-world, a deliverance of the
spirits of the Old Testament saints from a "Limbus" there. But certainly the words here *teach* nothing of the kind; only that He who suffered
for us entered the state of disembodied souls, "the Grave," "Sheol,"
"Hades." The mysterious passage 1 Pet. iii. 18, 19, will at once occur
in the question. But upon it we can only say here that it is too
isolated, and involves too many problems of interpretation, to allow any
great and *peculiar* article of belief to be built upon it; and, upon any
view, its only *explicit* reference is to the generation of the Flood. See
again Pearson. And for a different view from his, stated with great
ability and insight, see Note II. to *The Unsafe Anchor*, by the Rev.
C. F. Childe.

10. *He that descended*, &c.] As if to say, "Yes, He once descended,
as a step in the process, a means to the great end; but now we have to
dwell on the result; this Descender has now become by consequence the
Ascended One, giving gifts from the Throne." Both parts of the statement
are emphatic, the fact and wonder of the Descent, and the triumph and
result of the Ascent; and they are in deep connexion. But the main
stress is on the latter.

far above all heavens] Lit., **all the heavens.** Cp. Heb. iv. 14; vii.
26; where the ascended High Priest is revealed as "having passed
through the heavens," and as " become loftier than the heavens."—Scripture gives no precise revelation as to the number or order of regions or
spheres of the upper world, the unseen universe of life and bliss.
But its frequent use of the plural in regard of it, as here, whatever the
origin of the usage, sanctions the thought that the Blessed (angels and
glorified men), while from other points of view eternally concentrated

things.)   And he gave some, apostles; and some, prophets; **11**
and some, evangelists; and some, pastors and teachers;

and in company, and doubtless able, under their spiritual conditions of
existence, to realize and act upon their unity to a degree unimagined
by us, are yet distributed, classed, and ordered.   "The Rabbis spoke
of two heavens, or seven" (Smith's *Dict. of the Bible,* under the word
Heaven; and see Wetstein on 2 Cor. xii. 2).   St Paul himself speaks
(2 Cor. xii. 2) of a "third heaven," meaning, apparently, the immediate
presence of God; possibly with a reference to the *twofold* division
mentioned just above, and which, if so, is to some degree favoured
by Scripture.   The plain meaning of the present passage, in any case,
is that the Lord passed through and beyond all regions of created
blessedness into the region of the Throne.   That Throne (we can only
use the language of figure, permitted by the Scriptures,) is as truly "far
above" the highest sphere of created life as it is "far above" the lowest.
To both it stands in the mysterious relation of the uncreated to the
created.   Cp. Psal. cxiii. 5, 6.   See further above, note on i. 21.—
From another point of view, He who is "far above" the heavens is
(like His Father) "in heaven" (below, vi. 9).   In this view, heaven includes the whole state of blessed existence, uncreated and created alike.

that he might fill]   Possibly, *"fulfil";* i.e. every prophecy, of humiliation and glory.   But St Paul's usage favours the other version.   He
ascended that He might, not only in possibility but in act, "fill all
things," "with His presence, His sovereignty, His working by the
Spirit; not with His glorified body, as some have thought" (Alford).
"There is here no reference to a diffused and ubiquitous corporeity,
but to a pervading and energizing omnipresence...Christ is perfect God,
and perfect and glorified Man; as the former He is present *everywhere,*
as the latter He can be present *anywhere*" (Bp Ellicott).

11.   *And he gave*]   The *"He"* is emphatic; **it was He who gave.**
See above on ver. 7.—Immediately, the Holy Spirit is the Giver (1
Cor. xii. 8, &c.; cp. Acts ii. 4, and xiii. 2).   But His action is in Divine
union *with* that of the Son, and vicariously *for* Him.

some apostles]   I.e., **some men as apostles,** and so through the
passage.   Cp. 1 Cor. xii. 28.—The gift is to the Church, from the Lord,
of spiritually called and enabled human ministers.—" *Apostles"* :—see
above on i. 1.

prophets]   In the enumeration, 1 Cor. xii. 28, this "ministry" comes
second, as here.   On the "prophets" of the N. T. see above on ii. 20,
and Appendix F.

evangelists]   The word occurs thrice in N.T.; here, Acts xxi. 8, and
2 Tim. iv. 5.   It seems, like our word "missionary," to indicate not
a defined ecclesiastical order (for Timothy "does the work of an
evangelist," while also an authoritative superintendent of pastors and
churches), but rather a special kind of personal function in the ministry;
the work of one called and devoted to direct proclamation of the Gospel
message.   It was thus an elastic word, like "missionary," sometimes
and oftenest denoting a minister's special function, sometimes one only

12 for the perfecting of the saints for the work of the ministry,
13 for the edifying of the body of Christ : till we all come in

of his functions. "This passage," our present passage, "would lead us to think of the evangelists as standing between the two groups," (apostles and prophets, pastors and teachers,) "sent forth, as missionary preachers of the Gospel, by the first, and as such preparing the way for the labours of the second" (Smith's *Dict. of the Bible*, under the word *Evangelist*). "The omission of evangelists in the list of I Cor. xii. may be explained on the hypothesis that the nature of St Paul's argument there led him to speak of the settled organization of a given local Church" (*Ibidem*).

pastors and teachers] Not, "some pastors and some teachers." The two functions are regarded as coinciding and combining in the one settled guardian of a local flock ; an instructive fact.—Such a "pastor-teacher" had St Paul himself been at Ephesus (Acts xx.), where indeed he had also been so conspicuously the "evangelist."—On the pastoral aspect of the Christian ministry cp. Joh. xxi. 16 (Gr. "*shepherd* my sheep"); Acts xx. 28 (Gr., "*shepherd* the church of God"), 29; I Pet. v. 2, 3. See also Luke xvii. 7 (Gr., "a slave...*shepherding*"). And note the Lord's own references to His supreme Pastorate, Matt. xxv. 32, xxvi. 31; Joh. x.; and Heb. xiii. 20; I Pet. ii. 25, v. 4; and Matt. ii. 6 (Gr., "shall *shepherd* my people"). On the teaching aspect of the ministry, cf. esp. Acts xiii. 1, xv. 35; Rom. xii. 7; I Cor. xii. 28, 29; I Tim. iii. 2; 2 Tim. ii. 24.

12. *for the perfecting of the saints*, &c.] More lit., **with a view to the equipment of the saints for [their] work of service.** Latin versions, *ad consummationem sanctorum in opus ministerii*. The noun rendered *equipment* occurs only here in N.T. The kindred verb occurs *e.g.* Matt. iv. 21 (A.V., "*mending* nets"); Gal. vi. 1 (A.V., "*restore* such a one"); Heb. xiii. 21 ("make you *perfect*"; and so 2 Cor. xiii. 11; I Pet. v. 10). The idea is of mending a breach, completing a connexion, putting the dislocated in order.—The practical suggestion here is most important. The Divine gift of a Christian Ministry is to have its effect above all things in the fitting of "the saints" (true believers in general) for active "service" for the common Lord. Government, preaching, teaching, is to bear upon this. Nothing will be a more lawful result of a Divine ministerial commission than energetic efforts for Christ and His cause on the part of private Christians. These efforts, on the other hand, will never be made (in the true ideal of Christian work) in neglect or contempt of the ordered ministry.

for the edifying of the body] A special aspect of the "work of service" just mentioned. Each true believer is, by the spiritually enabled ministry, to be "equipped" to act as a "builder up" of the Lord's Body (on which see above, on ver. 4); to gather in new "living stones," new "members," by holy influence of word and work; and to compact and consolidate the cohesion. See below ver. 29 for a special form of such labours.—For the fusion of the metaphors of "building" and "body" see the closing verses of ch. ii., and below ver. 16.

the unity of the faith, and of the knowledge of the Son of
God, unto a perfect man, unto the measure of the stature

13. *till we all come in*] Render, **come unto**. The thought is of the
holy Community converging into the spiritual harmony of a developed,
equal, identical faith in and knowledge of the Son of God, under the
mutual influence of individual believers stimulated and guided by the
spiritual ministry. This would take place by growth and development
in the faith and knowledge of individuals; but the cohesion of the true
Church would bring these individual growths to converge and result in
the maturity of the collective faith and knowledge, so to speak, of
the whole Body, the ideal "fullgrown Man" of which the "fullgrown
men" were the elements and miniatures.

of the faith, and of the knowledge of] I.e., faith *in* Him and knowledge
of Him. "Faith *of*" often, in the N.T., means "faith *in*"; *e.g.* Gal.
ii. 20 (A.V., "the faith of the Son of God," identically as here). See
above on iii. 12.—"*Knowledge*":—the Gr. word indicates true, full,
developed spiritual knowledge, but too delicately, perhaps, to admit
translation. See above on i. 17.

the Son of God] This sacred Title belongs to the Saviour specially,
among other respects, as He is the Head of the Church, the Firstborn,
"in Whom" the "children" have adoption and regeneration; "in
Whom" they are one with the Father. Their progress in the regenerate
life and likeness will be largely effected through their "faith in Him
and true knowledge of Him" *as such*.

perfect] Better, as R.V., **full-grown**. The maturity of the life to
come is in view; the state in which the mutual "edification" of the
present life will have done its work.

man] The Gr. corresponds to the Latin *vir*, not *homo*. It indicates
man as against *child*. See next verse.

unto the measure of the stature] The metaphor is of height, not age,
though the word rendered "stature" means "age" as readily, by itself.
The imagery of *growth* in this passage decides the alternative here.—
"*The measure*":—the allotted, proper, standard.

the fulness of Christ] Cp. the phrases "fulness of the Gentiles" (Rom.
xi. 25), and "fulness of the time" (Gal. iv. 4), and note on i. 23. The
phrase here appears to be analogous: *the total, at length attained, of what
is meant by Christ*. And "Christ" in this passage (so full of the idea of
the oneness in and with the Lord of His mystical Body) is, in effect, Christ
and His Church (see above on i. 23); as in 1 Cor. xii. 12, "as the body
is one, and hath many limbs...so also *is Christ*." The Lord the Son
becomes in accomplished fact all that He wills, and is willed, to be,
only when He is the Head of a perfected mystical Body which lives by
His sacred Life and is His incorporate "limbs," His immortal vehicle
of action, if we may so speak. So He and they are guardedly and
reverently spoken of here and there as One Christ, with full reservation,
from other Scriptures, of the truth of the undying personality of each
individual "limb" of the glorious Head, and of His Divine Personality.
—See further above on i. 22.

14 of the fulness of Christ: that we *henceforth* be no more children, tossed to and fro, and carried about with every wind of doctrine, by the sleight of men, and cunning crafti-
15 ness, whereby they lie in wait to deceive; but speaking the

It is possible to explain the present phrase to mean "the fulness which flows from Christ," the full, ideal, supply of grace and glory derived to the members from the Head. But we think this less probable, in view of the passage above quoted, 1 Cor. xii. 12. See also below, vv. 15, 16.

14. *that we* henceforth, &c.] This verse takes up the thought of ver. 12. The mutual activity and influence of Christians, guided aright, is to result in, at once, fixity of principle and richness of power; both characteristic of spiritual maturity.

children] The same Gr. word as *e.g.* 1 Cor. iii. 1 (A.V., "babes"), xiii. 11; Heb. v. 13 (A.V., "babe"). By usage, it denotes the young child in the aspect specially of ignorance or mental weakness, "childishness." From another side the same word sometimes conveys ideas *commended* by the Gospel, the little child's simplicity of purpose and willingness to be taught, "childlikeness" (*e.g.* Matt. xi. 25, xxi. 16; 1 Cor. xiv. 20, where the kindred verb is used).

tossed to and fro] Lit., "*billowed*"; carried up and down as *on* waves. Another explanation of the (rare) Gr. word is "worked *into* waves," as the sea by the wind. But the next phrase is against this, and so is the analogy of a verb of similar form, Jas. i. 6 (A.V., "driven *with* the wind").

carried about] Like St Paul's own ship in Adria (Acts xxvii. 27, where the Gr. verb is closely akin to this).

of doctrine] Lit., **of the teaching**, the teaching in question, that described just below.

by the sleight] Lit., **in the dicing.**—"*In:*"—more than "*by.*" The thought is of "the evil atmosphere, as it were, *in* which the varying currents of false doctrine...exert their force" (Ellicott).—"*Dicing*":—the word was familiar in later Greek, in the sense of deceit, sharp practice, in general. It was thence borrowed, and similarly used, by the Rabbis.

of men] Not of Christ, nor for Christ. Cp. Gal. i. 1.

and cunning craftiness, &c.] More lit., **in cunning, with a view to the scheming of [their] deceit.** R.V., "*after* the wiles of error." But the Gr. preposition far more often means "with a view to" than "according to." The practical difference, however, is minute.

The Apostle here recognizes and exposes the sad fact of *intentional* misguidance on the part of these preachers of "another Gospel" (Gal. i. 6, 7). See the parallel cautions, Rom. xvi. 17, 18; Col. ii. 4.

15. *speaking the truth*] The Gr. (one word) is wider and deeper, including the thought of *living* and *loving truth*. Alford renders "*being followers of truth*." And the context is in favour of this. Not speaking truth, but avoiding false teaching, is in question. The Christian is to cultivate an instinct for Divine Truth, as against its counterfeits, in

truth in love, may grow *up* into him *in* all *things*, which is
the head, *even* Christ : from whom the whole body fitly ₁₆
joined together and compacted by that which every joint

thought and in life.—R.V., "speaking truth" and (margin) "dealing
truly."

in love] The holy condition under which alone the "follower of
truth" would follow it truly, free from bitterness and prejudice, intent
only on the will of God. It has been well said that some men find love
the easier precept, some truth; but that the Gospel enjoins the harmony
of both.

grow up] The metaphor of the living Body reappears. See above,
notes on ver. 12, 13.

into him] So as to deepen the realization of "in-ness" in Him, and
more richly to derive its blessings.—Just possibly we may render "*unto*
Him." In that case the Lord would be viewed as the Archetype to
which each believer, in his spiritual development and growth, grow-
ingly conforms. But this is less in harmony with the imagery of the
Body *and Head* which we have here.

in *all* things] Lit., "*as to all things*." Our growing sense of incorporation is to affect our whole being, not a part; "spirit, soul, and
body" (1 Thess. v. 23).

the head] See on i. 22.

16. *from whom*] He is the vital Source to which the whole complex organism now to be described wholly owes alike its *existence* and
its *action*.

fitly joined together] The Gr. participle is present, and indicates
a process going on. The Body, vitalized from and by the Head, is
evermore acquiring a deeper and truer contact of part with part, a
more harmonious ("*fitly*") inner union and action. See above on ii.
21, where the same Gr. word occurs.

compacted] Again a present participle. (The same word recurs
Col. ii. 19.) The idea of growth in harmony of structure (see last
note) here merges into that of growth in solidity and strength.

by that which every joint supplieth] Lit., **by** or **through every joint
of the supply.** It is possible to render "by every *contact* of the supply"; i.e., as explained by St Chrysostom here, "as the Spirit touches,
in order to supply grace, each limb of the Body"; or, perhaps, as
each limb, each believer, touches (by faith) the source of supply. But
the parallel passage Col. ii. 19 is decisive for the explanation "join*.*"
So the Latin Versions, *junctura*. The thought is of "supply" passing
to the limbs through the *nexus* of each with the source of life. Each
such *nexus* is thus a "joint *of* supply," "a junction designed for, made
for, conveyance" of life and power; as we speak of "a bond *of* union."
The metaphor must not be elaborately pressed. The essential idea
is mutual coherence and common growth of the limbs through individual connexion with the Head (1 Cor. vi. 17), not through connexion
with other limbs. The "joint" thus represents the man's spiritual
union with Christ, not union with church-organization, which is a

supplieth, according to the effectual working in the measure
of every part, maketh increase of the body unto the edifying
of itself in love.

17   This I say therefore, and testify in the Lord, that ye
henceforth walk not as other Gentiles walk, in the vanity

thing, however sacred, of another order. The life flow from the Head
to each spiritual Limb is individual and direct. The product of this,
not the cause or means of it, is the life of the Body.

according to the effectual working] Better, simply, **[the] working.**
The process in view takes place "according to," in the manner and
on the scale of, the life-power of the Head acting in the Limb. The
original noun (whence our "energy" is derived) occurs in N. T. only
in St Paul; Eph. i. 19, iii. 7 (where see note), and here ; Phil. iii. 21;
Col. i. 29, ii. 12; 2 Thess. ii. 9 (of the working of the Evil Power).
The article is omitted before the word here, perhaps because the
power referred to is unmistakable. Alford renders "according to vital
working."

in the measure of every part] Each limb has its own conditions of
larger or smaller capacity; age, circumstances, training, and the like
occasion very various "measures" in the allotments of the Divine life-
power which adjusts itself to each real need, while it can always fully
meet that need.

maketh] The form of the Gr. verb (middle) indicates fulness and
intensity of action.

increase] Lit., **the increase**, *the* growth contemplated as taking
place.

unto the edifying of itself] For illustration, see ii. 21, and notes.

in love] The inmost condition of the whole process. All takes
place "in," under the power and after the action of, "love"; for the
Source of the life-energy is "the Son of the Father's love" (Col. i. 13,
Gr.), and the recipients are "rooted and grounded in the love" of the
Father in Him (see above on iii. 17); from which "no created thing
shall separate them" (Rom. viii. 39).

17—24   PRACTICAL RESULTS: A SPIRITUAL REVOLUTION OF
PRINCIPLE AND PRACTICE. THE OLD MAN AND THE NEW

17. *testify*] A word of solemn appeal occurring elsewhere in N. T.
only Acts xxii. 26 (St Paul speaking) and Gal. v. 3.

in the Lord] As myself being "in Him," and as to those who are
in the same union. Cp. Gal. v. 10 ("I have confidence towards you
in the Lord," Gr.); below, vi. 1 ("obey in the Lord"); &c. The
phrase "in the Lord" occurs 45 times in St Paul; "in Christ," or
closely kindred phrases, nearly 80 times.

henceforth, &c.] More lit., **no longer walk.** At their conversion
"old things were passed away" (2 Cor. v. 17) as to principle. Let
this be now realized, continuously and ever more completely, in
practice. On the metaphor "*walk*," see above on ii. 2, 10.

of their mind, having the understanding darkened, being 18
alienated from the life of God through the ignorance that

other Gentiles] Read, probably, **the Gentiles**. (On the word see
above, on ii. 11.) In a spiritual sense the Ephesians were *no longer*
"Gentiles," for they were spiritual "Israelites" (Gal. vi. 16); hence
the true form of the phrase here.

vanity of their mind] "Vanity" here is not *self-conceit*, which
would require another Gr. word. It is the "emptiness" of *illusion*,
specially of the state of illusion which sees pleasure in sin. In Rom.
viii. 20 the word is used of evil, whether physical or moral, regarded
as (what all evil ultimately proves to be) delusion and failure.

"*Of their mind*":—the "mind" sometimes denotes specially the
reason, as distinguished *e.g.* from spiritual intuition (1 Cor. xiv. 14,
15). Sometimes (Col. ii. 18) it apparently denotes the rational powers
in general, as in the unregenerate state; and again those powers as
regenerate (Rom. xii. 2). Here the unrenewed "Gentile" is viewed
as living on principles which reason can approve only when the eternal
facts are hidden from it.

18. *having the understanding darkened*] Lit., **having been darkened in the understanding**. On "the understanding" see note above
on ii. 3 (where A. V., "mind"). The Gr. word may fairly be said to
mean the reason (*nous*) in action. Here accordingly the phrase defines,
so to speak, the phrase just previous; the general *illusion* of the reason
comes out in *obfuscated acts* of thought.—On the metaphor of darkness
cp. Matt. vi. 23; Joh. iii. 19, viii. 12, xii. 35, 46; Acts xxvi. 18; Col.
i. 13; 1 Thess. v. 4, 5; 1 Joh. i. 5, 6, ii. 8, 9, 11; and below, ch. v.
8, 11, vi. 12. It often combines the ideas of blindness and of secrecy;
here it gives only the former.

being alienated from the life of God] The words, Gr. and Eng.,
imply a fall from a state of union. See above on ii. 12 where "alienated" occurs in another connexion. Here, as there, the Human Soul
in the abstract is viewed as having shared, in its unfallen state, the
Life of God, and having lost it in the Fall. And this view is transferred
from the Soul to the souls in which it is individualized. Historically,
we begin our personal existence aliens; ideally, we began in union
and fell from it.

"*The life of God*":—the word "life" occurs here only in the Epistle.
The phrase here denotes the spiritual force given to the human spirit
by spiritual contact with God, resulting in the action and exercise of
holiness. The Christian believer finds "this life in His Son" (1 Joh.
v. 11). In Joh. xvii. 3 we have at once its secret and its issue; "to
know the only true God, and Jesus Christ whom He hath sent." It
is entered, from one point of view, by "justification of life" (Rom. v.
18), that acceptance of the guilty in Christ which is the *sine quâ non*
in Divine Law. Its development is the state of glory, which is
therefore very often called, in a special sense, "eternal life" (*e. g.*
Matt. xxv. 46), though that phrase is also fully true of the present
state of the believer (1 Joh. iii. 15, v. 13).—It is plain that the

19 is in them, because of the blindness of their heart : who
being past feeling have given themselves over unto lascivious-
20 ness, to work all uncleanness with greediness.   But ye have

word "life," in spiritual connexions, means very much more than "existence." See above on ii. 1.

through the ignorance] Better, **on account of,** &c. They lost connexion with the Life of God, and so remain, because of their ignorance
of the eternal facts about God and holiness. We have here still something of the idealization explained just above. As the Human Soul fell
through guilty "ignorance" of the supreme *right* and *joy* of absolute
submission to God, so the individual soul is viewed as, ideally, losing
union through the same "ignorance" of self-will. Historically, the
individual begins self-willed and therefore alienated; ideally, he breaks
an existing connexion. The practical aspect of the matter is that he
maintains disconnexion by the ignorance of self-will. He "wills not to
come that he may have life" (Joh. v. 40), "seeing no beauty" in Christ,
"that he should desire Him" in an effectual sense (Isai. liii. 2).

blindness] Better, **hardening** (so R.V.). The word denotes failure
of sensation in general. This clause is a re-statement of that just
previous. What took place "on account of ignorance" took place "on
account of hardening"; another aspect of the same moral state.

.heart] See on i. 18, iii. 17. Much more than the seat of emotion is
meant by this word in Scripture.—Phrases compounded of "heart" and
"harden" occur (in the Gr.) Mar. iii. 5, vi. 52, viii. 17; Joh. xii. 40. In
2 Cor. iii. 14 we have (Gr.) "their *thoughts* were hardened."

19. *who being past feeling*] The Gr. relative pronoun indicates a
certain conditionality; almost as if it were, "*as being those* who." But
the shade is too slight for translation.—"*Past feeling*":—lit., "having
got over the pain," as when mortification sets in; a deeply suggestive
metaphor.

have given themselves over] Lit., **did give over themselves.** An
ideal crisis is in view, reflected in many a sad actual crisis in individual
lives.—"*Themselves*" is emphatic by position. The perverted *will* is
the traitor, the "giver over." However deep the mystery of its per-
version, it is always *the will*, and speaks as such the decisive "yes" to
temptation.

lasciviousness] The Gr. word occurs in N.T. 11 times. See *e.g.*
Mar. vii. 22; Rom. xiii. 13 (A.V., "wantonness"); Gal. v. 19. The
root-idea of the word is not specially fleshly impurity, but rebellion
against restraint as such; petulance, wantonness, as shewn *e.g.* in
violence. Abp Trench (*N. T. Synonyms*, on this word), recommends
accordingly **wantonness** as a better rendering than "lasciviousness,"
which is but one manifestation of the tendency denoted.

to work] Lit., **to the working of.** The Gr. noun occurs elsewhere
in N.T. Luke xii. 58 (A.V., "diligence"); Acts xvi. 16, 19 (A.V.,
"gain"); xix. 24 (A.V., "gain"), 25 (A.V., "craft"). The idea of
business thus adheres to the word. The suggestion conveyed by it here
is that sin becomes to the deliberate sinner an earnest pursuit, an occu-

not so learned Christ; if so be that ye have heard him, and 21

pation. Cp. Rom. xiii. 14 (*"forethought* for the flesh"). The R.V. gives in its margin here, "to make a trade of."

uncleanness] The connexion of the Gr. word is mainly with fleshly impurity, and so probably here. But it is not quite confined to this; one passage (1 Thess. ii. 3) giving the thought rather of "impure motives" in the sense of insincerity.

greediness] The Gr. word is rendered "covetousness," Luke xii. 15. But it means much more than the desire of *money*, or *property*, with which we specially associate "covetousness." It occurs (or its cognate verb or adjective) in close connexion with the subject of *fleshly impurity* 1 Cor. v. 11; 1 Thess. iv. 6; and below, v. 3, 5. See too Col. iii. 5. "Greed" has a strong and terrible connexion with impurity, as is obvious. Bp Lightfoot shews (on Col. iii. 5) that the present word never *of itself* denotes "lust," while it is, of course, rightly used to denote the horrible grasp and plunder which lust involves.

In this verse the Apostle depicts, as universal among "the Gentiles," an abandoned licentiousness. Contemporary literature gives mournful testimony to the charge, as regards society in general, indicating a large social toleration of the most hideous vices, and a significant readiness to import vicious imagery into refined spheres of thought. But the accusation of this passage, surely, transcends the limits of any one age, or state of society; it is levelled at unregenerate Man. And the explanation of it, so viewed, is to be sought in the study of those *tendencies* of evil which reside in the fallen "heart" as such. The action of outrageous *sinning* does but illustrate the underlying principle of *sin;* a principle with which absolutely nothing but "the life of God" can effectually deal. See further Rom. iii. 10—18, and notes in this Series.

20. *ye*] Emphatic by position.

have not...learned] Better, **did not learn**; at their conversion.— "*Learn*" implies the *instruction* then received in the Lord's precepts, and in the holy bearings of His work. For a similar reference to the first apprehension by new converts of Gospel purity of principle, cp. 1 Thess. iv. 7; "God did not *call us* on terms of impurity."

Christ] Who is the Subject-matter of His own message.

21. *if so be*] The Gr. interrogative (used also above, iii. 2) does not imply any doubt, necessarily, but calls the reader to verify the statement.

have heard him, &c.] Better, as "Him" is emphatic by position, **If it was He whom ye heard**. The Gr. construction leads us to explain this not of listening *to* the Lord so much as of hearing *about* Him, or rather, of hearing "Him" as Truth rather than Teacher. "Christ" had been the Message they had received.—He does indeed, by His Word and Spirit, personally continue the "teaching" which in His earthly ministry He began (Acts i. 1); but that is not the point of the present words.

have been taught by him] Better, **if it was in Him that ye were taught**. The instruction was "in Christ," if the teacher's limit and rule

22 have been taught by him, as the truth is in Jesus : that ye put off concerning the former conversation the old man,

was the truth of His Person and Work, and if those who received it were, by living spiritual union, "in Him," and so capable of "spiritual discernment" (1 Cor. ii. 14). This clause defines and explains the previous clause.

as the truth is in Jesus] Better, **even as in Jesus truth is.** See last note, on the relation of spiritual "in-ness" to the standard and reception of spiritual truth. The emphasis here is as if to say, "If you were taught, as I say, in Him ; in the lines of eternal *fact* and spiritual *reality* which do so truly meet in Him."—The question arises, why does the Lord's designation change from "Christ," ver. 20, to "*Jesus*" here ? Probably to mark the fact that the prophesied Christ *is* the historical Jesus.

22. *that ye put off*] The Gr. verb is the infinitive aorist. The tense tends to denote singleness of crisis and action. Some would render "that you have" (or "did) put off." But the better explanation, or paraphrase, is, "with regard to your (definite) putting-off." The "instruction in Christ" had informed them *about* such ? "putting-off"; its principles, secret, effects, as well as its fact.—But the view of the "putting-off" as a definite crisis remains ; and the only question is, does this crisis appear here as a past or future one? The answer will be best given under the words "the old man," just below. For the present we refer to Col. iii. 9 as strongly favouring the reference here to a crisis past ; so that we may paraphrase, "you were taught in Christ with regard to the fact that your old man was laid aside."

concerning the former conversation] On "conversation" see on ii. 3 above. The word (noun and verb) happens to be almost always used by St Paul in reference to the unregenerate life-course.—The clause means that the "putting-off" *concerned*, had to do with, a former life-course ; it affected it, by being the close of it.—**As concerning your former manner of life** (R.V.).

the old man] This important phrase occurs elsewhere Rom. vi. 6; Col. iii. 9. In Rom. it appears as a thing which "was crucified with Christ"; in Col. as a thing which "was once stripped off" by the saints. (Cp. the remarkable parallel words Col. ii. 11, as in the best supported reading, "in the stripping off of *the body of the flesh.*") On the whole, we may explain the phrase by "*the old state.*" And under this lie combined the ideas of past personal legal position and moral position ; all that I was as an unregenerate son of Adam, liable to eternal doom, and the slave of sin. To "put off the old man" is to quit those positions, which, at the root, are one. It is to step into the position of personal acceptance and of personal spiritual power and victory; and that position is "in Christ." The believer, lodged there, enters definitely and at once upon both acceptance and spiritual capacity for victory and growth.—"*The old man*" is thus not identical with "*the flesh,*" which is an abiding element (Gal. v. 16, 17) in even the regenerate and spiritual, though it need no longer—even for an hour—be the ruling

which is corrupt according to the deceitful lusts; and be 23
renewed in the spirit of your mind; and that *ye* put on the 24

element; it may be continuously overcome, in a practical and profound
manner, in the strength of "the new man."—The phrases "old Man"
and "new Man" have a probable inner reference to the doctrine of the
First and Second Adam (Rom. v. 12—19; 1 Cor. xv. 21—58). The
"putting off" and "putting on" may be expressed by saying, "ye broke
connexion (in certain great aspects of connexion) with the First Adam,
and formed connexion with the Second," connexion both of acceptance
and of life-power[1].

corrupt] Lit., **corrupting, growing corrupt**; morally decaying, on
the way to final ruin. Such, from the Divine point of view, is the condition of ideal Man unregenerate, Man as represented by and summed
up in Adam fallen. And such accordingly is the actual condition, from
the same point of view, of unregenerate *men*, in whom the ideal is
individualized.

according to the deceitful lusts] Lit., **the desires of deceit**; desires
after the forbidden, full of *deceitful* promises of joy and gain. See Gen.
iii. for the great typical case, which perhaps is in view throughout this
verse.—"*According to*":—by natural result. Moral decay *must* follow
in their path.—Cp. 2 Peter ii. 19.

23. *be renewed*] A present infinitive in the Gr. The idea is thus of
progress and growth, the antithesis to the "corrupting" just above.
The decisive fact of new position in and connexion with Christ was to
result, and was resulting, in an ever developed spiritual experience, with
its ever new disclosures both of need and of grace. Cp. 2 Cor. iv. 16.—
We may paraphrase the clause (on the principle explained in the first
note on ver. 22), "*and with regard to* your being renewed."

in the spirit of your mind] I.e., practically, "in your spiritual life
and faculty, coming out in the phase of thought and understanding," as
distinct from *e.g.* the phase of emotion. "Spirit" can scarcely here
refer to the Holy Ghost; and it cannot bear the vague modern sense of
"sentiment," or the like. It is the human spirit, as the substratum, so
to speak, of every activity of the "inner man," and now specially of the
activity which sees and grasps truth ("your *mind*"). See above, last
note on ver. 17.—The Gr. may be rendered "*by* the spirit of your mind,"
as the instrument, or avenue, used by the Eternal Spirit in the process
of renewal. And cp. Rom. xii. 2 for a good parallel. But usage is on
the whole in favour of the rendering "in," in the sense of "with reference to."

24. *that* ye *put on*] See note on "put off," ver. 22. Here again is
an aorist infinitive in the Gr.; and we may correspondingly paraphrase,
"(you were taught) with regard to the fact that the new man was put on."

On the meaning of the phrase here, see notes on ver. 22, where it is
explained by contrast and implication. The "putting on the new man"

[1] On this aspect of Christian doctrine much excellent matter will be found in an old
book, *The Gospel Mystery of Sanctification*, by Walter Marshall, Fellow of New
College, Oxford (about 1670).

new man, which after God is created in righteousness and true holiness.

is the inseparable converse to the "putting off the old man." There is no neutral border; to step out of the old position and connexion, out of Adam, is to step into the new, into Christ.

Meantime, what is in covenant and in principle a thing done, is to be in realization and application a thing doing, a thing repeated. So we have Rom. xiii. 14; *"put ye on* the Lord Jesus Christ," an exhortation to a new act of realization. And cp. Col. iii. 12. The other side, the side (as we believe) of this passage, appears Gal. iii. 27; *"ye did put on* Christ."

the new man] Practically, the new position and power (legal and moral, see note on ver. 22) of the regenerated self. In a deeper analysis, we trace (as above on ver. 22) a reference to the Second Man, the Second Adam, Christ. (See the quotation from St Ignatius, *Introd.*, p. 28. See also, for another aspect of this phrase, ii. 15). By incorporation with Him His "members" become (in a sense needing reverent caution in the statement) repetitions of Him the glorious Archetype, as occupants of His position of Acceptance, and as "one spirit" with Him, and as enabled in Him to live a life whose principle is His—separation from sin to God. To come to be "in Him" is thus to "put on the New Man" in the sense of part and lot in the standing and in the power of the Lord as Second Covenant Head. But, we repeat it, the practical reference of the verse is to the "newness" of the believer's standing and power, acquired in regeneration.

which] Better, in modern English, **who.**

after God] "Answering His great Idea," His plan and will.

is created] Better, **was created.** This "creation" was accomplished, ideally, when the new Covenant Head of the regenerate Race was provided, in eternal purpose; historically, when He was "made Man," in time; actually, for individuals, when each believer "put on Christ," came to be "in Him." Cp. on the thought of spiritual "creation" ch. ii. 10, 15; 2 Cor. v. 17; Gal. vi. 15; and especially Col. iii. 10, a close and suggestive parallel here.

righteousness] Of which the essential idea is willing conformity to Law; "the keeping of His commandments."

true holiness] Lit., **sanctity of the truth.** We use "sanctity" rather than "holiness," to mark the fact that the Gr. word (*hosiotēs*) is not akin to that commonly rendered "holy." Its meaning is discussed by Abp Trench (*N. T. Synonyms* ii. § xxxviii). He shews it to be the virtue which "reverences everlasting sanctities, and owns their obligation"; the intuitive conviction, *e.g.*, of the sacredness of an oath, or of marriage, or, in the spiritual sphere, of God's absolute claims, wholly apart from a calculation of results. "*Piety*" would fairly, though not fully, represent the word. In two places (Rev. xv. 4, xvi. 5) the cognate adjective is used of God Himself. It there suggests His own inviolable regard for His own truth, in mercy and judgment.

The word (noun, adjective, or adverb) occurs (as here) with "right-

Wherefore putting away lying, speak every man truth 25

eous" or "righteousness" Luke i. 75; 1 Thess. ii. 10; Tit. i. 8. It
is the almost invariable rendering in the LXX. for the Heb. *châsîd;*
e.g. Psal. xvi. 10, quoted Acts ii. 27, xiii. 35 (A.V. *"thy Holy One"*);
and Is. lv. 3, quoted Acts xiii. 34 (where lit. *"the holy things* of David,"
the inviolable promises given to him[1]).

"Of the truth":—so lit., and so, looking at St Paul's usage, we translate; not *"of truth,"* as R.V. and marg. A.V. This "sanctity" or
"piety" is *"of"* the truth of the Gospel, because the Gospel explains
it, and it characterizes the Gospel; and this is equally so, whether the
thought is of its manifestation in Christ or in Christians, in Head or in
Members.

25—32 THE SUBJECT PURSUED: THE REVOLUTION COMING OUT
IN TRUTHFULNESS, KINDNESS, HONESTY, PURITY, PATIENCE,
FORGIVINGNESS

25. *Wherefore*] From these deep principles come now the more
detailed inferences of holy practice, and these fill most of the rest of the
Epistle. Here and there (as in this verse, and in ch. v. 23) the
basis of the whole in the truth of the relations of the Church to Christ appears
explicitly.

putting away lying] Cp. Col. iii. 9, 10, for a suggestive parallel.
There, as here, truthfulness is connected with "new creation." He
who is "in Christ" is, above all things, in a region of light and of right,
whose first result will be the aim to do and speak truth; the truth of
entire and unselfish sincerity.—"*Putting away*" carries on the imagery
of ver. 22. For the phrase, in reference to a definite break with sinful
principle and practice, cp. Col. iii. 8; Heb. xii. 1; Jas. i. 21; 1 Pet. ii.
1 (A.V., "*lay aside,*" in the last three places). And see below, ver. 31.
—This "putting away" may be viewed either as a thing *done,* in principle, for the member of Christ has, in respect of that union, definitely
"done with sin"; or as a thing *to be done* (Col. iii. 8, imperative), in
each application of sinless principle. The Gr. is an aorist participle,
and thus, grammatically, allows either view. We recommend the former,
as most in harmony with the previous context.

speak...truth] The application of the decisively accepted principle of
truth. Observe the sober and humbling practicality of the Apostle's
precepts; as necessary now as ever. And earnestly observe the uncompromising condemnation, by the Gospel, of all kinds and phases of
dishonesty. Nothing untruthful can possibly be holy. A pious fraud
is, in the light of true Christianity, a most grievous sin.—The emphasis
laid on truthfulness in Scripture is all the more significant of the
character and origin of Scripture when we remember the proverbial
Oriental laxity about truth. Lying is a vice deeply characteristic
of heathenism. An Indian missionary said of his first convert, "he

---

[1] The lit. rendering of the Heb. of Is. lv. 3 is "the mercies of David, the assured
(mercies)." The LXX. represents, but does not translate, this. In Ps. xvi. 10 render
lit., "Thy godly One," or perhaps, "Thy favoured, beloved, One." (Note by the
Dean of Peterborough).

with his neighbour: for we are members one of another.
26 Be ye angry, and sin not: let not the sun go down upon

would often come to me with tears in his eyes, saying, ' I told you a
falsehood, but it seemed nature to me to say *yes* when I should say *no*,
and *no* when I should say *yes*'." (Communicated by the Dean of
Peterborough).—Contrast Psal. xv. 2, 3.

his neighbour] Primarily, the fellow-Christian is in view; see the
next clause. But this first bearing of such a precept is pregnant with a
universal reference. For to the believer his fellow-Christian *is* a fellow-
member of Christ, his fellow-man *may be*.—On the word "neighbour"
it is obvious thus to compare the Lord's parable, Luke x. 29 &c.

for we are members one of another] Each vitally and directly joined
to the Head (see on ver. 16) and so, *through Him*, incorporated into one
another. And thus comes a profound correction to that selfishness which
inheres in falsehood. The interests of each member centre not in itself
but in the Head, and the Head is equally related to and interested
in each member. In Him, therefore, each is as important to each as
each to itself.—Cp. Rom. xii. 5; 1 Cor. xii. 12—27.—On the *universal*
application latent in this argument, see last note.

26. *Be ye angry, and sin not*] Another inference from co-member-
ship in the Lord. Anger, as the mere expression of wounded personality,
is sinful; for it means that self is in command. Anger, as the pure
expression of repugnance to wrong in loyalty to God, is sinless, where
there is true occasion for it. The Apostle practically says, let anger,
when you feel it, be *never* from the former motive, always from the
latter. "Ebullitions of temper," alike the greatest and smallest, the
seen and unseen, are wholly forbidden here.

The words are verbatim the LXX. version of Psal. **iv. 4.** The lit.
Hebrew there is, "tremble, *and sin not*." And the verb rendered
"tremble" may denote the tremor of grief, awe, or anger indifferently.
The question of interpretation thus becomes one of context, and it has
been suggested (by Dr Kay) that the reference is to the temptation to
David's followers, during Absalom's rebellion, to give way to unholy
wrath against the rebels. Dean Perowne, though saying that the LXX.
Gr. is "certainly a possible rendering," refers the words to the tremor
of awe before God. And he remarks that St Paul here gives the Gr.
version "not in the way of direct citation." This last remark is important. The N.T. does not necessarily endorse a certain version of
the O.T. by adopting its wording for a special purpose, *without* the
decisive formula "it is written," or the like. Still, the suggestion of Dr
Kay is noteworthy in itself, and its adoption would give a peculiar
point and force to the words here.

let not the sun go down] Wetstein quotes a curious parallel from
Plutarch, (*De Fraterno Amore*, p. 488 B.), who says of the Pythagoreans
that it was their rule, if betrayed into angry reviling, to shake hands
before the sun set.—It is possible that we have Ps. iv. still in view here;
"commune with your own heart *upon your bed*, and be still." As if
to say, "if you *have* sinned in the way here forbidden, see that at least

your wrath : neither give place to the devil. Let him that ²⁷ ₂₈
stole steal no more : but rather let him labour, working with
his hands the *thing which is* good, that he may have to
give to him that needeth. Let no corrupt communication ₂₉

the sin is reversed and renounced before night calls you to bid your
brother farewell and to meet your God in solitude."

your wrath] Better, perhaps, **your provocation**, as R.V. margin.
The Gr. denotes an occasion of anger, rather than the feeling. See
further on the cognate verb, vi. 4. The reasons, as well as the acts, of
quarrel were to be done with by set of sun.—The Gr. word is one
often used by the LXX. of the provocation of God by His unfaithful
people.

27. *give place to the devil*] The rendering suggested by some, "to
the calumniator," the heathen or Jewish slanderer, is quite untenable,
in view of St Paul's use elsewhere of the word *diabolos* (lit., "Accuser")
for the great Enemy.

" *Give place* " :—as to one who would fain intrude at a half-open
door, intent on occupying the house. Personal anger gives just such a
point d'appui to the Spirit of pride and hatred. " Wherever the devil
finds a heart shut, he finds a door open " (Monod). And this is true
not of individuals only, but of the Church and its life.

28. *him that stole*] Another moral inference from Christian incorporation. Here again, as above (see on ver. 25), and more obviously
than ever, the *Christian* aspect of the duty has also a *universal* reference.—The Gr. is a present participle, and may equally well be rendered
him that stealeth. It is possible, surely, that St Paul (like many a
modern missionary and pastor) was prepared to find inconsistency so
serious in the Christian community as to warrant the assumption of
present thieving in some cases. (See above on ver. 25). Such things
were surely to be found in the early *Corinthian* Church.

The duty of strict restitution is not explicitly mentioned here. But in
the Epistle to Philemon, written at the same time, it is both insisted
upon and acted upon.

his *hands*] Better, perhaps, **his own hands.** If personal activity has
been spent on wrong, let nothing less than personal activity be spent on
" working that which is good," with a view to honest getting and gain.

that he may have to give] Impartation of good is of the genius of the
Gospel ; and there would be a special call now to impart where there
had been unholy appropriation before. Christian morality, as Monod
remarks, is never satisfied with reform ; it demands conversion.

29. *no corrupt communication*] Or, better, **speech,** as R.V.—
Another moral inference from membership in Christ.

" *Corrupt*" :—lit., "*rotten, putrid.*" The Latin versions render
simply *sermo malus*, and the Gr. adjective *may* (by usage) bear this
merely general reference to "evil" of any sort ; worthlessness, uselessness, as well as impurity. But we recommend the narrower reference,
as certainly more native to the word, and as extremely likely *à priori*,

proceed out of your mouth, but that which *is* good to the use of edifying, that it may minister grace unto the hearers. 30 And grieve not the holy Spirit of God, whereby ye are 31 sealed unto the day of redemption. Let all bitterness, and wrath, and anger, and clamour, and evil speaking, be put

in view of the moral pollution of common conversation in heathen society.

the use of edifying] Lit., *"for edifying of the need,"* i.e., as R.V. well paraphrases, **for edifying as the need may be.** The thought of the spiritual influence of one "living stone," and one "limb of Christ's body," upon another, so largely illustrated in previous passages, is still present. See ii. 21, iv. 16, and notes.

minister grace] Lit., **give grace,** instrumentally.

Bp Burnet says that he had *never* been in the company of his master, Abp Leighton, without receiving spiritual benefit.

30. *grieve not*] A distinct indication of the Personality of the Blessed Spirit. "Grief is certainly a personal affection, of which a Quality is not capable" (Pearson, *On the Creed*, Art. VIII). Putting aside passages where "spirit" obviously denotes "breath" or "wind," the usage of the word in Scripture favours the interpretation of it as always denoting a personality, good or evil.—See further Bp Pearson's discussion.—This precept, in this context, seems to indicate that *polluting* words would be a special "grief" to the Holy One.

ye are sealed] Better, **ye were sealed,** at the definite crisis of reception. See above, i. 13 and notes.

the day of redemption] "the redemption of the purchased possession," i. 14, where see note.

31. *all...all*] Observe the uncompromising scope of the precept. Revolution in principle was to result in nothing short of *revolution* in temper and practice.

wrath...anger] The two original words occur together also Rom. ii. 8; Col. iii. 8; Rev. xvi. 19, xix. 15 ("*the wrath of the anger* of God"). The word rendered "wrath" denotes rather the *acute* passion, and the other the *chronic*. See Trench, *Synonyms*, § xxxvi.—There is no real contradiction here to ver. 26. The aim there was to limit the admission of anger only to the rare cases where it could be present "without sin." Here the question is not of the exception but of the rule. Personal irascibility, personal feud and quarrel, were to be things past and gone out of Christian life.

clamour] The violent assertion of rights and wrongs, real or supposed.

evil speaking] Gr. *blasphêmia.* Our word "blasphemy" is now confined to "evil speaking" against God and Divine things, but the Gr. word includes all kinds of slander and opprobrium. It is used (verb, noun, or adjective) of evil speaking against man, or human things, often in N.T.; *e.g.* 1 Cor. iv. 13 (A.V., "*defamed*"); x. 30; Col. iii. 8; Titus iii. 2.

away from you, with all malice : and be ye kind one to ₃₂
another, tender hearted, forgiving one another, even as God
for Christ's sake hath forgiven you.

be put away] Or, **taken away.** The verb is in the aorist imperative,
enjoining a decisive act, a definite and total rejection of these phases of
evil. Such an act, and the maintenance of its results, would be only
possible "in Christ"; but *so* it could be done. See the parallel passage,
Col. iii. 8, where the precept is as decisive and as inclusive as here.

malice] The Gr. word sometimes bears the sense of "evil," "ill,"
in general; *e.g.* "*the evil*" of "*the day*," Matt. vi. 34. But where, as
here, it forms one of a list of vices (cp. Rom. i. 29; Col. iii. 8; Tit. iii.
3; 1 Pet. ii. 1), it tends to mean the bitter and unjust habit of mind
which we denote by malice. (See Trench, *Synonyms*, § xi.) It is
here mentioned last, as the deeper and more subtle sin of which those
just mentioned are manifestations. Unkindness, in its inmost secret,
is to be a thing cast out.

32. *be*] Lit., **become**; shew yourselves, in the actions and developments of life.

kind] The Gr. word (noun or adj.) occurs in similar contexts, Luke
vi. 35; Rom. ii. 4; xi. 22 ("*goodness*"); 2 Cor. vi. 6; Gal. v. 22; Col.
iii. 12. Its primitive meaning is "*useful*"; hence "helpful," and so
"kindly."—It is the original of "easy" in Matt. xi. 30; the Lord's
"yoke" is a real yoke, but instinct with the lovingkindness of Him
who imposes it.

tender-hearted] The same Gr. word as in 1 Pet. iii. 8 (A.V., "*piti-
ful*"). It occurs nowhere else in N.T. **Kind-hearted** may perhaps be
a better rendering, as somewhat wider. The word carries the idea of
the previous word a little more into life and detail.

forgiving one another] Lit., "*forgiving yourselves.*" Usage and
common sense alike fully justify the rendering of A.V. and R.V. (which
reads, somewhat needlessly, "*each* other"). The "yourselves," as
a grammatical fact, indicates the solidarity of the body within which the
reciprocity takes place; though this fine shade of meaning must not be
exaggerated.

For a close parallel to the precept see Col. iii. 13. The holy duty of
heartfelt forgiveness, entire and unreserved, is prominent in the Lord's
teaching; cp. especially the Lord's Prayer (Matt. vi. 12; Luke xi. 4);
Matt. xviii. 21, &c. No duty is more readily owned in the abstract, none
more repugnant to the will in many a case in the concrete. But the law
of Christ knows no exceptions, and grace is able to meet every demand
for fulfilment.—It is humbling and instructive to see here, as in the
Lord's Prayer, that the *abiding need* for mutual forgiveness is assumed.

even as] The Divine pardon is at once supreme example and sacred
motive. Cp. just below, ch. v. 2.

God] The Father, "FOUNT of Deity," and as such styled often
simply GOD where Christ is also and distinctively named (Joh. xvii. 3;
2 Cor. v. 19, xiii. 13; Jude 21). The SON has also Deity, but as
in the Stream, not in the Fountain. See Pearson, *On the Creed*, Art. I.

5   Be ye therefore followers of God, as dear children ; and
2 walk in love, as Christ also hath loved us, and hath given

for Christ's sake] Lit. and better, **in Christ.** The reason of pardon,
and the process of it, are alike summed up "in Christ," " in " Whom
the Father reveals Himself as God of Peace : " in " Whom resides the
immediate atoning *reason* of Peace ; and " in " Whom, by grace and
faith, are the human objects of pardon, " very members incorporate " of
Him Who is eternally the Accepted One of the Father.—Cp. i. 7.

hath forgiven] Lit., and better, **did forgive** ; ideally and in covenant,
"before the world was " ; historically, when the Son was accepted and
glorified as the perfect Propitiation, raised from the dead ; in individual
experience, when each person believed (Rom. v. 1, &c.)   It is important
to observe how the Apostle bids them deal with Divine forgiveness not
as a hope but as a fact. Cp. 1 Joh. ii. 12.

you] There is considerable, but not preponderating, evidence for a
reading "us". The question between the two readings is not of practical importance.

CH. V. **1—14** THE SUBJECT PURSUED: CHRIST'S SACRIFICE THE
SUPREME EXAMPLE OF SELF-SACRIFICE: PURITY: REPROOF OF
DARKNESS BY LIGHT

1. *therefore*] The argument passes unbroken from the previous
words.

followers] Lit. "*imitators.*"   The A.V. consistently uses "*follow,*"
"*follower,*" to render the original verb and noun; 1 Cor. iv. 16, xi. 1;
1 Thess. i. 6, ii. 14; 2 Thess. iii. 7, 9; Heb. vi. 12, xiii. 7; 1 Pet. iii. 13;
3 John 11. For the thought here cp. Matt. v. 45, 48; Luke vi. 36;
1 Pet. i. 15, 16, ii. 21, iii. 13. (In this last passage the true reading gives
probably "emulators," not "imitators"; but this obviously is the same
thought intensified in expression.)   The "Imitation of God" is the true
sequel and index of Peace with God and Life in God. It is, from
another aspect, the Manifestation of God in His people.

of God] Who, in that supreme instance, set the example of forgiveness.

dear children] Better, **beloved children.** As children (see Matt. **v.**
45; 1 Pet. i. 17, where read, "*If ye invoke Him as Father*, &c.") they
were to shew the family likeness.   And as children who had become
such by a sacred act of *pardoning love*, they were to shew it above all
things in self-forgetting kindness.—Cp. on the whole subject 1 John;
esp. iii. 10.—The word rendered "children" is the word specially
appropriate to ideas not of adoption but of birth.

2. *walk*] On the metaphor, see above on ii. 2. It is just in the
steps of actual life that Divine grace is to shew itself, if it is indeed
present.

as Christ also] "*Also,*" as an Exemplar additional to the Father, and
in different though profoundly kindred respects. See next notes.—On
"God" and "Christ" thus collocated see above on iv. 32.

himself for us an offering and a sacrifice to God for a sweet-smelling savour.   But fornication, and all uncleanness, or 3

hath loved...hath given] Better, **loved...gave**. Cp. for a pregnant parallel, Gal ii. 20, "Who loved *me*, and gave Himself for *me*." And, again of the community, the Church, ch. v. 25; Rev. i. 5. On this holy Love see above iii. 19; Rom. viii. 35; 2 Cor. v. 14.

us] Considerable evidence, but scarcely conclusive, gives the reading "*you*." All the ancient Versions favour the received text.

given himself for us] as atoning, pacificatory, satisfactory Sacrifice. Thus we may safely interpret in the light of Scripture at large, and of the next following words here.   But the business of this passage is with the Lord's Example, and it does not enter in detail into His Sacrificial work, nor employ (in the Gr.) the strict formula for substitution, such as the Lord Himself uses, Matt. xx. 28, "to give His soul a *Ransom in place, instead, of* many."   The supreme Act of self-devoting love for others which, as a fact, the Atoning Death was, is here used as the great Example of all acts of self-devoting love in the Christian Church.   As the Father has just been named as the Ideal for the forgiving Christian, so here the Son is named as the Ideal for the self-sacrificing Christian.

"*Hath given*":—better, as R.V., **gave Himself up**, to the agents of death.—"*For us*"="on behalf of us," not here (see first paragraph of this note) "in place of us."   The phrase is the less precise and more inclusive.

offering...sacrifice]   Both Gr. nouns have a large and general meaning in many places and thus often "overlap" each other; but where, as here, they occur together we must look for some limit and distinction. "Offering" is, on the whole, the more general word, "sacrifice" the more particular.   "Offering" gives the thought of dedication and surrender at large to God's purposes; "sacrifice" gives that of such surrender carried out in altar-death.   Not that "sacrifice" necessarily implies death, but death is its very frequent connexion. Bp Ellicott here sees in "offering" a suggestion of the obedience of the Lord's life, in "sacrifice," of His atoning death.

a sweet-smelling savour]   The same Gr. occurs Phil. iv. 18 (A.V. "an odour of a sweet smell").   It occurs often in the LXX. of the Pentateuch; *e.g.* Gen. viii. 21; and see esp. Lev. i. 9, 13, 17, where the reference is to *atoning* sacrifices (see ver. 3).   It translates the Heb. *rêach nîchôach*, "a savour of rest."   In the picture language of typical sacrifices, the savour was "smelt" by the Deity as a welcome token of worship and submission, and thus it conveyed the thought of pacification and acceptance.   Pagan sacrificial language has many parallels; see, *e.g.* Homer, *Il.* I. 317, VIII. 549.   Cowper renders the last passage

> "Next the Gods
> With sacrifice they sought, and from the plain
> Upwafted by the wind, the smoke aspires,
> Savoury, but unacceptable to those
> Above, such hatred in their hearts they bore" &c.

The Lord's obedience and atonement "reconciled the Father unto

covetousness, let it not be once named amongst you, as be-
4 cometh saints; neither filthiness, nor foolish talking, nor
jesting, which are not convenient: but rather giving of

us" (Art. ii.), in that they perfectly met the unalterable demand of the
holy and broken Law. He thus sent up, as the result of His work for
us, the sacred "odour of rest;" becoming our "peace with God."

3. *but*] The word imports a sort of *a fortiori*. The Examples of
the Father and the Son oblige the believer to a uniform life of holy
unselfish love; how complete then is the condemnation, for the believer,
of all *gross* sins!

fornication] A sin lightly regarded by the heathen, and too often
palliated in modern Christendom, but utterly condemned by the Lord
and the Apostles. See esp. Matt. xv. 19; Acts xv. 20; 1 Cor. vi. 9,
13, 18; Gal. v. 19; Col. iii. 5; 1 Thess. iv. 3; Heb. xiii. 4; and below,
ver. 5. Regarding it, as regarding all sin, *total abstinence* is the one
precept of the Gospel; and the Divine precept will always be found,
sooner or later, to coincide with the highest physical law.

all uncleanness] Act, word, or thought, unworthy the children of
the All-Pure. Observe the characteristic *"all"*; and cp. last note, and
on iv. 31.

covetousness] The Gr. word has occurred iv. 19 (A.V. "greediness"),
where see note. Here as there the root idea is the grasp after another's
own, whatever it may be; money, person, wife. This passage, more
perhaps than any other, suggests that the word had acquired by
usage, in St Paul's time, a familiar though not fixed connexion with
sensual greed, just such as our word "covetousness" has acquired with
the greed of material property. It would scarcely otherwise be used to
denote an "unnamable" sin.

once named] Lit. and better, **even named**; obviously in the sense of
approving or tolerant mention. The Apostle himself here "names"
these sins for exposure and condemnation; and Christians may need, on
occasion, to do the same, and very explicitly. But let them beware
that it is done in the spirit of Scripture—in self-distrust, and as in God's
presence.—For the phrase, 1 Cor. v. 1 gives a parallel, in the A.V.; but
the word "*named*" is probably to be omitted there from the text. The
resolve not to "name" the Gods of Canaan (Psal. xvi. 4) is parallel and
illustrative.

4. *filthiness*] Lit. *"ugliness, deformity"*; vice in its aspect as
morally hideous. The Gr. word occurs here only in N.T. In the
classics some cognate words bear a special connexion with forms of
gross sensuality.

foolish talking] Talk about sin, in the spirit of the "fool" who gloats
and jests over his own or his neighbour's undoing. The word occurs
here only in N.T. It and its cognates occur in the classics, but not in
grave moral connexions.

jesting] Obviously, by context, in the sense of immoral pleasantry,
such as defiles some of the most brilliant pages of pagan literature,
not to speak of Christian, so called; and such as terribly impregnates

thanks.   For this ye know, that no whoremonger, nor un- 5
clean *person*, nor covetous man who is an idolater, hath *any*
inheritance in the kingdom of Christ and of God.   Let no 6

common talk in many strata and circles of society now.   It must have
been everywhere the fashion at Ephesus.   The passage does not deal
with the play of humour and wit in general.   This is not forbidden in
Scripture, and so far as it is the outcome of vigour, gladness, or (in the
case of humour) tenderness, it may be quite in harmony with the strict
piety of the Gospel.   But to remain so it must be watched; and see next
note but one.—The Gr. word denotes specially the *versatility* of clever
repartee; but it is wider by usage.

convenient]   Better, as R.V., **befitting**; the French *convenable*.   In
older English "convenient" could bear this meaning; but it has lost it.
Rom. i. 28 and Philem. 8 are parallel cases in the A.V.

giving of thanks]   as the far more "befitting" expression of the
buoyancy of the believing spirit.   See Col. iii. 16; Jas. v. 13.   Such
precepts, out of Scripture, have often been stigmatized as "puritanic,"
or the like; but they are nevertheless apostolic.   And the nearer the
conduct of inner life is brought to apostolic lines of principle the more
natural will such precepts be felt to be.

5. *ye know*]   More lit., **ye know with acquaintance**, or **recognition**;
as if to say, "you know it with full *recognition* of the fact and the right."
R.V. "ye know *of a surety*"; but the Gr. seems to imply, as above,
the *reasons* along with the certainty.

no whoremonger...hath]   Lit. **every fornicator...hath not**; a form
of phrase which perhaps *accentuates* the individual exclusions from the
kingdom.   But it must not be pressed.

who]   Read, **which**; the Gr. relative pronoun, in the probable
reading, being neuter.   As if to say, "which word means, or implies,
idolater."

an idolater]   See the close parallel Col. iii. 5.   Lightfoot there says,
"The covetous man sets up another object of worship besides God,"
or, more truly still, instead of God.   And this is so, whatever is the
object of his avarice.   Monod remarks that this clause points rather to
the *miser* than the *seducer*; and most certainly it includes the miser.
But there is a terrible fitness also in the other application; and we cannot but think that "covetousness" had, in the apostolic age, a familiar
reference, among other references, to immoral cupidity.   See on iv. 19.

inheritance]   On the Gr. word, see note on i. 18.   It conveys regularly
the thought of possession by title, whether actually enjoyed or in prospect.   An "inheritor" (*clēronomos*) may be thus either a present
occupant, or an expectant "heir," as context may indicate.   Here
probably the expected possession of glory is mainly in view, though
we cannot exclude some reference to the organic antecedent to glory—
the present possession of "life eternal."   See further next note.

the kingdom of Christ and of God]   the realm of the Son, Who
"gave Himself for our sins," that He might be our "Lord" (Gal. i. 4;
Rom. xiv. 9); and of the Father, Who gave the Son that the redeemed

man deceive you with vain words: for because of these *things* cometh the wrath of God upon the children of dis-
7 obedience.   Be not ye therefore partakers with them.   For
8 ye were sometimes darkness, but now *are ye* light in the

might "yield themselves unto God" (Rom. vi. 13).   The secret of admission to this kingdom, and of congenial life in it, is "to know the only true God and Jesus Christ Whom He hath sent" (Joh. xvii. 3). The more common phrase "kingdom of God" is here displaced by one specially suggestive of the holy *conditions* of membership implied in the mention of Christ.—See note on iv. 32, on the word "God" in such collocations.

What is the "Kingdom" here?   On the whole, the glorified state, the goal of the process of grace.   True, the word often, with obvious fitness, includes the period of grace in this life, in which most truly the Christian is a subject of the King (see *e.g.* Matt. xi. 11, xiii. 41, xxi. 43; Rom. xiv. 17; Col. i. 13).   But usage gives the word a special connexion with the final state, glory; cp. esp. Matt. xxv. 34 (specially in point here); 1 Cor. xv. 50.   See also the passages, closely akin to the present, 1 Cor. vi. 9, 10; Gal. v. 21; where the "*shall* not in-herit" (as in 1 Cor. xv. 50) points to the idea of a *coming* "kingdom." Doubtless the state of will and life here in view excludes man, from God's point of view, from the *present* phase of His kingdom, in its spiritual essence (see 1 Joh. iii. 6, 15 &c.; though the imagery is dif-ferent).   But the phase to come, that of perfect and eternal result and development, is naturally the predominant phase of the word.   The practical meaning here, then, is "no such moral rebel can be, while such, a citizen of and pilgrim to the heavenly city."   See Rev. xxi. 27.

6.   *Let no* man *deceive you*]   See for similar warnings Rom. xvi. 18; 1 Cor. iii. 18; 2 Cor. xi. 3; Col. ii. 8; 2 Thess. ii. 3; Jas. i. 26.

vain]   Lit., **empty** ; alien to the *solidity* of the immoveable *facts* that the body cannot sin without sin of the spirit; that body and spirit alike are concerned in eternal retribution; that the wrath of God is no figure of speech, and that His love cannot possibly modify His holiness. "Vain words" on these matters, and therefore such cautions as this, are never obsolete.   Human sin began (Gen. iii.) with exactly such deceits, and they are the subtlest ingredient still in the secret of tempta-tion.

cometh]   **is coming**; is on its way, till in "the day of wrath" (Rom. ii. 5) it falls.

the wrath of God]   For this awful phrase cp. Joh. iii. 36; Rom. i. 18, ii. 5, 8, v. 9, ix. 22; Col. iii. 6 (parallel here); 1 Thess. i. 10; Rev. vi. 16, xix. 15; &c.   And see note above on ii. 3 ("children of wrath").

children]   Lit., **sons.**   For the Hebraism, see above on the same phrase, ii. 2.

7.   *Be not*]   Lit., **Become not.**   *Nolite fieri* (Latin versions).

partakers]   in disobedience, and so in the coming wrath.

8.   *sometimes*]   Better, in modern English, **once, formerly.**   See on ii. 13 above.—He refers to the whole period of their unconverted life.

Lord : walk as children of light : (for the fruit of the Spirit 9
is in all goodness and righteousness and truth ;) proving 10
what is acceptable unto the Lord. And have no fellowship 11

darkness] Not merely "in the dark". So had the night of spiritual
ignorance and sin penetrated them that they were, as it were, night
itself, night embodied. On the metaphor of darkness see on iv. 18.

light] Again, not merely "in the light." The Divine Light of truth,
holiness, and resulting joy, had now so penetrated them that they
were, in a sense, light embodied; not seeing light only, but being light,
and emitting it (see below, on ver. 13). Cp. Matt. v. 14.

in the Lord] By your union with and knowledge of Him Who is the
Light.

walk] See above on ii. 2, &c., for the metaphor.

children of light] See above on ii. 2, for the phrase "*children*, or
sons, of."

9. *for*] The suppressed link of thought is, " Walk in a path wholly
unlike that of the disobedient ; *for* the path of the light must be such."

the fruit of the Spirit] Cp. Gal. v. 22. But the literary evidence
here supports the reading **the fruit of the light**. The metaphor
"fruit" (found here only in the Epistle) gives the idea not only of result
but of natural and congenial result ; growth rather than elaboration.
Christian virtue is, in its true essence, grace *having its way*.

is in] Consists in, comes out in.

all] Observe here, as continually, the absoluteness in idea of the
Christian character. It is an unsinning *character*. "Whosoever is
born of God, doth not commit sin " (1 Joh. iii. 9). The Christian, *as
a Christian*, sins not: a truth at once humiliating and stimulating.

goodness] The Gr. word occurs besides, Rom. xv. 14 ; Gal. v. 22 ;
2 Thess. i. 11. The Gr. word like the English, while properly meaning
the whole quality opposite to evil, tends to mean specially the goodness
of *beneficence*, or at least *benevolence*. Such, on the whole, is the
evidence of the LXX. usage. But the context here favours the wider
and more original reference ; all that is *anti-vicious*.

St Chrysostom sees in it here a special antithesis to *anger ;* but this
is surely too narrow a reference. See further on the word, Trench, *N. T.
Synonyms*, § l.

righteousness] See above on iv. 24. And cp. Tit. ii. 12. The special
reference here doubtless is to the observance of God's Law in regard
of the rights of others, in things of honesty and purity.

truth] The deep, entire reality which is the opposite to the state of
" the simular of virtue that is incestuous " (*King Lear*, iii. 3).

10. *proving*] Testing, by the touchstone of His declared and beloved Will ; putting every action, and course of action unreservedly to
that *proof*, and unreservedly *approving*, in action, all that passes it.
Cp. Rom. i. 28 (where lit. "they did not *approve* to retain God, &c."),
xii. 2 (a close parallel here) ; 1 Thess. v. 21.

acceptable] Better, as R. V., **well-pleasing**. The word is kindred

with the unfruitful works of darkness, but rather reprove
12 *them.* For it is a shame even to speak of those *things*
13 which are done of them in secret. But all *things* that are
reproved are made manifest by the light: for whatsoever

to the noun rendered "pleasing" Col. i. 10. The. whole. question was
to be, "What *pleases* GOD?"

11. *unfruitful*] "For the end of these things is death" (Rom. vi.
21). The metaphor of *fruit*, which we have just had (ver. 9), is almost
always used in connexions of good. See a close parallel, Gal. v. 19,
22, "the *works* of the flesh"; "the *fruit* of the Spirit."

darkness] Lit., **the darkness**, which you have left; from whose
"authority" you have been "rescued" (Col. i. 13). The metaphor
here (on which see on iv. 18) suggests rather the secrecy and shame
of sin than its blindness.

rather] **Rather even**, R. V., and so better; "rather, *go the length*
of positive reproof."

reprove] The verb, in classical prose, has always an argumentative
reference; it is, to question, confute, disprove. And though in some
N. T. passages this reference is not necessary to the sense, it is always
admissible, and lies, as it were, behind the meaning of mere *blame* or
censure. So here, the Christian is not merely to denounce evil, but by
holy word and life to *evince* its misery and fallacy, to *convict* it (R. V.
margin) of its true nature.

12. *even to speak*] See above on "not once named", ver. 12. Perhaps the suggestion here is that the "reproof" of ver. 11 was to come
more through a holy life, and less through condemnatory words. Not
that such should never be used; but that they are weak reproofs compared with those issuing from a life of unmistakable holiness brought
into contact with the unholy.

The verse was terribly in point at the time, as every reader of ancient
literature knows. Is it much less in point to-day, in the midst of our
nominal Christendom? Neither, then, is ver. 11.

13. *all* things *that are reproved*] More lit., **all things, when being
reproved**, or **convicted.**

doth make manifest] Render, certainly, **is made manifest**, or more
precisely, **is being manifested.** So the Lat. versions, and, with verbal
variations, all the older English Versions except the Genevan (1557),
which has, loosely, "it is light that discovereth all things." The Gr.
is decisive against this and the A.V.

The drift of this somewhat difficult verse, suggested by the context,
seems to be; "You are light in the Lord; use this character upon the
surrounding moral darkness, in order to the rescue of its victims, that
they also may become light. Nothing but light will do this work ; no
conquest over darkness, literal or spiritual, is possible except to light.
And one evidence of this is that every such real conquest results in the
subjects of darkness becoming now subjects of light, becoming lights."
More briefly; "You are light; keep pure then, but shine far into the

doth make manifest is light. Wherefore *he* saith, Awake 14
thou that sleepest, and arise from the dead, and
Christ shall give thee light. See then that ye walk 15

dark. And then other men, as already you, shall become light in the
Lord."

14. *Wherefore*] With regard to the fact that whatever is really
brought to light, in the sense of true spiritual conviction, becomes light.

he saith] Or possibly **it** (the Scripture) **saith**. See note on iv. 8.

Awake, &c.] These words occur nowhere in the O.T. verbatim. St
Jerome, on the verse, makes many suggestions; as that St Paul may
have used an "apocryphal" passage, exactly as he used words from
pagan writers (*e.g.* Tit. i. 12); or that he utters an immediate inspiration granted to himself, in prophetic form. Thomas Aquinas
(quoted by Vallarsius on St Jerome) suggests that we have here the
essence of Isai. lx. 1 ; where the Lat. reads "Rise, be enlightened, O
Jerusalem, for thy light is come &c." Surely this is the true solution,
if we add to it the probability that other prophecies *contributed* to the
phraseology here. Dr Kay (in the *Speaker's Commentary*) on Isai. lx.
1 writes, "In Eph. v. 14 this verse is combined, in a paraphrase form,
with li. 17, lii. 1, 2. The Ephesians had been walking in darkness, as
dead men...but the Redeemer had come and the Spirit been given.
Therefore they were to *awake* (ch. li. 17, lii. 1) out of sleep, and *arise*
from the dead, that Christ the Lord might *shine upon* them, and they
again shed His light on the Gentiles round."

To the believer in the Divine plan and coherence of Scripture it will
be abundantly credible that "the LORD" (JEHOVAH) of Isaiah should
be the "Christ" of St Paul (cp. Isai. vi. 5 with Joh. xii. 41), and that
the "Jerusalem" of Isaiah should have an inner reference to the True
Israel (Gal. iii. 29, vi. 16), in its actual or potential members.

Dr Edersheim (*Temple and its Services*, p. 262), suggests that the
Apostle may have had present to his mind language used in synagogue
worship at the Feast of Trumpets. Rabbinic writers explain the
trumpet blasts as, *inter alia*, a call to repentance; and one of them
words the call, "Rouse ye from your slumber, awake from your sleep,
&c." Some such formula may have been in public use. Bengel makes
a similar suggestion here. But this would not exclude, only supplement,
the reference to Isaiah.

Another suggestion is that the words are a primitive Christian "psalm"
(1 Cor. xiv. 26); perhaps "the morning hymn used each day by the
Christians in Rome in St Paul's lodging," or "a baptismal hymn."
Here again we have an interesting possibility, for such a "psalm" may
have given or influenced the phrase here. But the introductory word
"*He*, or *it, saith*," seems to us to weigh decidedly for the view that the
words are, in essence, a Scripture quotation.

sleepest...the dead] The sleep is more than sleep; the sleep *of death*.
But death itself is but as sleep that can be broken (Matt. ix. 24) to the
Lord of Life. On spiritual death see above, on ii. 1.

shall give thee light] Better, as R.V., **shall shine upon thee.**—The

16 circumspectly, not as fools, but as wise, redeeming the time,
17 because the days are evil. Wherefore be ye not unwise,

idea, by context, is not so much of the light of conviction, as of that of spiritual transfiguration (2 Cor. iii. 18, iv. 4—6). The thought of "*being light in the Lord*" runs through the passage. It is a light consequent *upon* awaking and arising.—Another, but certainly mistaken, reading gives, "*thou shalt touch Christ.*" The "Old Latin" followed it. It is due, in part at least, to the close similarity in form of two widely different Gr. verbs.

15—21   THE SUBJECT PURSUED: THE TALENT OF TIME: TEMPERANCE: SPIRITUAL SONGS: THANKSGIVING: HUMILITY

15. *See then*] The more general exhortation to a holy life-walk is resumed here, after the special entreaties thus given to avoid, yet influence, surrounding darkness.

walk] The seventh and last occurrence in the Epistle of this important metaphor.

circumspectly] Lit., **accurately**, remembering the importance of details of both duty and danger, and the presence of the will of God *in everything*.

The R.V. adopts here a Gr. text which requires the rendering, "*Look* therefore *carefully* how ye *walk.*" But the documentary evidence scarcely warrants this change. And it has the objection of making the order of words in the Gr. more easy, and so more likely to be a transcriber's correction.

Observe how the illuminated Christian is to *keep his eyes open.* No guidance is promised him which shall dispense with patient watchfulness.

fools] Lit., and better, **unwise**; spiritually unwise, blind to spiritual facts and consequences.

16. *redeeming the time*] Lit., **buying out** (from other ownership) **the opportunity**. So Col. iv. 5. The same phrase occurs (Aramaic and Greek) Dan. ii. 8; "I knew of a certainty that ye would *buy the time*"; where the meaning plainly is, "that ye would get your desired opportunity, *at the expense of* a subterfuge." Here similarly the meaning is, "getting each successive opportunity of 'walking and pleasing God' *at the expense of* steady watchfulness." In Col. iv. 5 the special thought is of opportunities in intercourse with "them that are without." So, perhaps, here also, in regard of verses 12—14.—Cp. Gal. vi. 10; where render "as we have *opportunity.*"

because the days are evil] As if to say, "Make this sustained effort of getting opportunity; for it will be needed. The 'days' of human life in a fallen world do not *lend themselves* to it. Circumstances, in themselves, are adverse, for sin attaches to them."

The Apostle very probably had in view the special difficulties of the then present time, but his words have a permanent bearing on each following period with its new phases of difficulty, all related as they are to the permanent underlying difficulty, sin.

but understanding what the will of the Lord *is*.   And be 18
not drunk with wine, wherein is excess; but be filled with

17. *be ye not*]   Lit., **become ye not**; let not unwatchfulness pull you
down.

understanding]   Better, probably, **understand**.

what the will of the Lord is]   "The good, and perfect, and acceptable
will of God" apprehended by the disciple who is "being *transformed* by
the *renewing of his mind*" (Rom. xii. 2, a passage much in point here).
Not independent reason but the illuminated perceptions of a soul awake
to God will have a true intuition into "His will," both as to that
invariable attitude of the Christian, subjection to and love of the will of
God, and as to the detailed opportunities of action in that attitude.—
Cp. on the Divine Will and our relation to it, Psal. cxliii. 10; Matt. vi.
10, vii. 21; Mark iii. 35; Joh. vii. 17; Acts xiii. 36, xxi. 14, xxii. 14;
2 Cor. viii. 5; Col. i. 9, iv. 12; 1 Thess. iv. 3, v. 18; Heb. xiii. 21;
1 Joh. ii. 17; below vi. 6.   And on the example of the Lord, cp. Psal.
xl. 8; Luke xxii. 42; Joh. iv. 34, v. 30, vi. 38.

18. *drunk with wine*]   Cp. for similar cautions, Prov. xx. 1, xxiii.
30, 31; Luke xxi. 34; Rom. xiii. 13; 1 Cor. v. 11, vi. 10; Gal. v. 21;
1 Tim. iii. 3.   "He fitly follows up a warning against impurity with a
warning against drunkenness" (Bengel).

wherein]   In "being drunken with wine;" in the act and habit of
intemperance.

excess]   R.V., **riot**.   The word recurs Tit. i. 6; 1 Pet. iv. 4; and its
adverb, Luke xv. 13.   By derivation it nearly answers the idea of that
which is "*dissolute*," i.e. unbound, unrestrained.   The miserable exaltation of strong drink annuls the holy bonds of conscience with fatal ease
and certainty.

but be filled]   As if to say, "Avoid such false elevation; yet seek instead not a dead level of feeling, but the sacred heights of spiritual joy and
power, in that Divine Love which (Cant. i. 2) 'is better than wine'."

filled with the Spirit]   Lit., "*in spirit*," and so margin R.V.   But
the text R.V., and the A.V., are assuredly right.   The definite article
may well be omitted here (see on i. 17, and ii. 22), without obscuring the
ref. to the Divine Spirit, if context favours it.   And surely the context
does so, in the words "*in which*" just above.   The two "*ins*" ("*in*
which," "*in* Spirit,") are parallel.   And as the first "in" points to
an objective cause of "riot," so surely the second "in" points to the
objective cause, not subjective sphere, of joy; to the Spirit, not to our
spirit.—On the phrase "in (the) Spirit" cp. Matt. xxii. 43; Rom. viii.
9; Col. i. 8; 1 Tim. iii. 16; Rev. i. 10.   The phrase "in the Spirit"
(def. article expressed) occurs only Luke ii. 27.   "In (the) Holy Spirit"
occurs frequently, and in many places where A.V. has "*by* &c."; *e.g.*,
1 Cor. xii. 3, 9.   The parallel phrase "in an *unclean* spirit" occurs Mar.
v. 2.   On the whole, the idea conveyed appears to be that the possessing
Power, Divine or evil, which from one point of view *inhabits* the man,
from another *surrounds* him, as with an atmosphere.—"If the Spirit be
in you, you are *in It*" (Jer. Taylor, *Sermon for Whitsunday*).

19 the Spirit; speaking to yourselves in psalms and hymns and

Thus, "be ye filled in (the) Spirit," may be lawfully paraphrased, "Let in the holy atmosphere to your inmost self, to your whole will and soul. Let the Divine Spirit, in Whom you, believing, are, pervade your being, as water fills the sponge." And the context gives the special thought that this "filling" will tend to that sacred exhilaration, "the Spirit's calm excess[1]", of which wine-drinking could produce only a horrible parody. See next verse.

19. *to yourselves*] R. V., **one to another.** The Gr. admits either rendering (see above on iv. 32); but the parallel, Col. iii. 16 ("teaching and admonishing, &c.") is clearly for the R. V. here, as the much most natural reference there is to *mutual* edification.

It has been thought that we have here a suggestion of responsive chanting. But this is most precarious, to say the least; the words being fully satisfied by the thought of the *mutual* spiritual help, most real and powerful now as then, given on any occasion of *common* spiritual praise. The first disciples thus "spoke *one to another*" in the united outburst of ascription and praise, Acts iv. 24. Still, it is interesting to remember that responsive hymn-singing was, as a fact, used very early in Christian worship. In the famous Letter of Pliny to Trajan (written between A. D. 108 and A. D. 114), where the worship of the Christians is described, we read; "they are used to meet before dawn on a stated day, and to chant (*carmen dicere*) to Christ, as to a God, alternately together (*secum invicem*)." See Alford's note here.

psalms...hymns...spiritual songs] It is impossible to fix precisely the limits of these terms; nor does the character of the passage, full of the spirit rather than the theory of praise, demand it. But there is probability in the suggestion that the *psalm* was generally a rhythmic utterance, either actually one of the O. T. psalms, or in their manner; the *hymn*, a rhythmic utterance of praise distinctively Christian; and the spiritual *song*, or spiritual *ode*, a similar utterance, but more of experience or meditation than of praise. The canticles of Luke i., ii., would thus rank as psalms; the inspired chant of the disciples (Acts iv.) as a hymn; and the possibly rhythmic "faithful words" in the Pastoral Epistles (see esp. 2 Tim. ii. 11—13) as spiritual odes.

Another suggested distinction is that a psalm (Gr., *psallein*, to *play*,) demanded instrumental accompaniment, a hymn did not. But this cannot be sustained in detail.

"Psalm-singing" (see further 1 Cor. xiv. 26; Jas. v. 13) is thus a primeval element in not only Christian worship but Christian common life; for the Apostle here evidently contemplates social gatherings rather than formulated services; similar occasions to those formerly defaced by "excess of wine."

The history of psalmody and hymnody in the Church cannot be discussed, however briefly, here. See articles on *Hymns*, in Smith's *Dictionaries* (of the Bible and of Christian Antiquities). We may

---

[1] St Ambrose ("*Splendor paternæ gloriæ*," tr. by Chandler).

spiritual songs, singing and making melody in your heart to the Lord ; giving thanks always for all *things* unto God and the Father in the name of our Lord Jesus Christ; submitting yourselves one to another in the fear of God. 20 21

just note that (1) Pliny (quoted above on this verse) speaks already of Christian hymnody, very early cent. 2; (2) St Justin, rather later cent. 2, in his account of Sunday eucharistic worship makes no distinct allusion to it ; but (3) a century later the allusions are frequent.   See *e. g.* Eusebius, *Hist. Eccl.* v. 28, vii. 30.   The "earliest known Christian hymn" is a noble Greek hymn, in anapæstic metre, to the Son of God, by St Clement of Alexandria, at the end of his *Pædagogus* (middle of cent. 3).

"Spiritual songs":—not necessarily "inspired," but charged with spiritual truth.

making melody] Lit. *"playing instruments"* (*psallontes, psalm*). This seems to assume the use of lute or flute on such occasions.

in your heart] Both voice and instrument were literal and external, but the *use* of them both was to be spiritual, and so "in the heart." No other use of either, in and for worship, can be truly according to the will of God (Joh. iv. 24).

to the Lord] Who is either directly or indirectly addressed in the song, and to Whom every act of the Christian's life is related.

20. *always for all* things] Because everything in hourly providence is an expression, to the believing heart, of God's "good, perfect, and acceptable will" (Rom. xii. 2).   In view of this, the Christian will be thankful, both generally and as to details.   St Chrysostom's habitual doxology was, " Glory be to God for all things"; and it was the last word of his suffering life.

unto God and the Father] Lit. **to the God and Father**; i. e. probably, of our Lord, and of us in Him.

in the name of our Lord Jesus Christ] For the same phrase, or the like, cp. *e.g.* Matt. x. 41, xxi. 9; Mar. xvi. 17; Luke x. 17 ; Joh. v. 43, xiv. 13*, 14*, 26, xv. 16, xvi. 23*, 24*, 26*, xvii. 11, 12 ; Acts iii. 6, ix. 27, x. 48; 1 Cor. v. 4, vi. 11 ; Phil. ii. 10; Col. iii. 17; Jas. v. 14 ; 1 Pet. iv. 14. Of these references, those marked * carry, like this verse, the idea of an approach to the Father through the Son.   The whole series (compared with parallel phrases of the O. T., *e. g.* Deut. xviii. 19; Ps. xx. 5, xliv. 5, lxxxix. 24) indicates, as an idea common to all the uses of the expression, that he whose "name" is in question is the basis or reason of the action.   Empowered by the "name" of JEHOVAH, His revealed glory and will, the prophet speaks.   Empowered by the "name" of Christ, going upon His revealed character as Mediator, the believer in Him offers praise and prayer to the Father.   And so in such phrases as Ps. lxiii. 4; "I will lift up my hands in Thy name"; the thought is of action upon a revelation of God and of the way to Him.—In Phil. ii. 10 we perhaps find combined the ideas of worship *of* and worship *through* Jesus Christ.

21. *submitting*] The primary point in the spiritual ethics of the

22 Wives, submit yourselves unto your own husbands, as
23 unto the Lord.   For the husband is the head of the wife,
even as Christ *is* the head of the church : and he is the

Gospel is humiliation; self is dethroned as against God, and conse-
quently as against men.   Here the special, but not exclusive, reference
is to fellow-Christians.   "[The precept] seems to have been suggested
by the humble and loving spirit which is the moving principle of thanksgiving " (Ellicott).

Special applications of this great principle now follow, in a study of
the relative duties of the Christian Home.

**22—32   Special Exhortations : the Christian Home : Wife
and Husband**

22.   *Wives*]   Cp. Col. iii. 18; 1 Pet. iii. 1—6.   In Col. the corresponding instructions about domestic duty are drawn expressly from the
truth (Col. iii. 1) that the believer lives, in the risen Christ, a resurrection-
life.

submit yourselves]   It is probable that the Gr. original has no verb
here.   R. V. accordingly reads *in italics* be in subjection to.   But it
is obvious that the thought if not the word is present, carried on from
the last verse.

The Gospel on the one hand recognizes and secures woman's perfect
spiritual equality with man, an equality which modifies and ennobles
every aspect of possible "subjection"; on the other hand recognizes
and secures man's responsible leadership.

your own]   Words of special emphasis, suggesting the holy speciality
of the marriage relation.

as unto the Lord]   Who is, in a peculiar sense, represented to the
wife by the husband.   In wifely submission to him she not only acts on
the general principle of the acceptance of the Will of God expressed
in circumstances : she sees in that attitude a special reflection, as it
were, of her relations to the Lord Himself.   Her attitude has a special
sanction thus from Him.

23.   *the head*]   See 1 Cor. xi. 3.   The husband and the wife are
"one flesh" (ver. 31), and the husband, in that sacred union, is the
leader.   So Christ and the Church are one, and Christ is the Leader.

even as]   Not, of course, that the headship of the husband embraces
all ideas conveyed by the Lord's Headship, but it truly answers to
it in some essential respects; see last note, and its reference.

Christ is the head]   See on i. 22, and last note but one here.

the church]   The highest reference of the word " Church " (see
Hooker, quoted on i. 22, where see the whole note) is the reference
proper to this passage.   The out-called Congregation, truly living by
the heavenly Bridegroom, in union with Him, and subject to Him, is in
view here.—The sacred truth of the Marriage-union of the Lord and the
Church, brought in here incidentally yet prominently, pervades (in
different phases) the Scriptures.   See not only the Canticles, but *e.g.*
Psal. xlv. ; Isai. liv. 5, lxi. 10, lxii. 4, 5 ; Jer. iii. 14, xxxi. 32; Hos. ii.

saviour of the body. Therefore as the church is subject 24
unto Christ, so *let* the wives *be* to their own husbands in
every *thing*. Husbands, love your wives, even as Christ 25

2—20; Matt. ix. 15, xxv. 1—10; Joh. iii. 29; Gal. iv. 21—31; Rev.
xxi. 2, 9, xxii. 17.—It is observable that in the Revelation as in this
Epistle the metaphors of building and of bridal appear in harmony;
the Mystic Bride is the Holy City and the Spiritual Sanctuary. Cp.
Psal. lxxxvii. 3, where a possible rendering is, "With glorious *offers* art
thou *bespoken* [*for marriage*], O *City* of God."

and he is, &c.] Read, with R. V., [being] himself the Saviour of the
Body. The reference to the Lord, not to the earthly husband, is
certain. And the emphasis (see on next ver.) is that Christ's unique
position, in this passage of comparison, must be remembered; as if to say,
"He, emphatically, is to the Church what no earthly relationship can represent, its SAVIOUR." Some expositors see in this clause, on the other
hand, an indirect precept to the husband to be the "preserver," the
loyal protector, of the wife. But the "*but*" which opens the next verse
decides against this.

saviour] So the Lord is called elsewhere, Luke ii. 11; John iv. 42;
Acts v. 31, xiii. 23; Phil. iii. 20; 2 Tim. i. 10; Tit. i. 4, ii. 13, iii. 6;
2 Pet. i. 1, 11, ii. 20, iii. 2, 18; 1 John iv. 14. Cp. for the word "save"
in connexion with Him (in spiritual reference), Matt. i. 21, xviii. 11;
Luke xix. 10; John iii. 17, v. 34, x. 9, xii. 47; Acts iv. 12, xvi. 31;
Rom. v. 9, 10, x. 9; 1 Tim. i. 15; Heb. vii. 25. Deliverance and
Preservation are both elements in the idea of Salvation. See further,
above, on ii. 5.

the body] See on i. 23, iv. 16. The Body is the Church, viewed as
a complex living organism. The Gr. words *Sôtêr* (Saviour) and *sôma*
(body) have a likeness of sound, and perhaps a community of origin,
which makes it possible that we have here an intentional "play upon
words."

24. *Therefore*] Translate, certainly, But. The Apostle has guarded
the husband's headship from undue comparison with the Lord's; but
now he enforces its true likeness to it.

their own] There is an emphasis in "*own*"; a suggestion at once
of a holy limit, as against wandering loves, and of the fact that not only
does the wife belong to the husband, but the husband to the wife
(Monod).

in every thing] In all relations and interests. This great rule will
always, of course, be *over*-ruled by supreme allegiance to Christ; but
its spirit will never be violated in the Christian home.

25. *Husbands*] Here the instruction is equally precise and more
full. Cp. 1 Pet. iii. 7.

love] "in deed and in truth" (1 John iii. 18), "giving honour unto
the wife as unto the weaker vessel" (1 Pet., quoted above). Monod well
says that the Apostle, true to the spirit of the Gospel, speaks to the wife
of the authority of the husband, to the husband of devotion to the wife:
each party is reminded not of rights, but of duties.

26 also loved the church, and gave himself for it ; that he might sanctify and cleanse *it* with the washing of water by

even as Christ] What a standard for the man's conjugal love, in point of elevation, holiness, and self-sacrifice ! "In Christian domestic life, Jesus Christ is at once the starting point and the goal of everything... We may even say that domestic life is the triumph of the Christian faith " (Monod).

loved the church, &c.] Cp. the same words of the individual soul, Gal. ii. 20, "Who loved *me* and gave Himself for *me*." The two places are in deepest harmony. Cp. also above, ver. 2.

"*Loved:*"—in the pre-mundane view and grace indicated *e.g.* i. 3—7. Cp. 2 Tim. i. 9.

gave] Lit. (and so Gal. ii. 20), **gave over, delivered up**, to suffering and death. The same word is used *e.g.* Rom. iv. 25, viii. 32.

himself] The supreme Ransom-gift. Cp. Tit. ii. 14 (where the Gr. verb is simply "*gave*.")

for it] Better, in this vivid context, **for her.**—On the preposition, see above on ver. 2.

25. *sanctify and cleanse* it] Better, again, **her.** And the pronoun is slightly emphatic by position ; as if to say, "It was in *her* interest that He did this, and so in the wife's interest the husband should be ready for sacrifice."

"*Sanctify and cleanse:*"—lit., **sanctify, cleansing** ; both the verbs being in the aorist, and being thus most naturally referred to one and same crisis, not, as R. V. seems to imply, ("sanctify, *having cleansed*,") to a sanctifying process consequent on a cleansing. The Church was decisively "sanctified," separated from the claim and dominion of sin unto God, when she was decisively "cleansed," accepted as guiltless.

It needs remembrance that the word "to sanctify" lends itself equally, according to context, to ideas of *crisis* and of *process*. In one aspect the human being, decisively claimed and regenerated by God for Himself, *is* sanctified. In another aspect, in view of each successive subjective experience of renunciation of self for God, he is *being* sanctified.—The sanctifying crisis here in view is that of regeneration. This is put before us ideally as the regeneration *of the Church*. The Idea is realized historically in the regeneration of individuals, with a view to the final total. —On this individual aspect of the matter, cp. John iii. 3, 5 ; 1 Cor. vi. 11.

with the washing of water] Lit., **by the laver of the water.** So Tit. iii. 5 ; "through the laver of regeneration," the only other N.T. passage where the noun rendered "laver" occurs.

Here, undoubtedly, Holy Baptism is referred to. It is another and most important question, what is the precise bearing of the Rite upon regeneration ; whether it is the special channel of infusion of the new life, or its federal and legal "conveyance," the Seal upon the Covenant of it, and upon the actual grant of it. But in any case there *is a* connexion, divinely established, between Regeneration and Baptism. For ourselves, we hold that Baptism is a true analogue to the sacrament of Circumcision, and that its direct and essential work is that of a Divine

the word, that he might present it to himself a glorious 27
church, not having spot, or wrinkle, or any such *thing*;

seal. This view we believe to be (1) the view in truest harmony with the
whole spirit of the Gospel, (2) the view most consonant with observed
facts, (3) the view which, under wide varieties of expression, was held,
in essence, by the pre-medieval Church (and not wholly forgotten even
in the medieval Church), and by the great Anglican Protestant doctors
of the 16th and 17th centuries. But it is to be remembered that this
view leaves untouched the fact of *a* profound and sacred connexion
between New Birth and Baptism. And it is entirely consonant with
language of high reverence and honour for the Rite, language often
applicable, properly, only to the related Blessing, under remembrance
that the Rite derives all its greatness from the spiritual Reality to which
it stands related.

by the word] Quite lit., **in utterance**, or **in an utterance**. The Gr.
is *rhêma*, not *logos*. We may translate (having regard to the N. T.
usage of "*in*," in similar cases), **attended by**, or **conditioned by, an
utterance**: as if to say, not a *mere* laver of water, but one which is what
it is only as joined to declared truth.—What is the "utterance" in question? The Gr. word (in the singular), occurs elsewhere in the Epistles,
Rom. x. 8, 17; 2 Cor. xiii. 1, below, vi. 17; Heb. i. 3, vi. 5, xi. 3;
1 Pet. i. 25 (twice). In almost every case it refers to a definite Divine
utterance, whether of truth or of will. We explain it here accordingly
as the utterance of that New Covenant of the Gospel of which Baptism
is the seal, or, to put it more generally, the revelation of salvation
embodied in "the Name of the Father, Son, and Holy Ghost" (Matt.
xxviii. 19), or in "the Name of the Lord Jesus" (Acts xix. 5). Baptism,
in connexion with that revelation and the reception of it, is "the laver
of new birth" (Titus iii. 5).

Cp. the parallel 1 Pet. iii. 21; in which we see the same care to
correct any possible inferences from the material aspect of Baptism, as
if the rite itself, apart from the moral surroundings of the rite, were
a saving thing.

27. *that he*] In the Gr. "*He*" is emphatic; "He to Himself;"
with stress on the Lord's personal action.

present] Cp. for similar use of the same Gr. word 2 Cor. iv. 14,
xi. 2; Col. i. 22, 28. In Jude 24 a similar word is used.—The thought
is of the heavenly Bridegroom welcoming the glorified Bride at the
Marriage Feast hereafter. True, she is now "His Spouse and His
Body;" but the manifestation then will be such as to be, in a sense,
the Marriage as the sequel to the Betrothal. The words "present to
Himself" suggest that the Bride is not only to be welcomed then by
her Lord, but welcomed as owing all her glory to His work, and as
being now absolutely His own.

a glorious church] Translate rather, **the Church arrayed in glory**.
Cp. Rev. xix. 7, 8. And see Canticles iv. 7. She "shall be like Him,
for she shall see Him as He is" (1 Joh. iii. 2). He who gave Himself

²⁸ but that it should be holy and without blemish. So ought men to love their wives as their own bodies. He that ²⁹ loveth his wife loveth himself. For no *man* ever yet hated his own flesh ; but nourisheth and cherisheth it, even as the ³⁰ Lord the church : for we are members of his body, of his

for her had also given Himself to her, and His nature shall now be manifested in her eternal state.

holy] Absolutely, without qualification, and for ever, consecrated to Him.

without blemish] The Gr. is cognate to that in Cant. iv. 7 ("there is no *blemish* in thee"). The holy and perfect principle, perfect at length in all the conditions of its working, shall come out in actual perfection of spiritual beauty.—Cp. for the same Gr. word, i. 4 (side by side there also with "holy"); Phil. ii. 15; Col. i. 22; Heb. ix. 14; 1 Pet. i. 19; Jude 24; Rev. xiv. 5.

28. *So*] With a love akin to the love of Christ just described. The Gr. word is one whose reference tends to *preceding* ideas.

as their own bodies] A clause explanatory of "So" just above. It was thus that Christ loved the Church. In eternal purpose, and in actual redemption and regeneration, she is at once His Bride and His Body. The husband is accordingly to regard his wife as, in a profound and sacred sense, part and parcel of his own living frame.

his wife] Lit., **his own wife**. The Gr. emphasizes the "*self*-ness," so to speak, of the relation : "his *own* wife...his *own self*."

29. *no* man *ever*] under normal conditions. True, in a distorted mental state a man may "hate his own flesh." And in obedience to the will of God a man may so act as to be *said* to hate it ; to choose that it should suffer rather than that God's will should not be done (see, for such a use of "hate", Luke xiv. 26). But under normal conditions it is not only man's instinct but his duty to protect and nourish that mysterious work of God, his body, connected by God's will in a thousand ways with the action of his spirit. "Self-love," whether in the direction of flesh or of spirit, acts sinfully only when it acts outside God as the supreme and all-embracing Reason and Good.

the Lord] Read, with full documentary evidence, **Christ**.

30. *members*] **Limbs**; the word used above iv. 25; and cp. Rom. xii. 4, 5; 1 Cor. vi. 15 (a strict parallel), xii. 27.

of his flesh, and of his bones] Three important MSS. (ABℵ) supported by other but not considerable authority, omit these words. It has been suggested that they were inserted by transcribers from Gen. ii. 23, as the next verse is certainly quoted from Gen. ii. 24. But the phrase here is not verbally close enough to that in Gen. to make this likely. A transcriber would probably have given word for word, while the Apostle would as probably quote with a difference, such as we find here. And the difference is significant. "We" are not said here to be "bone of His bone &c.," which might have seemed to imply that our physical frame is derived from that of the Incarnate Lord, but, more

flesh, and of his bones. For this cause shall a man ₃₁
leave his father and mother, and shall be joined
unto his wife, and they two shall be one flesh. This ₃₂

generally, "limbs of His body, **out of His flesh and out of His bones.**"
Our true, spiritual, life and being is the derivative of His as He is our
Second Adam, in a sense so strong and real as to be figured by the
physical derivation of Eve from Adam. "As for any mixture of the
substance of His flesh with ours," says Hooker (*Eccl. Pol.* v. 56, end),
"the participation which we have of Christ includeth no such gross
surmise[1]".

In brief, this statement, in the light of other Scripture, amounts to
the assertion that "we," the believing Church, as such, are, as in the
case of Eve and Adam, at once the product of our Incarnate Lord's
existence as Second Adam, and His Bride. This profound and precious
truth is not dwelt upon, however. Strictly speaking, it is only incidental
here.

31. *For this cause*, &c.] The Gr. in this verse is practically identical
with that of Gen. ii. 24. We may reverently infer that the Apostle
was guided to see in that verse a Divine parable of the Coming Forth
of the Lord, the MAN of Men, from the FATHER, and His present and
eternal mystical Union with the true Church, His Bride.

"*For this cause:*"—the cause of His (covenanted and foreseen) Union
with us as Incarnate, Sacrificed, and Risen; in order to realize that
Divine Idea.

joined] A kindred word is used in a kindred passage, full of importance here, 1 Cor. vi. 17.

32. *This is*, &c.] More precisely, **This mystery is great.** For the
word "mystery" see above, i. 9, iii. 3, 4, 9; and below vi. 19. The
word tends to mean something of the sphere of spiritual truth not dis-
coverable by observation or inference, but revealed. The thing answering
to such a description in this context is, surely, "the mystical union and
fellowship betwixt Christ and His Church." It can scarcely be the
marriage union of mortal man and wife. That, as this whole passage
bears witness, is a thing most sacred, Divine in institution, and, in the
popular sense of the word, "mysterious." But it scarcely answers the
idea of a revealed *spiritual* truth.

We paraphrase the verse, then; "This revealed mystery, the Union
of Bridegroom and Bride, is great; but I say so in reference to the Bridal
of Redemption, to which our thought has been drawn."

The Vulgate Latin, which forms in its present shape the authoritative Romanist version, translates here, "*sacramentum* hoc magnum
est, ego autem dico in Christo et *in ecclesiâ*"; from which the Roman
theology deduces that "marriage is a great *sacrament* in Christ and
in His Church" (see Alford here, and the Catechism of the Council

---

[1] The remarkable chapter which thus closes deserves very careful study. It will
be seen that Hooker's view of "Christ's body in ours as a cause of immortality" is
that it is "a cause by removing, through the *death and merit* of His own flesh, that
which hindered the life of ours."

is a great mystery : but I speak concerning Christ and the
33 church.   Nevertheless let every one of you in particular so
love his wife even as himself; and the wife *see* that she
reverence *her* husband.

6   Children, obey your parents in the Lord : for this is right.

of Trent, *pars* ii. *qu.* xv.—xvii). The "Old Latin" read "*in
ecclesiam*," "with reference to the Church."

but I]   The pronoun is emphatic, possibly as if to say, "I, as distinguished from the narrator of the marriage in Eden."

On this whole passage Monod's remarks are noteworthy. He declines
to see, with Harless, a mere accommodation of the words of Genesis.
For him, those words, narrating true facts, are also a Divinely planned
type. "When St Paul quotes, by the Holy Spirit, a declaration of the
Holy Spirit, it is the Holy Spirit's thought and not his own that he
gives us...The relation which he indicates between the two unions...is
based in the depths of the Divine thought, and on the harmony established between things visible and invisible...The marriage instituted
in Eden was really, in the plan of God, a type of the union of Christ
with His Church."

For a reference by the Lord Himself to the passage in Genesis,
though with another purpose, see Matt. xix. 4, 5; Mark x. 6—9. For
Him, as for His Apostle, the passage was not a legend but an oracle.

33. *Nevertheless*] The word recalls the reader from the Divine but
incidental "mystery" of the mystical Union to the holy relationship
which is at once a type of it and sanctified and glorified by it.

of you]   Add, with the Gr., **also**: "you Christian husbands, *as well
as* the heavenly Husband."

his wife]   **His own wife**, as above, ver. 28.

reverence]   Lit., "fear," and so R.V. The fear of respect, of reverence, is obviously meant, and we prefer the expression of this as in A.V.
The word "fear" is indeed continually used in Scripture of the holy and
happy reverence of man for *God*, and so has lost all *necessary* connexion
with painful ideas. But just because we have here a precept for a *human*
mutual relation, the word which best keeps painful ideas out seems to
be not only the most beautiful, but the most true to the import of the
Greek, in such a context.

CH. VI. 1—4   THE CHRISTIAN HOME: CHILDREN AND PARENTS

1. *Children*]   Cp. Col. iii. 20.

obey]   The Gr. word differs from that rendered "submit yourselves"
(ver. 22). It is the same as that below, ver. 5, rendered "be obedient."
The child, and the bondservant, are to render an obedience (so the
words seem to indicate) different in kind from that of the wife, which
is so largely tempered by equality in other respects.

"Disobedience to parents" (Rom. i. 30; 2 Tim. iii. 2) appears in
Scripture as a symptom of a state of the gravest evil. The example of
the Lord stands in sacred contrast to it, for all ages of the Church (Luke

Honour thy father and mother; (which is the first 2
commandment with promise;) that it may be well with 3

ii. 51). It is in the school of the well-ordered Christian home that the
true idea of the Christian's position, divinely filial in its freedom, yet
(1 Cor. ix. 21) *"law-abiding* unto Christ," should be first illustrated
as well as taught.

parents] Mothers as well as fathers (see next verse). Scripture
uniformly upholds the authority of the mother. Cp. Prov. i. 8, vi. 20.

in the Lord] I.e., let your *obedience be in Him;* rendered as by
those whose action gets its reason and secret from union with Him. No
doubt the Apostle assumes here a family in which the parents are
Christians; but he certainly would not limit the precept to such a case,
as it would be limited if *"your parents in the Lord"* was the verbal
connexion.

In the case of *Christian* parentage, the children, as such, would
certainly be reckoned as within the covenant, and, in this sense, "in
the Lord." Cp. 1 Cor. vii. 14 ("now are the children *holy*"). It would
be for their own consciences before God, none the less, to ask whether
they were also "in Christ" in that inner and ultimate sense which is,
spiritually, "new creation" (2 Cor. v. 17).

There is some evidence, but quite inadequate, for the omission of the
words "in the Lord."

right] Just; not merely beautiful, or better, but according to the Law
of God, both in Nature and in Revelation.

The Apostle does not deal here with the limits of filial obedience in
cases where the Divine Will crosses the parental will. He has the
great rule and principle wholly in view.

2. *Honour,* &c.] Exod. xx. 12; Deut. v. 16. The Gr. here is
verbatim that of the LXX. On the duty, cp. Matt. xix. 19; Mark vii.
10, x. 19; Luke xviii. 20. The "honour" is that not of mere sentiment
but of obedience. See for illustration, Matt. xv. 4—8.

which is] He adds a significant circumstance about the Commandment.

the first...with promise] In the Decalogue, to which here the
reference plainly is, it is in fact the *only* "commandment with" definite
"promise." But the Decalogue is, so to speak, the first page of the
whole Law-Book of Revelation.

"*With*":—lit. "*in*"; attended, surrounded, by promise.

3. *that,* &c.] The Gr. is nearly verbatim from the LXX. of Exod.
xx. and Deut. v. It is observable that the Apostle omits the last words
of the original promise. Is not this on purpose, to dilate the reference
to the utmost? The Sinaitic limitation was but a special application of
a perpetual principle of Providence, illustrated, we may observe, in the
remarkable instance of the durability of the Chinese race and empire in
its "land." Not for Jews only, nor for Christians only, is the promise,
but for man, with such modifications of the meaning of "the earth,"
or "land," as circumstances may bring.

To seek a reference here to "the better country, that is, the heavenly"

4 thee, and thou mayest live long on the earth. And, ye fathers, provoke not your children to wrath: but bring them up in the nurture and admonition of the Lord.

(Heb. xi. 16), is a lawful and beautiful accommodation, but not in point as an interpretation.

mayest live] Quite lit., "*shalt* live." And it may be so read. But usage makes it at least probable that the A.V. (and R.V., text) repre sent rightly the intention of the Greek.

Observe, in passing, the hint given in these verses of the familiarity of the Gentile converts of St Paul with the O.T., and of the Divine authority which, he takes it for granted, they recognized in the Deca- logue. See further, Appendix H.

4. *fathers*] We may equally well render, **parents**. Moses' parents are called (Heb. xi. 23, Gr.) his *fathers*. The expression is found in the classics, Greek and Latin.—The father is the head of authority in the home, but the oneness of husband and wife, to speak of that only, secures the high authority of the mother also. This is assumed in the Fifth Commandment.

provoke not...to wrath] The same word occurs Col. iii. 21, and the cognate noun above, iv. 26, where see note. In Col. the suggestive words follow, "lest they be discouraged." The precept and the reason are both full of holy wisdom.—Here, as in the section on Marriage, observe how the two parties are reminded each exclusively of his own *duties*.

At the present time, undoubtedly, parental authority is at a low ebb in English Christendom. Its revival will depend, under God, on the active recognition of the whole teaching of such a Scripture as this, full of the warrant of parental government, and of the wisdom of parental sympathy.

bring them up] The Gr. conveys the idea of *development* (here in the sphere of character and principle) by *care and pains*. The same word has occurred ver. 29, with reference to bodily development.

nurture] Better, **discipline**. "Chastening" (R.V.) seems to us too narrow a word, at least in its ordinary sense of *punitive* discipline. It is true that in the leading N.T. passage of the kind (Heb. xii. 5—10; and cp. Rev. iii. 19) the word (or its kindred verb) obviously conveys that idea. And the verb is used of the terrible "chastisement" of the Roman scourge (Luke xxiii. 16, 22). But a wider meaning is, by usage, quite lawful, and it is certainly in point here. All the wholesome *restraints* of a wise early education are in view; all training in the direction of a life modest, unselfish, and controlled. Such will be the discipline of the true Christian home, and of its partial extension, the true Christian school.

admonition] The Gr. noun recurs 1 Cor. x. 11; Tit. iii. 10. For the kindred Gr. verb, see Acts xx. 31; Rom. xv. 14; 1 Cor. iv. 14; Col. i. 28, iii. 16; 1 Thess. v. 12, 14; 2 Thess. iii. 15. It will be seen that the noun relates to the warning side of instruction, a side too often neglected.

Servants, be obedient to *them that are your* masters ac- 5
cording to the flesh, with fear and trembling, in singleness
of your heart, as unto Christ; not with eyeservice, as men- 6

of the Lord] On His revealed principles, learnt of Him, and for His
sake. HE is everywhere in the Christian home.

5—9 THE CHRISTIAN HOME: SERVANTS AND MASTERS

5. *Servants*] **Bondservants, slaves.** Cp. Col. iii. 22—25; and see
1 Cor. vii. 21, 22; 1 Tim. vi. 1—2; Tit. ii. 9—10; Philemon; 1 Pet. ii.
18—25. The Gospel nowhere explicitly condemns slavery. But both
O.T. and N.T. state principles which are fatal to the extreme forms
of slavery familiar in the Roman world, forms which allowed no
rights whatever, in theory, to the slave. And the Gospel, in the act of
proclaiming the complete spiritual equality of slave and freeman, revealed a principle which was sure ultimately to discredit slave-holding
even in its mitigated forms. See Bp Lightfoot's *Introduction* to the
Ep. to Philemon, and the pamphlet (by Prof. Goldwin Smith) quoted
there, *Does the Bible sanction American Slavery?*

We may observe further that the great Gospel doctrine of the believer's "slavery" to his Master, Christ (cp. *e.g.* 1 Cor. vii. 22), when
once made familiar to the conscience and will, would inevitably tend to
a peculiar mutual *rapprochement* between Christian masters and slaves
while the institution still legally survived, and would do infinitely more
for the abolition of slavery than any "servile war." Prof. G. Smith
well observes, "Nothing marks the Divine character of the Gospel more
than its perfect freedom from any appeal to the spirit of political revolution" (*Does the Bible*, &c., p. 96). With impartial hands it not only
sanctions, but sanctifies, subordination to constituted authority (Rom.
xiii.), and meanwhile ennobles the individual, in respect of all that is
highest in the word liberty, by putting him into direct and conscious
relations with God.

The Gospel won many of its earliest converts from the slave-class.
This is less wonderful, when the vast number of slaves is remembered.
The little territory of Corinth alone contained nearly half a million slaves.

In the present and similar passages the primary reference to slavery
will, of course, be remembered. But there is a secondary and permanent reference to ordinary service, of all varieties.

according to the flesh] With the implied thought that they were not
the masters of their bondmen's *spirits*, and that the bondmen were
themselves, spiritually, the slaves of Christ. So Col. iii. 22.

with fear and trembling] With earnest, conscientious care and reverence. For the phrase, and this as its meaning, cp. 1 Cor. ii. 3; 2 Cor.
vii. 15; Phil. ii. 12.

singleness of your heart] The honest desire to do right for its own
sake, or rather for the Lord's sake; as against the self-interested seeking
for praise or promotion. Cp. for the word rendered "singleness",
Rom. xii. 8; 2 Cor. i. 12 (perhaps), viii. 2, ix. 11, 13, xi. 3; Col. iii. 22.

unto Christ] Cp. Rom. xiv. 7—9; a suggestive parallel.

pleasers; but as the servants of Christ, doing the will of
7 God from the heart; with good will doing service, as to the
8 Lord, and not to men : knowing that whatsoever good
thing any man doeth, the same shall he receive of the Lord,
9 whether *he be* bond or free.   And, ye masters, do the same

6. *eyeservice*] The word is found elsewhere only Col. iii. 22, and
was possibly coined by St Paul. It is the "service" which works for
another only under the compulsion of inspection, and only in external
action.

menpleasers] With no higher aim than the personal comfort of
getting, anyhow, the master's approval or indulgence. Cp. Gal. i. 10
for a close parallel. The underlying fact is that the earthly master can
be "pleased" by a merely specious service, but that the Christian is
really enslaved to One who sees infallibly whether the service rendered
Him is service of the heart. This comes out in the following clauses.

the will of God] expressed in the present fact of your servile duty.

Thus did the Gospel dignify the lowest walk of human life, in the
act of imposing the yoke of Christ on the whole being of the Christian.

> "A servant with this clause
> Makes drudgery divine;
> Who sweeps a room as for Thy laws
> Makes that and th' action fine."

Herbert, *The Elixir.*

the heart] Lit., **the soul.** So (Gr.) Col. iii. 23. A spring of inner-
most good-will, alike to the Heavenly Master and the earthly, must
work within. Cp. 1 Tim. vi. 1, 2.

8. *knowing*] as a certainty of the Gospel. For the Christian's
prospect of "reward," cp. Matt. v. 12, vi. 1, 4, xvi. 27; Luke vi. 35,
xiv. 14; Rom. ii. 6—10; 2 Cor. v. 10; Heb. x. 35; Rev. xxii. 12; &c.
The essence of the truth is that the obedience of love is infallibly welcomed and remembered by Him to whom it is rendered. "Well done,
good and faithful servant" (Matt. xxv. 21, 23), is His certain ultimate
response to every true act of the will given up to His will. This prospect, taken along with the conditions to it, has nothing that is not
deeply harmonious with our justification for Christ's Merit only, embraced by faith only. It is the recognition of love by Love, of grace by
the Giver. From another point of view it is the outcome of a process
of growth and result (Gal. vi. 7—9).

the Lord] Christ. Cp. among many passages Matt. xxv. 34—36;
2 Cor. v. 9, 10. In view of the context, the point would be still clearer
if the Gr. were rendered **the Master.**

9. *masters*] The Gr. is lit. "Lords." But English usage forbids
that word here. See last note; and the parallel passage, Col. iv. 1.

do the same things] Faithfully consult their true interests, be loyal to
your responsibilities in regard of them. These are "the things" you
look for from them towards yourselves.

things unto them, forbearing threatening : knowing that your Master also is in heaven ; neither is there respect of persons with him.

Finally, my brethren, be strong in the Lord, and in the 10

forbearing threatening] More lit., "**giving up your threatening,** 'the too habitual threatening'" (Ellicott).

your Master also] Better, in view of the true order of the Gr., **their Master and yours.**

respect of persons] Cp. Acts x. 34; Rom. ii. 11; Col. iii. 25 ; Jas. ii. 1, 9.

10—20 THE SPIRITUAL COMBAT: THE SECRET OF STRENGTH; THE ANTAGONISTS; THE ARMOUR; INTERCESSORY PRAYER

10. *Finally*] Lit., "*for the rest;*" "*for what remains.*" This may possibly mean "for the future," "from henceforth" (R. V. marg.). But the more probable reference is to "what remains of thought and precept." Had the Epistle dwelt on spiritual *weakness* as a previous characteristic of Ephesian Christian life, the other alternative might have been preferable; but it has not. For the Gr. phrase (identically, or nearly so), cp. Matt. xxvi. 45 (A. V. "now"); 1 Cor. vii. 29; 2 Cor. xiii. 11; Phil. iii. 1, iv. 8; 1 Thess. iv. 1; 2 Thess. iii. 1; 2 Tim. iv. 8; Heb. x. 13.—"Wisely does the Apostle, after the special injunctions to husbands and wives, &c., now in general enjoin it on all together to be strong in the Lord" (St Jerome). And observe that the deep secrets of spiritual victory now to be spoken of are necessary to the spiritual performance of the *common duties* just enjoined.

my brethren] These words are probably to be omitted; a possible insertion by transcribers from Phil. iii. 1, iv. 8.—The documentary evidence is scarcely decisive, but the absence elsewhere in the Epistle of the address " Brethren" is in favour of omission.

be strong] The Lat. versions have *confortamini;* a reminder of the true idea of "comfort," "comforter," in older English usage. See on ver. 22 below. For the same Gr. verb, in the (same) middle voice, cp. Acts ix. 22; Rom. iv. 20; 2 Tim. ii. 1; and in the active voice, Phil. iv. 13; 1 Tim. i. 12; 2 Tim. iv. 17. The tense here is present, not aorist, and suggests rather the maintenance than the attainment of strength. Their "Strength" (see *e.g.* Psal. lix. 17) was already and permanently theirs; let it be continuously used.—Cp. 1 Cor. xvi. 13 (where, however, "be strong" represents another Gr. word), and 1 Pet. v. 8—11, for close parallels to the thought and precept here.

in the Lord] This phrase, or its strict equivalents, occurs about 35 times in the Epistle.—The whole secret of spiritual strength resides in union with "the Lord." "In Him," and there alone, is there "no condemnation" (Rom. viii. 1); "in Him" is the fountain of spiritual vitality, to be made our own, in practical efficacy, only as we "abide in Him" (Joh. xv. 4—7). And these two aspects of benefit "in Christ" constitute together the believer's cause of strength; a strength the only alternative to which is spiritual impotence (Joh. xv. 5).

¹¹ power of his might. Put on the whole armour of God,
that ye may be able to stand against the wiles of the devil.

and in the power &c.] See i. 19 (and note there) for the same Gr.
The Gr. rendered "might" tends to denote strength rather as substratum or resource; the Gr. rendered "power", rather as outcome or exercise. We may paraphrase, "in the energy of Him the Strong."—The
phrase defines, so to speak, that aspect of the Lord in Whom they were
which was to be specially used in the great conflict. Elsewhere (1 Joh.
v. 20) the prominent thought is, "We are in Him that is TRUE,"
Veritable, Real. Here it is, "Ye are in Him that is ABLE."

11. *Put on*] For the word, cp. Rom. xiii. 12, 14 (a close parallel);
1 Cor. xv. 53, 54; 2 Cor. v. 3; Gal. iii. 27 (a parallel); above, iv. 24;
below, 14; Col. iii. 10, 12; 1 Thess. v. 8 (a close parallel). In 1 Thess.
and Rom. (just quoted) we have, so to speak, the germs of the developed imagery of this later-written passage. In them, as here, the believer,
already (from another point of view, that of covenant and possession)
clothed and armed with his Lord, is exhorted so to realize and to use
what he has that it shall be like a new clothing and arming.

the whole armour] One word in the Gr., *panoplia*. It occurs in
N.T. elsewhere only Luke xi. 22 and here ver. 13. In the Apocry-
pha it is not infrequent. Cp. esp. Wisdom v. 17 &c., a very close
parallel here as regards the picture:—"He (the Lord) shall take
His zeal as a panoply, and make the creature His weapon for the
defeat of His enemies; He shall put on righteousness as a breastplate,
and shall make true judgment His helmet; He shall take sanctity as
His invincible shield, and shall whet severe wrath as His sword, &c."
These words may very possibly have been in the Apostle's memory.
But far more certainly he had present there Isai. lix. 16, 17, itself the
probable ground of the imagery in Wisdom.

The word *panoplia* admits no doubt of a looser application in usage;
it may mean armour, complete *or not*. But its strict meaning, "*whole*
armour," is precisely in point here, where the stress of thought is on
the *one* secret of spiritual strength; the need of Divine safeguard, and
nothing less, for the *whole emergency*.

Cp. again 1 Thess. v. and Rom. xiii. for parallels, or rather germs, of
this passage. There, as here, the image of "putting on" is connected
with that of "armour." And in Rom. distinctly, and in 1 Thess. im-
plicitly, the armour is seen to be reducible ultimately, as here, to the
Lord Jesus Christ Himself. St Jerome says here, "From what we read
in the passage following, and from the things said in all the Scriptures
concerning the Lord (our) Saviour, it most clearly results that by 'all
the arms of God'...the Saviour is to be understood."

of God] Supplied by Him, having been wrought by Him. For
such a conflict nothing less will do than what is wholly HIS in origin
and gift.

that ye may be able] It is implied that thus, while only thus, the
militant Christian *shall* be able. No inadequacy in his equipment is to
be feared.

For we wrestle not against flesh and blood, but against 12

to stand] The key-word of the passage. The present picture is not of a march, or of an assault, but of the holding of the fortress of the soul and of the Church for the heavenly King. Bunyan's "Mr Standfast" is a portrait that may illustrate this page.—So again below, vv. 13, 14.

wiles] Lit., "*methods*"; **stratagems**. The Gr. word occurs (in Scripture) only here and above, iv. 14 (where R.V. "*wiles*"). For the formidable fact of the deliberate and subtle *plans* of the great Enemy, carefully concealed but skilfully combined on weak points, cp. 2 Cor. ii. 11; 1 Pet. ii. 11, (where render "*carry on a campaign* against the soul"). In this respect, as in so many others, the Temptation of the Lord Himself is a picture of that of His followers; a series of veiled attacks, upon points thought weak, by the most subtle of created intellects.—In 1 Pet. v. 8 the same Enemy appears acting, as he sometimes does, in another way; by violence and terror.

the devil] See on ii. 2 for considerations on his personality as recognized by St Paul. This designation (*diabolos*, accuser,) appears above, iv. 27, and elsewhere in St Paul, Acts xiii. 10; 1 Tim. iii. 6, 7, 2 Tim. ii. 26; besides Heb. ii. 14. It is frequent with St Matthew, St Luke, and St John. In the LXX. it is the regular equivalent, though not the precise translation, of the Heb. *Sâtân* (the *Adversary*); *e.g.* Job i.—ii.; Zech. iii. 1, 2. One of the terrible characteristics of the Adversary of the Son of God is the aim and effort to bring believing man into *condemnation*; hence his accusations of the saints. Cp. the Book of Job especially, and Rev. xii. 10 (where, however, another word than *diabolos* is used). Nor let it be forgotten that his first assault on man (Gen. iii. 5) was made by means of accusation *against God*, as grudging a good gift to man.

12. *we wrestle*] Lit., **our wrestling is.** War and the games are associated in the language of 2 Tim. ii. 4—5. But here, as Ellicott observes, there need be no mingling of metaphors. War involves wrestling, in many a hand to hand encounter.—The Gr. word (*palê*, wrestling) is found only here in Gr. literature, but is cognate to *palæstra*, and other familiar words.

The Apostle takes it for granted that the Christian life *is*, from one point of view, essentially a conflict. "We" obviously, by context, means all Christians as such. Cp. 1 Cor. ix. 25, &c. But it is a conflict maintained, in Christ, with Divine power and from a dominating position.

flesh and blood] Lit., "*blood and flesh*"; but English usage makes the other order better, as a rendering. The phrase occurs (in the opposite order of words) Matt. xvi. 17; 1 Cor. xv. 50; Gal. i. 16; Heb. ii. 14. It denotes (as 1 Cor. xv.) humanity in its present mortal conditions, or (other reff.) humanity simply. "Man," *as now constituted*, will not inherit the eternal kingdom; "man" did not illuminate St Peter; "man" did not teach the Gospel to St Paul; Christ so became "Man" as to be able to taste death. The thought here is not that we are not

principalities, against powers, against the rulers of the

wrestling with our bodily desires, or weaknesses, but that we are not wrestling with *mere mortal men*. True, they may be our ostensible and immediate enemies or obstacles, but behind them is the central force of evil in the spirit-world. See the language of Rev. ii. 10, and Abp Trench's note upon it (*Epistles to the Seven Churches*, p. 104). It will be observed how forcible is the testimony of the Apostle here to the objective existence of the world of evil spirits. He not merely takes it for granted, but carefully distinguishes it from the world of humanity. See further, Appendix G.

principalities...powers] Lit., **the principalities**, &c. See i. 21, iii. 10; and notes. Here, as Rom. viii. 38; Col. ii. 15; the ref. obviously is to personal *evil* spirits as members and leaders of an organized spirit-world. For allusions to such organization, under its head, cp. the visions of the Revelation, esp. xii. 7, 9. And cp. Matt. xxv. 41; 2 Cor. xii. 7. Note also the "*Legion*" of evil spirits (Mar. v. 9, 15; Luke viii. 30), compared with the "more than twelve *Legions* of (holy) angels", Matt. xxvi. 53. Great numbers and organized action are at once suggested by the military word; a word used on both occasions with profound earnestness and appeal to fact.

The *leaders* of the host of evil are alone mentioned here, and in the parallels, as are the leaders of the host of good in i. 21, &c. The "plebeian angels militant" (*Par. Lost*, X. 442), are taken for granted, represented in their chiefs.

the rulers of the darkness of this world] Lit. as R. V., **the world-rulers of this darkness**. The words "of this world" (or rather "age") are probably an explanatory insertion.

"*This darkness*" is the present order of things on earth, in its aspect as a scene of sin. As such it is *dark*, with the shadows of delusion, woe, and death. See Luke xxii. 53 (a suggestive parallel) and other reff. under iv. 18.

"*The world-rulers*":—the context obviously points to personal evil spirits, exercising rule, in some real sense, over the world; and the question is, what does the world (*cosmos*) mean here? See in reply ii. 2 and note. "The world" here, as very often in St John, and often in St Paul (esp. in 1 Cor.), denotes not the Universe, nor the earth and sea, but humanity as fallen and rebel. As such, it is the realm of these powers of evil. Their Head is the usurping, but permitted, Cæsar of this empire, which is not so much local as moral; and his subordinate spirits are accordingly "imperial rulers" within it, for him.—The Gr. word (*cosmocratôr*) appears in Rabbinic literature, transliterated (see Ellicott here). It is used sometimes there as a mere magniloquent synonym for "king." But we may be sure of a more special meaning in a passage like this.

For allusions to the mysterious "authority" of the Evil Power over the human "world," in its ethical aspect at least, cp. Luke iv. 6; Joh. xiv. 30, xvi. 11; 2 Cor. iv. 4; 1 Joh. v. 18. It has been asked whether this authority is connected with a *previous lawful* presidency of the great Spirit now fallen, over this region of the Universe.

darkness of this world, against spiritual wickedness in high
places. Wherefore take unto *you* the whole armour of God, 13
that ye may be able to withstand in the evil day, and having

But "God knoweth" is the best answer to such enquiries, till the veil
is lifted. The fact of the present authority is our chief concern; and in
this respect we are plainly warned that there is a real antagonism
between the Kingdom of God and the Kingdom of the Evil One, and
that in both cases we have the phenomenon of a spiritual dominion
expressing itself through human organization and institution. See
further on ii. 2, above.

spiritual wickedness in high places] Lit., **the spiritual** things **of
wickedness in the heavenly** places. R. V. paraphrases "the
spiritual *hosts*, &c."; and this well gives the meaning. The idea
is of beings and forces, spiritual as distinguished from material, belonging to and working for "wickedness." Wickedness is viewed as
having its visible and invisible agents, and these are the invisible.

"*In the heavenly places*":—the fifth occurrence of the phrase in this
Epistle (cp. i. 3, 20, ii. 6, iii. 10). The adjective occurs also Matt.
xviii. 35; Joh. iii. 12; 1 Cor. xv. 40, 48, 49; Phil. ii. 10; 2 Tim. iv. 18;
Heb. iii. 1, vi. 4, viii. 5, ix. 23, xi. 16, xii. 22. The connexion of it
with anything evil is confined to this passage, and is confessedly
startling. Of the several expositions offered, the oldest, given by
St Jerome here, seems best to meet the case; that which interprets
"heaven" as the large antithesis to "earth" (cp. Matt. vi. 26, "birds
of *the heaven*"; &c.), and "heavenly," accordingly, as "un-earthly,"
super-terrestrial, belonging to the region of things unseen and (in
power) superior to man, of which the impalpable sky is the parable.
See above on ii. 2, "the authority *of the air*." The import of the
words, then, is that we have to deal, in the combat of the soul and of
the Church, with spiritual agents of evil occupying a sphere of action
invisible and practically boundless.—In St Ignatius' *Ep. to the Ephesians*, c. xiii., the same Gr. adjective is used, with an almost certainly
similar reference. See Bp Lightfoot there (*Ignatius*, vol. ii. p. 66),
and our *Introduction*, p. 28.

13. *take unto* you] Lit., **take up**, even as Æneas (if the illustration
may be reverently offered) took up, and examined, and girt on, the
god-wrought panoply brought him by his Mother, on the verge of war
(*Æn.* VIII. 608, &c.). The Divine armour, perfect, and perfectly
ready, lies at the Christian's feet, and is his own. Let him, by the
grace of God, appropriate it *in act*.

withstand] See above on "stand," ver. 11. The verb here occurs
in the same connexion, Jas. v. 6; 1 Pet. v. 9. See on the other hand
Matt. v. 39, where perhaps render, "*withstand* not the Evil One,"
(represented by evil men). To the cruelty of the Enemy the believer
meekly *submits;* his spiritual stratagems he *withstands*, in Christ.

the evil day] The dark crisis of the campaign, whenever it may be.
And this will practically mean *any* felt crisis of the soul's resistance.
So in a familiar hymn:

14 done all, to stand. Stand therefore, having your loins girt
about with truth, and having on the breastplate of righteous-

> "[We] ask the aid of heavenly power
> To help us in *the* evil hour."

The definite article in such a phrase· does not isolate a solitary occasion, but denotes distinct occasions of the one class in question.

Some expositors see here a reference to the final conflict of the Church.
But the whole passage is concerned with a present and normal "wrestling" against present enemies. Cp. the words ch. v. 16, "the days
are evil."

having done] More precisely, the verb being compound, "having
wrought out," "*quite* done." This compound verb is a common one
with St Paul, however, and its special etymology must not be greatly
pressed (see it, *e.g.* Rom. vii. 8, 13, 15, 17). Still, an intensity of
meaning is in place in this context: "having **accomplished** all things,
all things demanded for equipment and action."—The verb bears the
meaning "to subdue," sometimes in the classics, and once or twice in
LXX.; but not in other N.T. passages.

to stand] unmoved at your post, ready for the next assault of the
unseen foe. It is important to bear in mind through the whole context
that the central idea is fixity, not progress or conquest; ideas of which
the Gospel is full, but which are not present *here*. The scene is filled
with the marshalled hosts of the Evil One, bent upon *dislodging* the
soul, and the Church, from the one possible vantage-ground of life and
power—union and communion with their Lord.

14. *Stand*] See last note. Here, as throughout the passage, the
tense of this verb is aorist. A decisive act of *taking a conscious stand,*
or a succession of such acts, is implied.

having your loins girt] Lit., and far better, **having girded your
loins** (R. V.). The girding is the own act, by grace, of the regenerate
will.

"*Your loins*":—cp. Exod. xii. 11; Job xxxviii. 3, xl. 7; Psal. xviii.
39; Isai. xi. 5; Luke xii. 35; 1 Pet. i. 13. The well-fastened girdle
kept together the soldier's dress and accoutrements, and added conscious vigour to his frame.

with truth] Lit., "*in* truth"; and the "in" may very possibly keep
its direct meaning; for the girded body is within the girdle. But this
meaning would be conveyed in English by "with."

"*Truth*":—not "*the* truth"; a phrase which would decisively mean
"the true message of the Gospel." The absence of the article leaves
us free to explain the word of the sincerity, reality, and simplicity of
the regenerate man. For this use of the word in St Paul see *e.g.* 1 Cor.
v. 8; 2 Cor. vii. 14, xi. 10; above, ch. v. 9; Phil. i. 18. The grasp on
revealed Truth is indeed all-important, but it must be made "in truth,"
in personal sincerity, if it is to avail in the spiritual struggle. And
this meaning of the word well corresponds to the imagery. Un-
reality, whether in trust or self-surrender, is fatal to the *coherence* of the
Christian life. Meanwhile it must be remembered that the "panoply"

ness ; and *your* feet shod with the preparation of the gospel 15

is "*of God*," and that "truth" is here, accordingly, a supernatural grace, that simplicity of attitude and action towards God, His word and His will, which is a gift of regeneration alone.—In Isai. xi. 5 "righteousness" and "faithfulness" are Messiah's girdle.

having on] Lit., and far better, **having put on**; the same verb as ver. 11. The tense is aorist. The believer is summoned to a decisive *renewal* of his exercise of grace.

the breastplate] Cp. Isai. lix. 17; 1 Thess. v. 8. And see note above on ver. 11 for the apocryphal parallel.—The breastplate covers the heart. Here the heart in its figurative and spiritual sense (see on i. 18, iii. 17) is in question ; how to protect it and its action, in the great conflict.

righteousness] Cp. 2 Cor. vi. 7.—One leading explanation of this word here is Christ's Righteousness as our Justification. According to this, the warrior is to oppose the Divine fact of JEHOVAH TSIDKENU (Jer. xxiii. 6; cp. Rom. iii., iv; Phil. ii.) to the strategy of the Accuser (Rom. viii. 33, 34). But this class of truth falls rather under the figures of the shoes and the shield (see below). Here (in view esp. of Isai. lix. 17, where "righteousness" is JEHOVAH'S breastplate), it is better to explain it of the believer's personal righteousness, i.e. his loyalty in principle and action to the holy Law of God. For clear cases of this meaning of the word (the root-meaning with reference to all others) in St Paul, cp. Rom. vi. 13, xiv. 17; 2 Cor. vi. 14, ix. 9, 10; above, iv. 24, v. 9; Phil. i. 11; 1 Tim. vi. 11; and see Tit. ii. 12.

The idea is closely kindred to that of "truth," just considered. But it is strictly defined by the correlative idea of Law. The believer is armed at the heart against the Tempter by definite and supreme reverence for the Law, the revealed preceptive Will of God. So Daniel was armed (Dan. i., vi.), and the Three (Dan. iii.).

Here, as under the word "truth," remember that the armour is "*of God*." See note on "truth," above.

In 1 Thess. v. 8 the breastplate is "*faith and love.*" There is no discrepancy in the difference. Loyalty to the Divine Law is inseparably connected with trust in the word of God and love of His will.

15. your *feet shod*] Lit., and better, **having shod your feet**. See note above, on "having on."—If the warrior is to "*stand*" he must have no unprotected and uncertain *foot*-hold.

the preparation] The Gr. word occurs here only in N.T. In the LXX. it occurs several times, and tends, curiously, to denote equipment in the special form of base or pedestal (*e.g.* Ezra iii. 3; A.V. "bases"). Such a meaning is obviously in point here, where the imagery suggests not readiness to run, but foothold for standing. **Equipment** will be a fair rendering.

the gospel of peace] Cp. Isai. lii. 7; Nahum i. 15; and the quotation, Rom. x. 15. Those passages are closely linked to this by the concurrence in them of the words "feet" and "message of peace." But in them the imagery distinctly suggests movement, message-bearing; in this, as

16 of peace; above all, taking the shield of faith, wherewith ye shall be able to quench all the fiery darts of the wicked.

distinctly, steadfastness in personal spiritual warfare. Here, accordingly, we interpret "the Gospel, the glad message, of peace," to mean the Divine revelation of peace as heard and welcomed by the Christian for himself. See above, ii. 17 (and note), where the words "Gospel" (in the Gr.) and "peace" also concur; and, for other mentions of the Gospel message and work in the Epistle, i. 13, iii. 6, 8, and below ver. 19.

The paradox here, "*peace*" as part of the panoply of the holy *war*, is as significant as it is beautiful. The warrior's foothold needs to be settled, sure, and restful, just in proportion to the stress around him. "Peace *with* God" (Rom. v. 1), the peace of justification, and its holy sequel and accompaniment, "the peace *of* God, keeping the heart and thoughts in Christ Jesus" (Phil. iv. 7), are just then most necessary to the saint's spirit, and most real to his consciousness, when put to the proof "in the evil day." Christ, in Himself, is the Rock of vantage; a clear view and personal hold of Him revealed is the secret of a true foothold upon Him.—The Apostle himself stood in this strength when he wrote, "I know Whom I have believed, &c." (2 Tim. i. 12).

16. *above all*] The Gr. admits the renderings, "*over* all things"; "*besides* all things"; "*on occasion of* all things, (on all occasions)"; "*against* all things." We incline to this last, as suitable to the imagery of the shield *shifted to meet* any and every stroke.—Another reading gives "*in* all things"; at every turn of the conflict. But the evidence is far from conclusive. "It has not sufficient external support, and may have been a correction for the ambiguous [preposition in the text]" (Ellicott).

taking] Lit., **having taken up.** See note on ver. 13 above.

the shield] The Gr. is one of two familiar words for "shield," and denotes a large oblong shield (such as that used by the heavy Roman infantry) about 2½ × 4 feet in size. (See Smith's *Dict. Class. Ant.*, under the word *Scutum*). The significance of the choice of word is obvious. In the parallel apocryphal passage (see note on ver. 11 above) the Gr. word for "shield" is the other alternative, denoting a circular and lighter shield. But this is no proof (as some expositors have thought) that the present word was not deliberately chosen, in a passage like this, where the idea of protection, and the need of it, is pressed to the utmost.

faith] "That faith whereby we resolutely rely on God and His word for deliverance from temptation" (Monod). The true safeguard in the evil day lies ever, not in introspection, but in that look wholly outward, Godward, which is the essence of faith (see Psal. xxv. 15).

wherewith] Lit., and perhaps better, in this vivid picture, **in which.**

ye shall be able] Observe the certainty of the promise, good for the whole future of the conflict.

to quench] before the soul's living frame, so to speak, is reached and burned.—It may be, and very often is, impossible for the Christian

And take the helmet of salvation, and the sword of the 17

to detect the point where temptation passes into sin; a fact which should secure humble caution in all language about personal spiritual victory. But this verse warrants the reverent expectation of very true victories in the real exercise of enlightened and simple faith. The word "*all*" is important.

the fiery darts] Lit., "*the darts, the ignited* darts." The metaphor is taken from the fire-arrows of ancient warfare. Wetstein here gives abundant illustration, from Thucydides, Livy, Vegetius, Ammianus, and many other authors. Ammianus (about A.D. 380) describes the Roman *malleoli* as arrows carrying a perforated bulb, like a distaff, just below the point; the bulb filled with burning matter; the arrow discharged from a slack bow, lest speed should kill the flame. Another variety was simpler; the shaft near the point was wrapped in burning tow.

The imagery is sternly true to the experience of injections into the soul of polluting ideas, or of doubts of God, or of unchastened anger.

the wicked] I.e., as R.V., **the Evil One**; the great General of the besieging host.

17. *take*] Lit., **receive**, as from the hands of Another, who presents it to all His soldiers.

the helmet] Cp. Isai. lix. 17; 1 Thess. v. 8. See also Psal. cxl. 7. The head needs protection not only as a vital part, but as the seat of sight. The believer "looks up, and lifts up his head, as his redemption draweth nigh" (Luke xxi. 28).

salvation] The Gr. is not the common word so rendered, *sôtêria*, (which is used 1 Thess. v. 8), but *sôtêrion*, which occurs Luke ii. 30, iii. 6; Acts xxviii. 28. It is frequent in the LXX.; occurring *e.g.* Psal. li. (LXX. l.) 12, xci. (LXX. xc.) 16; Isai. xxvi. 1, lix. 17, lxi. 10. If the difference between the two forms is to be pressed, it may be suggested that *sôtêrion* tends to denote "salvation" (deliverance from judgment and sin) as it is in the Divine Person who saves; *sôtêria*, "salvation" as it is applied and received. But the difference often vanishes.

In Isai. lix. the Divine Warrior wears this helmet; doubtless in the sense of His being the Worker of deliverance, clothed and armed, as it were, with His great purpose. The Christian warrior here wears it in the sense of his being the receiver and possessor of deliverance, clothed and armed in the victory of his Head. In 1 Thess. v. "*the hope of* salvation" is the helmet: the sure prospect of the final and absolute deliverance (cp. Rom. xiii. 11), a deliverance of which the present peace and victory of faith is but the outline or prelude, "covers the head" of the soldier. The two passages supplement each other; the hope is based on the actual possession of the thing in its present phase; the sense of possession is vivified by the hope.

the sword] The one offensive weapon in the picture. The fight is stationary and defensive, but it continually requires the thrust and cut of the defender. The assailant is himself to be assailed; the accusing

¹⁸ Spirit, which is the word of God : praying always with all

tempter to be *silenced*. Cp. Heb. iv. 12 for the only other N.T. passage
where the "sword" appears in spiritual imagery. There, as well as
here, the "Word" is the sword-like thing. In the O.T., cp. Psal. lxiv.
3; Isai. xlix. 2.

of the Spirit] The great Conveyer of the "word of God," as the
Inspirer of the Prophets, under both O.T. and N.T. (above iii. 5; Heb.
iii. 7, ix. 8, x. 15; 1 Pet. i. 11; 2 Pet. i. 21) Thus the sword is of
His forging; and as He works in the believer as the Spirit of truth
(Joh. xiv. 17), and faith (2 Cor. iv. 13), He puts the sword into his
grasp and enables him to use it. See next note.

the word of God] The sure *utterance* of Revealed Truth. The Gr.
word (as in ch. v. 26, where see note,) is not *logos* but *rhéma*. Doubtless
the reference is not to be limited to the very words of Scripture; for true
conclusions from them, in the Creeds for example, are "utterances" of
Divine truth. But the evidence of Scripture itself, as it indicates historically the principles and practice of the Lord and the Apostles in regard of
the Written Word, is altogether in favour of interpreting the phrase here,
as to its main and permanent meaning, of the believing use, in spiritual
conflict, of the Scriptures; the Written Word, revealing the Living
Word. It is true that when this Epistle was written, the Spirit, Whose
work in producing Scripture was still in progress, was also speaking
direct to the Church in other modes (see *e.g.* Acts xi. 28; 1 Cor. xiv.; &c.).
But that this was a great *passing* phase of the Church's experience is
indicated by 1 Cor. xiii. 8, and by the broad facts of history. And
meanwhile both Christ and the Apostles appeal to the Written Word
for proof and certainty in a manner altogether peculiar, and which
calls for the close personal study of the Christian disciple.

Above all, observe that the Lord Himself, in His Temptation, the
history of which should be compared carefully with this whole passage,
uses exclusively verbal citations, written "utterances," from the Scriptures, as His sword; and this immediately after His Baptism and the
Descent of *the Holy Spirit* (Matt. iii. 16—iv. 11; Luke iv. 1—13).
No suggestion could be more pregnant than this as to the abiding position of the Written Word under the Dispensation of the Spirit.

With this verse the imagery of the passage gives way to unfigurative
spiritual precepts. The writer is careless of literary symmetry, in
favour of a higher order and beauty.

18. *praying always*] Lit., **praying on every occasion**, every incident of life, especially every incident of temptation. Cp. the yet broader
and deeper precept, 1 Thess. v. 17, "pray *without intermission*." See
too Luke xviii. 1; Phil. iv. 6; Col. i. 3, 9, iv. 2. The attitude of
the believer's mind is to be one of perpetual prayer, in the sense of
continuously maintaining a trustful and humble reference of all parts of
life to his Lord's will and grace. This will express itself in acts, if
only momentary and wholly internal acts, of adoration and petition at
each felt crisis of need. See Heb. iv. 16.

with] Lit., **by means of**; the expressions being the *instruments* of
the spiritual state.

prayer and supplication in the Spirit, and watching there-
unto with all perseverance and supplication for all saints ;
and for me, that utterance may be given unto me, that *I* may 19

all prayer and supplication] "*All:*"—every variety; deliberate, ejacu-
latory; public, private, secret; confessing, asking, praising. Or again,
more simply, with a full, not partial and niggardly, employment of the
privilege and resource of prayer.

"Prayer" is the larger word, "supplication" the more definite. The
former includes the whole attitude and action of the creature's approach
to God; the latter denotes only petition. "Prayer," however, is very
often used in this narrower sense. See out of many passages Matt. v.
44; Luke xxii. 40.—The two words occur together, as here, Phil. iv. 6;
1 Tim. ii. 1, v. 5.

in the Spirit] So also R. V. Lit., "*in spirit*;" but see last note on
ii. 22 above.—The Holy Spirit was to be "the Place" of the prayer, in
the sense of being the surrounding, penetrating, transforming atmosphere of the spirit of the praying Christian. Cp. Zech. xii. 10; Rom.
viii. 26; Jude 20.

watching] **Keeping awake.** The Gr. word occurs also Mark xiii.
33; Luke xxi. 36; Heb. xiii. 17. There was to be no indolent, som-
nolent oblivion of the need of prayer, or of the fact of offered prayer.
For similar precepts (with another Gr. word) see Matt. xxvi. 41; Col.
iv. 2; 1 Pet. iv. 7.

with all perseverance] Lit., **in** (as R. V.).—"*All:*"—that is, "*full,*"
"utmost;" so "all faith" (1 Cor. xiii. 2).—For a close parallel to the
thought see Rom. xii. 12; where lit., "in the (matter of) *prayer,
persevering.*" Our Lord's parable (Luke xviii. 1, &c.), makes it plain
that persistency as well as trust has a mysterious value in the efficacy of
prayer.

supplication] "*All* supplication;" the "all" being implied from the
previous words. "*All:*"—with the full particularity and thoughtfulness
proper to faithful intercessions.

for all saints] Lit., **for all the saints.** With a noble abruptness the
thought, long detained upon the combat and resources of the individual,
and of the single community, now runs out to the great circle of the
Church. The inner connexion of ideas is close and strong. The Christian cannot really arm himself with CHRIST, and use his armour, without getting nearer in sympathy to the brotherhood of the saints of
Christ. Cp. 1 Pet. v. 9 for the same connexion otherwise indicated.

"*Saints:*"—see on i. 1 above.

19. *for me*] Lit., **on behalf of me.** This change of phrase, by
change of preposition, is perhaps due to the Apostle's strong personal
sense of his need of the *help* of intercessory prayer.—He wisely covets
for his apostolic work the prayers of the obscurest militant believer.
Cp. Rom. xv. 30; 2 Cor. i. 11; Phil. i. 19; Col. iv. 3; 2 Thess. iii. 1;
Philem. 22; Heb. xiii. 18.

utterance] Lit., "*word*" (*logos ;* Latin versions, *sermo*); a special
deliverance of the Gospel. Cp. 1 Cor. i. 5.

open my mouth boldly, to make known the mystery of the
20 gospel, for which I am an ambassador in bonds: that therein
I may speak boldly, as I ought to speak.

given] by the inspiring and enabling Spirit. Cp. Acts ii. 4; 1 Cor.
xii: 8. The Apostle was still as entirely dependent on the heavenly
Gift as when his work began.

that I may open] Lit., "*in opening of.*" "In" such "opening," as
opportunity came by God's providence, and power came by His grace,
the "gift" would be seen.

boldly] Lit., **in boldness of speech.** The Gr. word has occurred iii.
12, where see note. Cp. Phil. i. 20. St Paul was not insensible to the
difficulty of a full and open utterance of the Gospel, not least in the
Capital of the world. Cp. Rom. i. 15, 16, and notes in this Series.

the mystery] The sixth occurrence of the word in the Epistle; cp. i.
9, iii. 3, 4, 9, v. 32. On the meaning, see on i. 9. The special reference here is fixed by the previous occurrences; it is to Divine Redemption in its world-wide scope and eternal issues. Cp. 1 Tim. iii. 16.

20. *for which*] **On behalf of which,** in the interests of which.
The Gospel is, so to speak, the *Power* whose envoy he is. Cp. 2 Cor.
v. 20 for the same phrase and image with express mention of the
Sovereign, Christ, represented by His envoys.

an ambassador] Cp. 2 Cor. just quoted. And see Philem. 8, where
Bp Lightfoot renders (and so R. V. margin) "*an ambassador*, and now
also a prisoner, of Jesus Christ;" giving this passage, so closely parallel
and exactly contemporary, as a main reason for the rendering. See his
note there. This is not the place to discuss the question.

in bonds] Lit., **in a chain.** The Gr. word occurs elsewhere in St
Paul's speech or writings, Acts xxviii. 20; 2 Tim. i. 16.—Prisoners
detained upon appeal to the Emperor, as was St Paul, were sometimes
"coupled by a slight chain round the right wrist to the left of a soldier,
and, thus shackled...if they could afford it, were at liberty to hire a lodging for themselves without the walls, but within the prescribed limits"
(Lewin, *Life, &c., of St Paul*, ii. 236. See too Bp Lightfoot, *Philippians*,
p. 8). Cp. Josephus, *Antiquities*, xviii. c. 6, for similar custody (though
not upon appeal) in the case of Agrippa, the Herod of Acts xii., in his
earlier life in Italy in the reign of Tiberius. For St Paul's allusions to
the "bonds" of this Roman imprisonment, see Phil. i. 7, 13, 14, 16;
Col. iv. 18; Philem. 10, 13; and above, iii. 1, iv. 1.

Wetstein calls attention here to the paradox; "an *ambassador* in
chains."

therein] I.e., in "the mystery of the Gospel." This was the field or
sphere of his speech. The Gr. makes it plain that the reference is to
this, and not to the "bonds."

speak boldly] The verb is cognate to the noun in ver. 19. See note
above on "boldly" there. The tense is aorist, and suggests that he
prays for grace to take, as it were, a "new departure" in outspoken
testimony and exposition.

But that ye also may know my affairs, *and* how I do, ²¹
Tychicus, a beloved brother and faithful minister in the

I ought] under the holy obligation of my commission. Cp. 1 Cor.
ix. 16.

speak] The Gr. verb indicates specially the *wording* of the message.
He prays for grace to be perfectly explicit in terms.—The tense is aorist;
see last note but one.

21—22   THE MISSION OF TYCHICUS

21. *ye also*] as well as my other friends, near or distant. Perhaps
the emphasis has to do with Col. iv. 7, words written so nearly at the same
time: Ephesus as well as Colossæ should be kept informed. This, however, opens the question (not to be discussed here) which Epistle was
first written, this or the Colossian.

my affairs] Lit., **the things concerning me**. So Phil. i. 12; Col.
iv. 7. The phrase is common in later classical Greek.—Omit "*and*",
supplied by A. V. after these words.

how I do] Lit., "*what* I do." But Gr. usage confirms the rendering of A.V. and R. V. The "doing" is *faring*; exactly as in the
English phrase.

Tychicus] Named elsewhere, Acts xx. 4; Col. iv. 7; 2 Tim. iv. 12;
Tit. iii. 12. An examination of these passages and their surroundings
shews that Tychicus belonged to the province of Asia, and makes it
likely that he was an Ephesian. His character is drawn in noble
outlines here and in Col. We see in him one who attracted the
Apostle's love and reliance, in the fellowship of Christ, in a high
degree; and the words in 2 Tim. shew that his faithful readiness for
service was maintained into the last trying days of St Paul's life.—It
is suggested that Tychicus, and his brother Asian, Trophimus, were
the two "brethren" associated with Titus in the management of the
collection (2 Cor. viii. 16—24) for the poor Christians in Judea.—
Tradition makes Tychicus afterwards bishop of Chalcedon in Bithynia,
or of Colophon, or of Neapolis in Cyprus.

See the art. *Tychicus* in Smith's *Dict. of the Bible;* Ellicott here; and
Lightfoot on Col. iv. 7, and p. 11 of his *Philippians*. Lightfoot shews
that the name Tychicus, though not common, occurs in inscriptions and
on coins belonging to Asia Minor.

This is the one individual personal allusion in the Epistle.

a beloved brother] Lit., and better, **the**, &c. The allusion is to a
person well-defined by acquaintance. On the word "brother" see
below, on ver. 23.

minister] Gr. *diaconos:* so in Col. iv. 7. See on iii. 7 above for the
essential meaning of the word. In this passage, as in Col., the probable reference is to the activities of Tychicus as St Paul's helper. Cp.
Col. i. 7 for the word in a similar connexion. In Phil. i. 1; 1 Tim.
iii. 8, 12, iv. 6; the word is used to denote holders of a subordinate
office in the Christian ministry. And cp. Rom. xvi. 1, where it is used
of a Christian *woman* holding a recognized position in the work of

²² Lord, shall make known to you all *things:* whom I have
sent unto you for the same purpose, that ye might know
²³ our affairs, and *that* he might comfort your hearts. Peace
be to the brethren, and love with faith, from God the Father

the Church. Here, however, such a meaning is unlikely, the person
being of a calibre, and in a connexion with the Apostle, which do
not suggest an inferior grade of work. In no passages of the N.T.
save Rom., Phil., and 1 Tim., quoted above, has the word *diaconos*
any necessary connexion at all with organized ministry as such. E. g.
in Joh. ii. 5, 9, it denotes a "servant" in the commonest sense;
in Rom. xiii. 4, a "servant" of God in civil magistracy; in 2 Cor. iii. 6,
a "servant" of the New Covenant, as an active agent in its promul-
gation. In Rom. xv. 8; Gal. ii. 17; it is used of the Lord Himself.

in the Lord] The last occurrence in the Epistle of this sacred
and pregnant phrase. The life, and the life-work, of Tychicus were
altogether conditioned, characterized, and animated, by his union with
Christ, and the people of Christ.

22. *I have sent*] Lit., "*I did send.*" The aorist is "epistolary";
it speaks from the time of the arrival, not the sending, of the messenger. Cp. 2 Cor. viii. 18, 22; Phil. ii. 28; Col. iv. 8 (where see
Lightfoot's note); Philem. 12, &c.

our affairs] The circumstances of St Paul and his fellow Christians
at Rome. There are passages (see esp. 1 Thess. iii. 1, 2) where he
obviously uses "we" in the sense of "I"; but this is not likely here,
in view of the "how *I* do," just before (ver. 22).

comfort] The word is rendered "beseech," iv. 1, above, where see
note. By derivation and usage it has more in it of *exhortation* than
consolation; though the two ideas run often into one another. "Comfort" by derivation (*confortatio*) means rightly, "strengthening." If
this is borne in mind, the A. V. gives a true interpretation.

your hearts] See, for collocation of the words "heart" and "comfort," Col. ii. 2, iv. 8; 2 Thess. ii. 17.

23—24 BENEDICTION

23. *Peace*] The Apostle returns to his opening benedictory prayer.
See on i. 2 and note.—We may remark here that the phrase "Grace
and peace," in apostolic salutations, though no doubt connected with
ordinary Greek and Hebrew greetings, is not to be explained by them.
Both nouns are surely used in the fulness of their Christian meaning.
It is "the grace of our Lord Jesus Christ;" "the peace of God."

the brethren] The only certain occurrence in this Epistle (see note
on ver. 10 above) of this word in the plural. In the singular it has
occurred once, ver. 21. As children of God, Christians are brothers
of one another in a sense full of Divine life and love. See Rom. viii.
29; 1 Joh. v. 1.

love] The Divine gift of love in all its aspects. He prays that
"the love of God may be poured out in their hearts" (Rom. v. 5),

and the Lord Jesus Christ. Grace *be* with all them that ₂₄ love our Lord Jesus Christ in sincerity. Amen.

¶ Written from Rome unto the Ephesians by Tychicus.

and that they may "walk in love" (above, ch. v. 2) as its result. For the word "love" in benediction or salutation, cp. 2 Cor. xiii. 11; Jude 2.

with faith] As if to secure the reality and purity of the experience of love by its *co-existence with* faith, holy reliance, in God through Christ by the Spirit. Here "faith," as well as "love" and "peace," is *invoked* upon them; it is a "*gift* of God." See on ii. 8 above.

from God the Father] Cp. i. 2, and notes. There "*our* Father" is the wording. For the present phrase, cp. 2 Tim. i. 2; Tit. i. 4. The probable reference of the word "Father" in such an invocation (having regard to the far more frequent other form) is to the Father's Fatherhood as towards the brethren of His Son, rather than directly towards His Son. But the two aspects are eternally and indissolubly united.

and the Lord Jesus Christ] See on i. 2.

24. *Grace*] Lit., "*the* grace." So in the closing benedictions of Col., 1 Tim., 2 Tim., Tit., Heb. In Rom., Cor., Gal., Phil., Thess., Philem., Rev., the benedictions are in the full form (or nearly so), "the grace *of our Lord Jesus Christ.*" The shorter form is very probably the epitome of the larger; "*the* grace" is *His* grace. On the word "grace," see note on i. 2. It is nothing less than God Himself in action, in His Son, by His Spirit, in the salvation of man.

with all them that love, &c.] In this short clause, at once so broad and so deep in its reference, so exclusive from one point of view, so inclusive from another, we find the last expression of those great ideas of the Epistle, the local Universality and spiritual Unity of the true, the truly believing and loving, Church. All who answer this description are, as a fact, in contact with the Fountain of Grace, and on all of them the Apostle invokes "grace for grace" (Joh. i. 16), the successive and growing supplies of the gift of God.

"*Our Lord Jesus Christ*":—the full name and style of the Object of love is given. In this lies the needful warning that the Object must be no creature of the individual's, or of the community's, thought, but the Redeemer and King of history and revelation.

in sincerity] Lit., (as R.V.,) **in uncorruptness.** The word is the same as that in Rom. ii. 7 (A.V., "immortality"); 1 Cor. xv. 42, 50, 53, 54 (A.V., "incorruption"); 2 Tim. i. 10 (A.V., "immortality"). The cognate adjective occurs Rom. i. 23: 1 Cor. ix. 25, xv. 52; 1 Pet. i. 4, 23 (A.V., in each case, "incorruptible" and so, practically, 1 Pet. iii. 4); and 1 Tim. i. 17 (A.V., "immortal")[1]. Thus the word tends always towards the spiritual and eternal, as towards that which is in its own nature free from elements of decay. "In *spiritual reality*" would thus

---

[1] The Genevan English Version (1557) renders the words in the text here, "*to their immortalitie.*" The preposition ("to") cannot stand, but the noun conveys part of the true meaning.

represent a part, but only a part, of the idea of the present phrase. The whole idea is far greater in its scope. The "love of our Lord Jesus Christ" in question here is a love living and moving *"in"* the sphere and air, so to speak, of that which cannot die, and cannot let die. GOD Himself is its "environment," as He lives and works in the regenerate soul. It is a love which comes from, exists by, and leads to, the unseen and eternal. "Thus only," in Alford's words, "is the word worthy to stand as the crown and climax of this glorious Epistle."

Amen] See note on iii. 21, above.—The evidence for the omission of the word here is considerable, though not overwhelming. The early Versions, and the Fathers (in quotation), retain it, almost without exception in both cases. Some very important MSS. omit it.—What reader will not supply it from his own spirit?

THE SUBSCRIPTION

Written from Rome, &c.] Lit., **(The Epistle) to (the) Ephesians was written from Rome, by means of Tychicus.**—It may safely be assumed that no such Subscription appeared in the original MS. of the Epistle, and the question of various forms has, accordingly, an antiquarian interest only. In the oldest Gr. MSS. the form is the same as that of the Title (see note there); TO (THE) EPHESIANS. Old, but later, MSS., along with some early Versions and some Fathers, read, exactly or nearly, as the A.V. Among other forms we find, (HERE) ENDS (THE EPISTLE) TO (THE) EPHESIANS, (AND) BEGINS (THAT) TO (THE) COLOSSIANS (*sic*), or, THAT TO (THE) PHILIPPIANS.

The Subscriptions (to St Paul's Epistles) in their longer form (as in the A.V.) are ascribed to Euthalius, a bishop of the fifth century, and thus to a date later than that of the earliest known MSS. (See Scrivener's *Introduction to the Criticism of the N.T.*, ed. 1883, p. 62.)

The Subscription here is obviously true to fact, (assuming the rightness of the words *"at Ephesus,"* i. 1). In this it resembles those appended to Rom., Phil., 2 Tim. Other Subscriptions are either (1 Cor.; Galat.; 1 Tim.) contradictory to the contents of the respective Epistles, or (Thess.; Titus) difficult to be reconciled with them.

ADDITIONAL NOTE (see p. 54)

The Rev. C. T. Wilson, M.A., of Jerusalem, has favoured the Editor with the following remarks:

"The word ἀρραβὼν occurs in the colloquial Arabic of Palestine, in the form *arraboon*, and is frequently used…for the sum of money paid in advance to a tradesman or artizan to seal a bargain. It is also used to signify a sum deposited as a pledge for the fulfilment of a bargain. When engaging a muleteer, it is usual to take a small sum from him as a pledge that he will be forthcoming at the appointed time. The *arraboon* is forfeited if he fails."

APPENDICES

A. HEADSHIP OF CHRIST WITH RELATION TO THE UNIVERSE

In the Commentary, on ch. i. 10, we have advocated the restriction of the reference of the Headship to the Lord's connexion with the Church. This is by no means to ignore His connexion with the whole created Universe; a truth expressly taught in the Holy Scriptures (see esp. Joh. i. 3, and Col. i. 16, though the latter passage makes its main reference to personal existences, not to merely material things). The connexion of the Eternal and Incarnate SON with the created World is indicated to us, directly and indirectly, as a profound and manifold connexion. But on a careful view of the whole teaching of the Ephesian Epistle we think it will be seen that the Epistle does not, so to speak, *look this way* with its revelations and doctrines, but is occupied supremely with the Lord's relations with His Church, and with other intelligent existences through it. And we doubt whether the imagery of the *Head* is anywhere (if not here) to be found used with reference to the Universe at large, material and immaterial alike.

B. ST AUGUSTINE ON THE CHURCH   (Ch. I. 22.)

HE is describing with general approval Tichonius' *Book of the Seven Rules*[1] (for the elucidation of Scripture mysteries), and writes thus (*De Doctrinâ Christianâ*, III. 32):—"The second Rule is that concerning the Lord's *twofold Body (de Domini corpore bipartito)*. The phrase is unsuitable, for that is not really the Lord's Body which will not be with Him eternally.   He should have said, 'concerning the Lord's true and commingled Body,' or 'true and feigned Body,' or the like ; for not only eternally, but now, hypocrites are not to be described as being with Him, however they may seem (*quamvis videantur*) to be in His Church.   This rule demands a watchful reader; for [often] the Scripture, turning from one party to speak to, or about, another, seems to be still speaking to, or about, the first, as if the two constituted one Body, by reason of their temporal commingling and their equal share in sacraments."

In allusion to this passage Bp Ridley writes (*Works*, Parker Society Ed., pp. 126—127):—"That Church, which is His Body, and of which Christ is the Head, standeth only of living stones and true Christians, not only outwardly in name and title, but inwardly in heart and in truth.   But forasmuch as this Church...as touching the outward fellowship, is contained within that great house [2 Tim. ii. 20] and hath, with the same, outward society of the sacraments and ministry of the word, many things are spoken of that universal Church (which St Augustine calleth the mingled Church) which cannot truly be understood but only of that purer part of the Church.   So that the rule of Tyconius concerning the mingled Church may here well take place, &c."

C. ORIGINAL SIN   (Ch. II. 3.)

THE theological literature, ancient and modern, of this great subject (the title of which we owe to St Augustine), is very extensive.   The English reader will find information in Commentaries on the XXXIX Articles, such as those of Bps Beveridge and E. H. Browne.   Art. ix deals expressly with the subject, and its statements underlie those of several following Articles, especially x, xi, xiii, xv, xvii.   Among English discussions of the subject we specially recommend three of the late Prof. Mozley's *Lectures* (one of which is quoted in the notes) ; "*Christ alone without Sin*," "*Original Sin*," and "*Original*

---

[1] This book is extant.   See Migne's *Patrologia Latina*, Vol. XVIII.

Sin asserted by Philosophers and Poets." To the quotations given in this last Essay we may add the lines of Mr Browning:

"I still, to suppose it" [the Christian faith] "true, for my part,
   See reasons and reasons; this, to begin;
'Tis the faith that launched point-blank her dart
   At the head of a lie—taught Original Sin,
The Corruption of Man's Heart."

Gold Hair; a story of Pornic.

See, for some admirable pages on Original Sin, Prof. Shedd's *Sermons to the Natural Man*, especially Sermons v. and xiv. On the Pelagian Controversy, see Hagenbach's *Dogmengeschichte*, or English Translation (*History of Doctrines*), 2nd Period, B., i. 2 ; Shedd's *Hist. of Christian Doctrine*, Book iv. ch. iv. ; Cunningham's *Historical Theology*, Vol. i. ch. xi. A popular but able account of the controversy is given in Milner's *History of the Ch. of Christ*, Cent. 5, cch. iii., iv.

D. "WITHOUT GOD" (Ch. II. 12.)

"The vulgar believed in many Gods, the philosopher believed in a Universal Cause ; but neither believed in God. The philosopher only regarded the Universal Cause as the spring of the Universal machine, which was necessary to the working of all the parts, but was not thereby raised to a separate order of being from them. Theism was discussed as a philosophical not as a religious question,...as no more affecting practice than any great scientific hypothesis does now... Nothing would have astonished [the philosopher] more than, when he had proved in his lecture hall the existence of a God, to have been told to worship Him. 'Worship whom?' he would have exclaimed, 'worship what? worship how?'"

Mozley, *Lectures on Miracles*, Lect. iv.

E. THE UNSEARCHABLE RICHES OF CHRIST (Ch. III. 8.)

The following passage, referred to in the notes, is extracted from "A Sermon preached in the Parish Church of St Paul's, Deptford, on Sunday, May 7, 1786, on the lamented occasion of the death of Richard Conyers, LL.D., late Rector of that Parish," by the Rev. John Newton.

"When he entered upon his ministry at his beloved Helmsley, in Yorkshire, he found the place ignorant and dissolute to a proverb... With much zeal and diligence, he attempted the reformation of his parish, which was of great extent and divided into several hamlets. He preached frequently in them all. He encouraged his parishioners to come to his house. He distributed them into little companies, that he might instruct them with more convenience; he met them in rotation by appointment. In this manner...I have been assured that he often preached or exhorted, publicly or more privately, twenty times in a week. These labours were not in vain; a great, visible, and almost universal reformation took place. About the time I am speaking of, a clergyman in his neighbourhood made very honourable mention of Mr Conyers, in a letter to the Society for Promoting Christian Knowledge (which I have seen in print), as perhaps the most exemplary, indefatigable and successful, parochial minister in the kingdom. Yet, in the midst of applause and apparent success, he was far from being satisfied with himself. He did what he could; he did more than most others; but he felt there was something still wanting, though for a time he knew not what; but he was desirous to know. He studied the Scriptures, and he prayed to the Father of lights. They who thus seek shall surely find. Important consequences often follow from a sudden, involuntary turn of thought. One day an expression of St Paul's, 'the unsearchable riches of Christ' (Eph. iii. 8), engaged his attention. He had often read the passage, but never noticed the word '*unsearchable*' before. The Gospel, in his view of it, had appeared plain and within his comprehension; but the Apostle spoke of it as containing something that was 'unsearchable.' A conclusion, therefore forced itself upon him that the idea he had hitherto affixed to the word '*Gospel,*' could not be the same with that of the Apostle....Thus he was brought, with the Apostle, to account his former gain but loss. The 'unsearchable riches of Christ' opened to his mind; he received power to believe; his perplexities were removed, and he 'rejoiced with joy unspeakable and full of glory.'...He, from that time, preached Jesus Christ, and Him crucified, as the only ground of hope for sinners, and the only source from whence they could derive wisdom, righteousness, sanctification and redemption. 1 Cor. ii. 2, i. 30....This change in his sentiments, and manner of preaching, though it added efficacy to his moral instructions, and endeared him to his people at home, lost him much of that high estimation in which he had been held abroad. But he knew the gospel of God too well to be ashamed of it: whatever disgrace he suffered in such a cause he could bear with patience[1]."

F. APOSTLES AND PROPHETS (CH. II. 20.)

ON this collocation of Apostles with (Christian) Prophets some interesting light is thrown by early non-canonical Christian literature. The "Prophet" appears as a conspicuous and most important element in the life and work of some Christian communities in the closing years of

[1] Conyers' name occurs in Cowper's *Truth*:

"[Heaven's] open, and ye cannot enter—why? Because ye will not, Conyers would reply."

cent. 1. The recently discovered *Teaching of the Twelve Apostles*, often referred to with high respect by the Christian Fathers (St Clement of Alexandria even seems to quote it as Scripture, *Strom*. I. c. xx.), belongs most probably to cent. 1, and to the Churches of Syria. Of its sixteen chapters, five (x., xi., xiii., xiv., xv.) explicitly speak of the Prophets of the Church. We gather that they were usually itinerant visitors to the Churches, but sometimes resident, and then supported by firstfruits. They presided at Divine worship, particularly at the weekly "Thanksgiving" (Eucharist), and had the right (as apparently the ordained "Bishops" and "Deacons," ch. xv., had not) of using their own words in conducting the sacramental service (cp. perhaps Justin Martyr, *Apol*. I. c. 67). They are called "high priests" (ch. xiii.). They were to be tested (cp. 1 John iv. 1) by known standards of truth, and by their personal consistency of life, but then, so long as their teaching did not contravene those tests, they were to be heard with the submission due to inspired oracles (ch. xi.). To sit in judgment on them was to incur the doom of blasphemy against the Holy Spirit. The local "Bishops" and "Deacons" were in some respects inferior to them. The language of ch. xv. indicates, perhaps, that this inspired superior ministry was gradually passing away, and the regularly ordained ministry taking more and more its place.

The same document (ch. xi.) mentions other Visitors called "Apostles;" so entirely itinerant that a stay of three days in one place would betray the man as a "false prophet." The notice of these "Apostles" is very brief. They were evidently a rarer phenomenon, and of less practical influence, than the Prophets. No reference to the Great Apostles is to be sought in the passage. It *may* be illustrated by Rom. xvi. 7 (where however see note in this Series); and seems to indicate the existence of a class of constantly moving, and inspired, superintendents and instructors of the Churches, who, as such, would bear a likeness to the Great Apostles. No function of superintendence seems to be assigned to the Prophets.

In the *Shepherd of Hermas* (first half of cent. 2), 'Commandment' xi., is a passage referring to the Christian Prophet and his credentials. These credentials were especially a deep personal humility, a renunciation of gain, and the refusal to "prophesy" in answer to consultations and questions. The Prophet was regarded as "filled by the angel of the prophetic spirit," when it pleased God, and he then spoke not to individuals but to the congregation.

In the "First" Epistle[1] of St Clement of Rome to the Church of Corinth (probably about A.D. 95) there is ample allusion to the ordained ministry, but none to the Prophets. The same is the case in the Epistles of St Ignatius and the Epistle of St Polycarp (early cent. 2). In the *Epistle of Barnabas*, written probably somewhat later than the *Teaching*, and possibly based upon it in some measure, no allusion to the "Prophets" occurs.

---

[1] The "Second Epistle" is probably by another and later writer. It contains nothing to the point here.

G. THE CONFLICT WITH PERSONAL EVIL SPIRITS

(Ch. VI. 12.)

WE have remarked in the notes on the strong testimony given by this verse, with its exact wording, to the real and objective existence of such personal beings. We may add that such testimony still gains in strength when it is remembered that it was first addressed (at least among other destinations) to Ephesus, and that Ephesus (see Acts xix.) was a peculiarly active scene of asserted magical and other dealings with the unseen darkness. Supposing that the right line to take in dealing with such beliefs and practices had been to say that the whole basis of them was a fiction of the human mind, not only would such a verse as this not have been written, but, we may well assume, something would have been written strongly contradictory to the thought of it. As it stands, the passage is in full accord with main lines of Scripture doctrine, in both Testaments.

H. OLD TESTAMENT QUOTATIONS AND REFERENCES

IN THE EPISTLE

GENESIS	ii. 24,	quoted	Eph.	v. 31.
Exodus	xx. 12,	,,	,,	vi. 2.
Psalm	iv. 4,	,,	,,	iv. 26 (see note).
,,	viii. 6,	referred to	,,	i. 22.
,,	lxviii. 18,	quoted	,,	iv. 8.
,,	cxviii. 22,	referred to	,,	ii. 20.
Canticles	iv. 7,	,,	,,	v. 27 (possibly).
Isaiah	lvii. 19,	,,	,,	ii. 17.
,,	lx. 1,	quoted	,,	v. 14;

with probable recognition also of Isai. li. 17, lii. 1 (see note).

In view of the fact that the Church addressed in the Epistle is a Church of *Gentile* converts, these quotations and allusions illustrate instructively the degree to which the Apostle took it for granted that all his converts would study the Old Testament as the Word of God.

J. CHRISTOLOGY OF THE EPISTLE

MORE by way of suggestion than with any claim of completeness we subjoin a study of the view given by the Epistle of the Person and Work of the Lord Jesus Christ.

He is the Son of God: i. 3, iv. 13; His Father being also His God: i. 3, 17.

The Beloved One (of the Father): i. 6.

With the Father before Creation: i. 4.

Incarnate: ii. 15.

Slain, by crucifixion: i. 7, ii. 16.

Propitiatory Sacrifice, self-offered: v. 2, 25.

Redeemer from condemnation: i. 7. See iv. 32.

Raised from the dead: i. 20. See ii. 6, iv. 9.

Exalted "far above all heavens," to the Throne of the Father: i. 20 —22, iv. 8—10. See ii. 6.

Giver, on His ascension, of spiritual gifts from thence: iv. 7, 8.

Perpetual Giver, with the Father, of grace and peace: i. 2. See vi. 23.

He fills all things in His exaltation: iv. 10.

King, with the Father, of the spiritual Kingdom: v. 5.

Absolute Master of His own: i. 1, vi. 6.

Head of His Church, which is His Body: i. 22, 23, iv. 12, 15, 16, v. 23, 30.

Saviour of the Body: v. 23.

Mystic Bridegroom of the Church, His Bride: v. 25—27.

Corner-stone of the spiritual Temple: ii. 20.

Indweller in the saints' hearts: iii. 17.

Object of spiritual knowledge (iv. 13); faith (i. 15); hope (i. 12); love (vi. 24).

Treasury of unsearchable riches: iii. 8.

His Love passes knowledge: iii. 19.

He is the Secret of spiritual strength: vi. 10.

Mediator of Divine pardon: iv. 32.

In Him, the Son and Gift of the Father, the Father is eternally glorified: iii. 21;

As in Him the pre-mundane Plan of Redemption was laid by the Father: iii. 11.

Other lines of doctrine may be similarly worked out. Let the Epistle, by an effort of imagination, be regarded as a *newly discovered* Scripture, and interrogated accordingly.

Such interrogations will need, of course, to be pursued with humility and reverence, and with the remembrance that each section of the Scriptures is but part of an ordered whole. And the enquirer will never lightly forget the great definitions of doctrine, above all the catholic Creeds, produced within the Church in the past, and which are in fact authoritative collections and summaries of Scripture teaching. But none the less such direct and personal enquiries into the Divine Word in its parts will be as rich in suggestive interest as they will conduce to settlement in faith.

"Since you desire to learn concerning the doctrine, let me set forth, to the best of my powers, some few things concerning the faith of Christ. You are indeed competent to ascertain that faith from the Divine Oracles, although you are thus pleased to learn also from other teachers. For the Divine and inspired Scriptures are of themselves sufficient (αὐτάρκεις) for the proclamation of the Truth."

ST ATHANASIUS, Oratio contra Gentes, § 1.

"Perhaps we act rashly, in wishing to discuss and examine the words of GOD. Yet, why were they spoken, if not to be known? Why were they uttered, if not to be heard? Why were they heard, if not to be understood? May HE therefore strengthen us, and grant us somewhat, even as much as HE is pleased to grant."

ST AUGUSTINE, In Joannem, Tract. xxi.

"Do not only bend over [the Scriptures]: embrace them, and keep them upon your minds. Not to know the Scriptures is the cause of all evils." ST CHRYSOSTOM, Hom. IX. in Ep. ad Coloss.

INDEX